T0365312

MAGNOLIAS AND CORNBREAD

An Outline of Southern History for Unreconstructed Southerners

Leslie R. Tucker

iUniverse, Inc.
New York   Bloomington

Copyright © 2010 by Leslie R. Tucker

All rights reserved. No part of this book may be used or reproduced by any means, graphic, electronic, or mechanical, including photocopying, recording, taping or by any information storage retrieval system without the written permission of the publisher except in the case of brief quotations embodied in critical articles and reviews.

iUniverse books may be ordered through booksellers or by contacting:

iUniverse
1663 Liberty Drive
Bloomington, IN 47403
www.iuniverse.com
1-800-Authors (1-800-288-4677)

Because of the dynamic nature of the Internet, any Web addresses or links contained in this book may have changed since publication and may no longer be valid. The views expressed in this work are solely those of the author and do not necessarily reflect the views of the publisher, and the publisher hereby disclaims any responsibility for them.

ISBN: 978-1-4502-4147-2 (sc)
ISBN: 978-1-4502-4146-5 (hc)
ISBN: 978-1-4502-4145-8 (ebook)

Library of Congress Control Number: 2010909472

Printed in the United States of America

iUniverse rev. date: 08/17/2010

To all my Southern ancestors, especially Lt. Henry H. King of Company F, 6th Arkansas Infantry. The family stories about him helped instill in me a desire to preserve my heritage.

Also, to my wife, Dr. Phebe M. Tucker, who has been with me through most of my life. Together we have been lucky enough to find a life in which we can do more than simply survive.

TABLE OF CONTENTS

PREFACE

Today there are many people who attack not only the Confederate flag but also other symbols of the Old South. They claim they are offended. Many Southerners have surrendered to this for the sake of harmony. I am not one. I am offended by their attitude. These are symbols of my ancestors and my heritage. I feel that they are saying that my ancestors were so evil that they do not deserve to be remembered and honored. Not only am I offended by this anti-Southern bigotry, but I also believe that the North was wrong and that they were guilty of crimes against humanity. They killed my ancestors; burned their homes, farms, and towns; raped their women; and denied them the right to self-determination. I am an unreconstructed Southerner.

I am proud to be a Southerner, but I have not always felt that way. I was born in New Mexico, the son of Okies, and was then raised in California. When I started school out on the West Coast, hillbilly was my native language. By the time I started middle school, I spoke Californian fluently. I was like Jethro Bodine of the *Beverly Hillbillies*; my parents were rubes and hayshakers, but I was a sophisticated international playboy because I was from California. Later I got involved with genealogy. I learned that all my people came from the South. By the time of the American Revolution, all my ancestors were living below the Mason-Dixon line. I have five great-great-grandfathers who were Confederate soldiers, and when I number their brothers and nephews, I have more than a hundred who fought for the South. Some deserted, some even went to the other side, but nonetheless they were Southerners. Then I began to think about my religious upbringing, about the food I was fed, and the music I like. I was raised in a Southern colony, just like Merle Haggard, Buck Owens, and Dwight Yokum. I am a Southerner.

When I moved back to Oklahoma in 1981, I was proud to see a display of the Fourteen Flags that have flown over our state during its colorful history. Some of them seemed to be a bit of a stretch, but we accomplished our goal of having more flags than the six that Texas boasted of. In 1960, Governor Henry Bellman asked Muriel Wright for suggestions on how to represent Oklahoma at the New York World's Fair. Muriel had been active for years in Oklahoma history; her grandfather is the one who came up with the name for our state. Muriel researched what became known as the Fourteen Flags. After the fair ended, the flags were arranged around the entrance to the state capitol building. The Fourteen Flags could also be found in the plaza of the Liberty Bank building, in front of the Myriad Convention center, and at the main plaza of the state fairgrounds. Today the poles in front of the capitol are all Oklahoma state flags. The ones at the convention center, now called the Cox Convention Center, were changed to colorful banners and then later removed altogether, and the poles at the now Chase Building are adorned with only the American or state flags. Despite attempts to change those at the fairgrounds, they still defiantly fly. These changes are the result of a direct attack on one of those flags, the Confederate flag. It matters not that all but one of the other flags, including the Stars and Stripes, also represented nations that had slavery. It is only the Confederate flag that has been singled out for removal.

Every American-schooled child is taught to be proud of their heritage. We see communities celebrating Cinco de Mayo, Saint Patrick's Day, or Kwanza. We are encouraged to be proud of the fact that we are all Americans, but we all have another heritage—a hyphenated heritage. We may be African-American, Irish-American, or simply Native American; but we are all part of the "diversity" that is America. There is an exception—Confederate Southern American. We are supposed to be ashamed and believe that our ancestors fought for racism and bigotry and that they had to be defeated so that the diversity that is the United States of America could come into being.

This view is wrong. I am proud to say that my ancestors have lived in the South since the first English colonies, which were in Virginia, not Massachusetts. Some of my Southern ancestors arrived more than ten thousand years before that since I am also part Cherokee and Choctaw Indian. My ancestors fought for independence in 1776, and their grandsons fought for the same cause in 1861. Some of them owned slaves, but the majority didn't. There are those who have the absurd idea that the Confederate soldier is in the same class as the Nazi who gassed innocent civilians in Germany. Such thinking is based on a distortion of history that is nothing short of propaganda.

Recent Attacks and Interpretations

Attacks on Confederate symbols, especially the battle flag, have increased since a 1991 resolution by the National Association for the Advancement of Colored People (NAACP). They claimed that the "tyrannical evil symbolized in the Confederate Battle Flag is an abhorrence to all Americans and decent people of this country, and indeed, the world and is an odious blight upon the universe."[1] The liberal revisionist historians do not use the same language but do seem to condone the sentiment.

I cannot prove it, but I believe there are ulterior motives for this attitude. For the NAACP it is simply politics. As discrimination against blacks in America decreased, the need for the NAACP did also. Any organization must justify its existence. Since 1991, this group has called for boycotts, marches, petitions, and other actions against the Confederate battle flag. They have lost some, but for the most part, the flag and other symbols continue to disappear throughout the land.

My explanation of the liberal revisionist's motivations is more complicated. I call it my "scapegoat theory." First, the liberals like to endorse anything sponsored by the NAACP. However, they also like to think of America as the land of diversity. They tend to complain about the racism in American history, but they still like to boast of the diversity. They like to think of the Declaration of Independence and the Constitution as documents which foster diversity. This is a contradiction to the reality of American history, which is full of racism. How do we reconcile these facts with the dream of diversity? A simple way out is to put the sins of racism on Southerners. Since bleeding heart liberals are also concerned about the poor, they have even found a way to lift the burden of racism off of them. I am talking about the poor whites of Appalachia and the Populist and the ones like Woody Guthrie. We

---

1 NAACP Resolutions, 1991.

can't think of them as evil. Again, the solution is simple. We blame only those Southerners who defended the Confederacy. That is why the revisionists like to try to show that the poor whites were not loyal Confederates. According to them, it was mainly the planters, the slave owners, the rich. This is very similar to the old planter conspiracy theory that helped to bring about the war in the first place. By putting the sins of racism on the Confederate battle flag, we can then sacrifice that flag to the rubbish pile of history. This is classic scapegoating.

Though many of us have fought to preserve our heritage, it seems we are losing much more than we are winning. I could fill a volume with examples. The only car banned by NASCAR was one sponsored and decorated with the Sons of Confederate Veterans logo. The voters were able to restore part of the battle flag to the Georgia state flag, and Mississippi kept theirs, but as a result, the NCAA has called for a boycott of any bowl games being played in either of those states. Theme parks from Oklahoma City's Frontier City to Tennessee's Dollywood have removed it. I can remember when every fair and carnival in the South, as well as other states, used to sell the battle flag. It is getting so that now many of our young do not even know what it is. There are even many examples of where the hated banner has been eliminated from battlefield paintings so that Union soldiers carrying the Stars and Stripes battle a bannerless enemy.

Us unreconstructed Southerners diminish in numbers as more and more of our own people abandon the defense of our Confederate history. Many give the subject lip service, but they have assigned priority to other issues. The NAACP and their allies have found it a successful tactic to convince the Chambers of Commerce that they are going to look like a bunch of rednecks and lose business if they display Confederate pride. Recently the Republican Southern strategy has become a major force. Richard Nixon started what is called the Southern strategy of the Republican Party. The conservative party that traditionally supported big business in the northeast has convinced Southerners that they are now the party of the social issues which they agree with, such as public prayer, opposition to gay marriage, or antiabortion. The Republican Party has embraced the agenda of the religious right, but they would never defend our Confederate heritage. I remember shortly after September 11, President Bush visited Columbus Day festivities, met with Hispanics, and even courted Muslim-Americans. I know that neither Bush nor any other high-ranking Republican would ever visit a meeting of the Sons of Confederate Veterans or United Daughters of the Confederacy. I even have serious doubts that he would attend a meeting of the Sons or Daughters of the American Revolution. One of the main reasons that the Republican Party would never be seen at any event in support of our Confederate heritage is that they are also trying to recruit more black voters, and they do not want to jeopardize this goal. They also know that the liberal media would attack them for showing support to anything Confederate. Even Southern Republicans are willing to set aside their Confederate pride if it will help them achieve the Republican agenda.

A historiography is quickly growing around the issue of Confederate heritage. As far back as 1960, C. Vann Woodward addressed the *Burden of Southern History*; but of course, that was before the direct attacks on Southern icons. Some books defending our heritage have turned to the traditional romanticized view, such as Mike Grissom's *Southern by the Grace of God* while others have taken a more radical approach, such as *The South Was Right* by James R. and Walter D. Kennedy. Meanwhile, the liberal revisionists have entered the fray. They like to claim objectivity and even seem to recognize that our defenders are not all Klansmen but in the end, agree it is time to furl the flag forever. This would include Tony Horwitz with *Confederates in the Attic* or David Goldfield in *Still Fighting the Civil War*, and K. Michael Prince with *Rally Round the Flag, Boys!: South Carolina and the Confederate Flag*. Anyone interested in preserving our heritage should read these books. Know the enemy. You may even accept that some of what they have to say is true and that they do have some good points. We must also realize the truth in what James C. Cobb said: "In the century that lies ahead, dedicating so much attention to the lower right corner of the United States will be increasingly difficult to justify unless we realize that for future generations the value in studying the South's experience may actually lie not in what seems unique about it but in what seems universal."[2] What is universal about this issue is that we need to appreciate and accept people of different cultures. White

---

2   James C. Cobb, *Redefining Southern Culture: Mind & Identity in the Modern South*. (Athens: University of Georgia Press, 1999), 211.

Southerners have taken great strides in understanding and accepting black Southerners. It is reasonable to expect the same. We deserve to be accepted for what we are, which means accepting what our ancestors were. Some of us still believe the words of the old song, "And I don't want no pardon for what I was and am, and I won't be reconstructed, And I don't give a damn."[3] Our ancestors did not do anything that they need a pardon for, and we do not need a pardon for honoring them.

This is not intended to be an essay for academia but rather for the Southern people. I have a PhD in history, and I know how to do the kind of research expected for one in that profession. I have done proper historical research; however, I sometimes feel that if history does not get to the people then something is missing. As a professional historian, I am often frustrated by the distortion of historical fact that is used to support one's politics and philosophy of life. I have had students who have openly expressed contempt for the general education requirements that put them in my class. Nonetheless they use historical fact to support their views on contemporary issues. The problem is that they are only using what they believe to be the facts of history. We all make basic assumptions, but they should be based on fact. That is why it is critical to have a complete and accurate understanding of history. We will have differences in how to interpret historical facts, and no doubt bias will tend to creep in, but we should strive for accuracy as much as possible. When it comes to the Confederate flag, I believe that even the professionals are distorting the facts because of the liberal Northern bias that dominates intellectual America. No doubt they consider us to be the biased ones, therefore my main objective is to offer an alternative to their interpretation. Much of the liberal arrogance is based on an assumption that our alternative view is due to ignorance. It is not.

Since I am a professional historian well schooled in the liberal biased view of history, I hope to pass on my advice to the defenders of Confederate heritage. I am not presenting a complete history of the South but only an outline of history with an emphasis on those topics most relevant to the condemnation of our heritage. I will point out the liberal revisionist teachings and discuss why their view is not necessarily the only one. I want the unreconstructed to understand the viewpoint of the liberal revisionist historians so that they can better

---

3   Major James Randolph, *O, I'm a Good Old Rebel*

defend our position. I am not doing original historical research, and so this is an essay, not a true history. I will not use footnotes except in the case of direct quotes. I will include an appendix with bibliographical essays on the books depended on most by the liberal revisionist. I will present my conclusions, which I know some, if not most, professional historians will disagree with. Generally, their disagreement will be over my interpretation, not the facts that I present. They will say that my view is biased, but I say that theirs is. Academic historians live in a culture of liberalism, which most of them defend, but I am not writing for professional historians; I am writing the general reader. More specifically, I am writing for the unreconstructed Southerner.

As I do my outline of Southern history, I will consider the point of view of the four main classes of our society. The liberal revisionists are correct in their identification of these classes in Southern history. The dominant one and the one romanticized by books and movies such as *Gone With the Wind* is the planter class. The largest white population is the middle class or what the historians call the Yeoman farmer. Historians have labeled the lower white classes pine-barrens folk instead of a more offensive term, such as hillbilly, redneck, or peckerwood. The fourth is black Southerners who were slaves, then freedmen, and now African-American. This is why I have titled my book *Magnolias and Cornbread*. Southern culture is not just the planters and the romantic stuff of which movies are made, but also the toil and sweat of the Southern farmers and working class. I will try to cover the point of view of these main classes in Southern history, including black Southerners. I consider the latter important since if I can help them realize that this is their history too, maybe they will not be so determined to obliterate it. I feel a necessity to discuss the middle- and lower-class whites since the Revisionist trend is to say that they did not support the Confederacy.

INTRODUCTION

Three Main Objectives

While others are honored with various holidays and festivals, Southerners are supposed to stand by as all signs of our Confederate heritage are erased from the pages of American history. In 1996, I visited the California high school I graduated from. As we entered the auditorium, the principal, a former classmate of mine, pointed out a display of more than one hundred flags and boasted that they represented the diversity of his student body. I did not see a Confederate flag nor would I ever expect to see one. It is not just that our heritage and ancestors are ignored but that they are quite often vilified.

I have three main objectives that I hope will assist the defenders of our heritage. The professional historians have now entered the battle, and they speak with such authority that many will assume them to be correct. I am a professional historian, and so I am familiar with the current historical interpretations relevant to Southern history. With this essay, I hope to provide information that will help those who are still proud of their Southern heritage to better defend it against those who are determined to bury it.

My first objective is to inventory the relevant interpretations of the liberal revisionist historians, who I will refer to as the Librevs. I understand that they are professional historians and that we must accept the fact that they are right more often than they are wrong. They have correctly identified numerous myths and inaccuracies and, as a result, have given us a more accurate American history. I certainly have no desire to discredit their work or to give the impression that they do not know what they are talking about. However, I do not believe they are correct in the position that most have taken in wanting to deny us our past or in creating the impression that our ancestors were evil. It is important for us to understand what they have to say before we criticize them.

My second objective is to correct some of the common myths that the Dixie defenders have. If we counter professional historians with rhetoric, they will not even bother to respond. We must be able to defeat them with a factual history of not only our Southland, but also of the United States. The Librevs may not agree with us, and most of the time, we will not be able to prove them wrong, but we should be able to reduce our disagreements to opinion. Therefore it is important that our opinion be based on historically accurate facts. We should even be willing to concede when the Librevs are right for the sake of credibility while standing firm on those areas in which the professionals are wrong.

My third objective is to include the history of the black Southerner. Traditionally, Southern history has been the story of white Southerners. In the meantime, blacks have been put into the field of African-American history. At least a third of Southerners are of African ancestry, and most blacks in America have Southern ancestors. It seems to me that it is a distortion of history to separate the two. In the past, the majority of Southern whites have been racist and thus believed themselves to be superior to the blacks, but nonetheless they have lived together for centuries. Of course, I also hope to convince many blacks that Confederate heritage is part of their past too and not something they should seek to destroy. There is no denying that most of our white Southern ancestors were racist and that blacks were not treated fairly; however, there is more to the story. I also want to recognize that even though blacks were slaves, they made many contributions to Southern culture and that they deserve our respect for their contributions. If we make it clear that our heritage is the heritage of all Southerners, then it will be more difficult for the politically correct to condemn our past.

Librevs

History is written by the winners, everyone realizes this. This is why the Northerners have been portrayed as more righteous than Southerners. We have another problem in America—the liberal bias in academia. The most influential scholars come from Harvard, Yale, and other prestigious Northern universities. This has created a Northern slant with a liberal bias. Academic liberalism has become a self-justifying system. Those who step too far over the line of liberalism could never hope to be accepted into one of these institutions, and therefore their views will never be incorporated into their academia. The academic elite equate liberalism with intelligence and conservative views with ignorance. Unfortunately, this has spilled over to secondary and primary education also, and from them to the general public. Even the majority of Southern academic historians have embraced this liberalism. I cannot say if it is due to self-esteem or simply the desire to be recognized by the Northern-dominated academic elite. I also believe that this liberal bias has led many of the professionals into the ranks of the politically correct.

Librevs have identified Southern patriotic groups such as the Sons of Confederate Veterans and United Daughters of the Confederacy as defenders of that they call the Lost Cause myth. There is definitely much to the early views of Southerners that reek of filial piety; however, the liberal revisionists are too quick to reduce us to two choices— the old over-romanticized "lost cause" view or theirs. That is a main reason that I find it necessary to write this essay. I believe that we can accept accuracy in Southern history without sacrificing the honor and memory of our ancestors. The mothers, daughters, and widows of the Confederate soldiers sacrificed much when they literally collected their pennies to construct monuments to their sons, brothers, fathers, and sweethearts, who bravely defended their homes from foreign invaders. We should feel shame every time one of these memorials is destroyed in the name of political correctness. These people were our ancestors, our culture, and our heritage. They need not be sacrificed for the sake of historical accuracy or political correctness. I am glad that we no longer have slavery. I am glad that blacks have made considerable progress toward achieving equality. However, my white ancestors were victims of their times as much as the blacks were. In hindsight, I see that much of their thinking was wrong, but I will not hate them for it nor will I deny them the respect they deserve.

We have much to be ashamed of in our history. However, we must not be too harsh in judging those who lived by different rules. Before World War II, most Americans believed in white superiority. When most Americans of the early twentieth century saw *The Birth of a Nation*, they saw it as factual. Today few of us look at the world this way, and we are all better off because of the change. But I will not condemn our ancestors for being wrong about this anymore than I would condemn them because they did not know as much about math or science as we do now. I am sure that we do things today that will be considered wrong in the future. I hope we will not be held accountable for not following the moral standards of the future. We should study history to understand where we came from and how this made us what we are today. We should not study history to find someone to blame.

I will not attempt to deny that my Southern forefathers were racist, and I am certain that if I could meet them today, there would be much that I would disagree with them about. But the sin of slavery, if it could be considered a sin at a time when most of the world practiced it, cannot be put solely on the shoulders of Southerners. The Stars and Stripes defended slavery for much longer than the stars and bars. The racism that justified slavery in the South also justified the extermination of Indians throughout America. It made immigrant slums acceptable and made it easier to kill brown-skinned natives whether they be from America, Puerto Rico, Hawaii, or Philippines. This attitude was not limited to Americans as the slaughter of nonwhites occurred around the globe as Europeans conquered the world and expanded their empires. It is not even limited to Europeans as the study of almost any other culture would quickly reveal. Conquerors usually consider themselves superior to the conquered. This not only justifies their aggression but to them it explains their success.

Librev Issues

Entire philosophies can be reduced to a handful of assumptions. There are a few main topics that the Librevs take a position on that are relevant to the defense of our heritage. It is these that I will focus on in my outline of Southern history. There are six of these which I consider crucial, as well as a few lesser ones.

The first topic is the most obvious. Generally, the Librevs have agreed with those who seek to remove the Confederate flag. They understand that we look at the flag as a symbol of our heritage rather than the racist icon that some have used it for. Nonetheless, they realize that it represents something negative to many black folks, and therefore we should be willing to sacrifice this symbol for the sake of harmony and to make amends for past sins of racism. Much of their position on this is relevant to the other issues that I will be discussing.

The second topic is the question of Southern distinctiveness. They see this as related to what they call "the lost cause myth." Because of this, they believe that the Confederate flag and other symbols are not part of our heritage since we did not have a heritage before the war. I do not agree with this idea. I firmly believe that the differences between the North and South are great, and in fact, I feel a greater affinity with those of the West Indies than with New Englanders. Grady McWhiney wrote about what is called the Celtic Fringe theory. To simplify, he said that the difference between North and South existed in the British Isles before the American colonies were founded. It dates back to the conflict between the Celtic population that lived there before the Roman occupation and the Anglo-Saxons who arrived in conjunction with the Romans. The Celts were pushed off to the fringes of England, Ireland, Scotland, and Wales while the Anglo-Saxons dominated in the South. The theory works on the assumption that the Anglo-Saxons settled in New England while the Celts settled in the southern United States. Thus, according to this theory, there were social differences from the very beginning. I believe in the Celtic fringe theory, and this theme will run throughout. In other words, I believe that the North and South were different from the start, and the differences have continued through today. We may have much in common with the North, but we are different in other ways. I also accept the theory that the South has more in common with West Indies culture than with the North.

The third topic has been a big question in American history since 1860—the cause of the war. They still argue that the Civil War was fought over slavery, and of course, this is a big part of the reason they agree with the view that the flag is a symbol of slavery. This interpretation is largely based on a book by David Potter, although there are others. In his book, Potter traced the growing sectional crises after the Mexican War, saw that most issues revolved around slavery, and then concluded that the war was fought over slavery. The Librevs think this is a brilliant and conclusive argument. The key here is in the way the question is posed. If we ask the question "Was the war fought to free the slaves?" then the answer would be no. If we ask "Did slavery cause the war?" then the answer would be yes. I can recall seeing Potter's argument in the *Confederate Military History* written by a Southerner way back in the 1890s. The author did not do as extensive a job but still reached the obvious conclusion that the conflict came about because of slavery. I can only say that those leading the fight for the North said they were not fighting to free the slaves and that 75 percent of those in the South did not own any slaves. I cannot believe that the average Southerner would have fought so long and hard so that the rich guys could keep their slaves. I do believe that the rich slave owners caused secession, but once Lincoln invaded the South, it was a different issue. It seems to be important to the Librevs to insist that the war was over slavery; they find this critical if we are to buy into their belief that Confederate symbols are bad.

The fourth topic is an attitude that Northerners are morally superior as well as intellectually and culturally. It is true that the North has supported reform more than the South throughout American history. However, Northern liberals seem to have developed an attitude of self-righteousness, which suggest that they are not quite as open-minded as they claim to be. There is an element in America today that fosters an image of the liberal Northerner as charitable toward minorities and that conservatives, especially Southern conservatives, are stingy. Southerners do tend to be more resistant to change, and they do have a strong work ethic, but that does not mean they are morally bankrupt. Southern morality is based on their strong religious views. These are not generally accepted by liberal society as legitimate and are even condemned for not being politically correct. The Librevs believe Northern humanist morality to be superior to Southern religious morality.

The fifth topic is the nature of Reconstruction. Since they see the war as a war to end slavery and that they think of Northerners as morally superior, then the logical conclusion would be that Northerners were the good guys during Reconstruction. This is a big part of what they call the "lost cause myth." They claim that it was during the Reconstruction years that Southerners developed their Southern identity but that their objective as "redeemers" was to establish their cast society where the whites would continue to dominate over blacks and that the freedmen would end up back in the cotton fields. They recognize that some cases of Yankee corruption can be documented, but for the most part, the invaders were simply trying to insure the equality of the African-Americans. According to them, the main objective of the Ku Klux Klan was to intimidate the freedmen into submission and that the scallywags were hapless Southerners who wanted to join the carpetbaggers but ended up targets themselves. I do believe that some of the carpetbaggers such as the young school teachers, wanted to contribute in helping the freedmen in making the difficult transition from slavery to freedom. However, the main motivation of the Republicans was to guarantee the future of their political party, which gained victory in 1860 with less that 40 percent of the American population.

When it comes to the sixth topic of slavery, there are a number of subtopics the Librevs like to pursue. Some are relevant to the flag controversy and some are not. The number one relevant issue is the question of whether the slavery system was harsh or benign. There seems to be an unspoken assumption that most unreconstructed Southerners still defend slavery, or at least the system their ancestors had, with statements such as "our family treated their slaves well." I know I have grown up with these kinds of sayings and admit the Librevs are right to attack this view. I believe that the majority of the slaves did not hate their masters and that many of the owners did have a paternalistic attitude toward their slaves. I am also sure that some were beaten, raped, mutilated, and even killed by cruel masters. It is hard to determine how many fit into each category, and in all probability, most fell in varying degrees in between. I also believe that regardless of how benign the experience was that the vast majority, if not all, would have preferred their freedom over slavery. They may have faced new challenges as freedmen, but most people prefer difficult freedom over a gilded cage. We Southerners need to shed the old rationalizations for slavery.

There are a number of related topics in which they seem to be trying to refute the idea of a benign system and seem to have the notion that Confederate slavery was worse than even other Europeans. They accept the reality that slavery existed in Africa before Europeans brought it to America. However, they have the attitude that the way the Europeans did it was much worse. There is no doubt that the demand for slaves greatly expanded when the whites entered that market; everything the

Europeans did in the modern age was on a much greater scale that what had been done before. As to whether they did it worse is debatable, and the fact remains that they did what they did with the help of African chiefs and kings. As to the way those in the United States did it, even the Librevs accept that there must be something to the fact that the slave population in the United States grew because of natural population growth. This indicates that the system may have been more benign than in other American colonies.

There are those who like to explore the preservation of African families, religion, or culture. This is a topic I enjoy myself. I lived in Africa for a year, and not only do I believe that African-Americans have preserved many African ways, but also that the Africans had a significant influence on the white population of the South. I will discuss this topic in greater detail later.

Southern History Myths

There are a few myths that we Southerners cling to which we need to abandon if we can expect to have any credibility with the professional historians. If one attends a Sons of Confederate Veterans or United Daughters of the Confederacy function, they will find plenty of those who get lost in the *Gone With the Wind* fantasies. This is what the Librevs attack first, this is what they refer to as the "lost cause myth," and for that matter, it is something that I find to be a major block in understanding Southern history. It is in effect supporting the old theory that the South was resisting modernization, which includes holding on to slavery. These myths will be discussed in my outline of Southern history.

As stated earlier, many of the Librevs refer to the traditional view of Southerners as the "lost cause myth." They claim that the South did not have a strong regional identity until shortly before the war and that it became stronger after. This is why they separate the Confederate symbols from Southern culture. In other words, they argue that the Confederate battle flag is more of a symbol of the postwar redeemers than of our Southern heritage. The Librev consensus is that Southern distinctiveness did not exist until after the war and that the main objective was to rebuild their white-dominated Southern society. They see the present day members of the Sons of Confederate Veterans and the United Daughters of the Confederacy as the torch bearers of the lost cause myth.

Southerners have had a somewhat unrealistic self-image, and so we deserve some of the criticism that has been laid on us by the Librevs. The Sir Walter Scott or the *Gone With the Wind* view appeared in the antebellum years. By this I mean the view of the South as the last bastion of aristocracy. It was mainly the planter class who saw themselves in this way, although some of the lower classes also found this delusion attractive. They see their ancestors as the cavaliers who fled England after the puritans took over during the English Civil War. The Yankees were the descendants of the puritans. Margaret Mitchell went with that image, and the movie referred to the feudal way of life as that which was "gone with the wind."

The Compromise of 1877 rid the South of the Yankee occupation, but unofficially, it also gave them their "lost cause" interpretation. Though modern Yankee historians now call this a mythology, it was the Columbia University historian William A. Dunning (1857-1922) who gave his name to this interpretation. He accepted the nobility of the Confederate soldier, recognized the superiority of the white race, and laid the foundation for tales of Southern history that included such classics as *Gone With the Wind* and *The Birth of a Nation*.

The Dunning School accepted the Southern idea that those involved with Reconstruction were corrupt, and the blacks elected to office were incompetent. The revised view is just the opposite. I believe that both views are wrong, Reconstruction was a power struggle in which the Republicans fought for survival while the Southern Democrats sought to end Union occupation. It was not really a matter of morality as much as a political contest. Our Southern forefathers were not morally superior, but neither were they inferior.

Another myth in Southern history is the idea of the "new South." Southerners have contributed as much to this myth as Northerners have. It is related to the notion that the South resisted modernity while the North encouraged the Industrial Revolution, but after the war, they not only surrendered to the Union army but to Northern modernization. It is true that the North exceeded the South in urban and industrial development; however, the South was also on the road of progress. They had cities, factories, and railroads. Most in the South were farmers but so were most Northern Americans. The planters were not feudal lords, but many were developing agribusiness similar in many ways to what we see in agricultural America today. This is an important issue because some see this as a justification in their condemnation of the South; after all, they retarded American progress. Northerners feel justified in their invasion because not only did they free the slaves, but they also began the process of modernizing the South.

Some U.S. History Myths

In order to obtain an accurate picture of Southern history, we need to have an accurate picture of American history. There are a number of myths that continue to be passed on in the textbooks and thus passed on by high-school teachers. These myths have been carried into adult life by many Americans of the North as well as the South. Most Americans have a self-image that has been forged by patriotic fervor. The work of the revisionist has helped to correct many of these misconceptions; however, they continue to survive. In this essay, I am only concerned with those which apply to Southern history. Many conservative Southerners hesitate to abandon these myths too; however, we need to recognize the revisionist corrections that are valid. Remember that these historians are professionals and that there have been numerous aspects of American history that needed to be corrected. Ironically, the rejection of these United States historical myths can help us in defending our Southern culture. Librevs have been more than willing to be critical of the domination of western or American civilization over others. The way I see it, the South is one of those who have been victimized by American imperialism. Now we are subjected to the cultural imperialism of American liberals. There are three that I feel are very important.

First is that people came to America for religious and political freedom. Some did come for religious reasons, and in some cases even for religious freedom; however, most did not. This is important because many Northerners use this as a justification for their invasion of the South. They see the South as a stumbling block to the American dream. Most came for economic opportunity, and most of those who came for religious reasons were not terribly interested in general religious freedom. We Americans have liked to place some kind of higher purpose to our being, starting with the widely accepted myth of religious freedom. It is crucial to my defense of our Southern culture to realize that most Americans, Northern or Southern, black or white, Indian or European, operate on Adam Smith's principle of self-interest. I will attempt to show that those in the South are no worse or better than those in the North. I will not deny our selfishness, but neither will I accept the blame for something all people are guilty of.

The New England Puritans came for religious reasons. However, the fact is that it would be difficult to be less tolerant than they were. By the 1630s, they made it clear that any deviates were not welcomed. Those in Massachusetts Bay Colony did not even get along with the Plymouth pilgrims. Roger Williams and his friends such as the Quakers had to leave town because of Puritan intolerance. The New England Puritans believed themselves to be about the Lord's work, building a "city upon a hill," as proclaimed by John Winthrop, to serve as an example for all other Englishmen. This is an attitude that they took with them into the first reform period of the early nineteenth century, including the crusade against slavery. The religious origin of the New England Puritans does not mean that they had a moral superiority—the moral superiority that many abolitionists claimed as well as those who condemn our Southern heritage today.

The Thanksgiving holiday is an example of how they worked. As all Americans partake of this feast, we have been conditioned to think of the Pilgrims and the Mayflower and the first settlers. This is the main reason why I have difficulty convincing some people that the first Anglo-American colonists were in Virginia, not Massachusetts. This holiday started as a "Civil War" propaganda tool. The first national holiday for Thanksgiving was during the war. The stories created an image of the religiously and morally motivated pilgrims and associated them with the beginnings of our nation. No doubt this inspired belief in the righteousness of the Northern cause during the war, as well as a view that these pilgrims were the founders of the America, which became the United States. Many Americans have come to look at the Pilgrims as those who believed in religious freedom and have become a symbol of those who believe in all freedom and thus represent what America stands for. The descendants of these Pilgrims fought the South because they stood in the way of the freedom that Americans love.

I have no doubt that not only do many Northerners still think this way, but also many other Americans buy into it. The majority of the Americans descend from the immigrants who came after the war, but their ancestors settled in the Northern cities. They were raised on the Northern propaganda and identify with the region where they were born and where their families have lived since coming to this country.

I had an experience which summarizes the image created by the puritan founding fathers myth. I sat on a plane next to a gentleman from Massachusetts. I do not recall his exact background, only that he came from immigrants that arrived in this country after the war of Southern independence. He clearly had an American identity, and it was equally clear that he felt he was as much a part of New England as any Mayflower descendant. In the course of our conversation, I pointed out to him that Virginia was established before Massachusetts. He had a hard time accepting this fact. He confessed that his interpretation of American history was that the colonists first arrived in his New England homeland and from there spread out across the continent. In other words, the Pilgrims were the founders of the United States. This is an inaccurate interpretation of our history, but it is a very common one.

The second myth is that America is a classless society. Class conflict was part of European history before and after the age of exploration and has also been part of American history. Most of the time, this class conflict has taken the form of the rich attempting to acquire cheap labor. This is critical for us, as the issue of slavery was the Southern form of class conflict. The North was not morally superior to the South when it comes to the exploitation of workers; it is just that they found a different source for cheap labor. In both regions, there were those who had privileges, and they often took advantage of those underneath them. American history involves stories about slaves, indentured servants, immigrant laborers—in other words, those who worked while others accumulated most of the profits. The world economy has generated a growing middle class, but that was a function of modernity, not of American or Northern exceptionalism. Though we prefer to ignore it, America has had its class struggle. In the South, those of the white lower classes quite often ended up on the frontier so that much of conflict between them and the rich takes the form of frontiersmen versus the planters or tidewater people. In reality, it was a class conflict. Most of those of African ancestry were slaves; and thus, it seems to be a racial conflict when, in fact, it was more of a class conflict. In the North, it was the working classes who were most in conflict with the middle and upper classes. There, too, racism was still a factor since most of the lower classes were immigrants and most Northerners looked down on them as inferiors in the same way those in the South considered Africans as inferior. John C. Calhoun argued the slaves were better off than the Northern workers. There was a lot of truth in this claim, a claim upheld by the research of the recent liberal historians Fogel and Engerman. They later made it clear that slavery was terrible; however, they never changed the view on the overall living conditions. Charles Dickens and Karl Marx clearly saw the nineteenth-century working classes as oppressed. I understand that the workers were free, and the slaves were not. However, I believe the freedom of the workers was more of an illusion than a reality. The bottom line is that in each region, the rich found their own way to meet the demand for cheap labor, and their choices were based on economic advantage not morality.

North or South, many described the war as a rich man's war but a poor man's fight. There is certainly some truth to this in both cases. As early as Bacon's Rebellion, we see that the interest of the common man is contrary to the interest of the wealthy. In the North, a larger percentage of the colonists seem to have been middle class; nonetheless they did have growing numbers of those not accepted as equals. At the time of the Revolution, the number of working class was insignificant, but they did exist. The demand for cheap labor increased considerably by 1860 and would really take off after the war. There is no evidence that the preference for the immigrant laborers was based on anything other than economic advantage, though there was a growing distaste for slavery. The appearance of the moral superiority of the Northerners is mainly due to the fact that their need for cheap labor did not exist on a large scale until after the rise of the abolitionist sentiment. In other words, those of the South inherited a cheap labor system developed at a time when slavery was not considered morally wrong by most Europeans. Those of the North did not have a great need for cheap labor until after the Enlightenment thinking had changed the mind of many regarding slavery.

The third myth so many Americans cling to is that the United States is not, nor has ever been, an imperialist power, and the American people never had imperial ambitions. The United States started with thirteen states hugging the Atlantic coast; by 1850 they reached the Pacific Ocean. There is no power on earth that expanded more in the nineteenth century than the United States. The colonists clearly had a strong interest in land from their first days on the new continent. In the early days of the United States, it is the Southerners who were most aggressive. We will see that after the Civil War, the thrust for expansion came from the Northern businessmen while the Southern farmers struggled to survive. In the colonial period, it is the Indians who were victims of imperialism; in the 1860s, it was the Confederacy. If we deny American imperialism, we will not understand the main reasons the United States conquered the Confederate States.

Black Southerners

There is no wonder that many blacks do not have the same pride in being Southern as whites. They were brought here in chains either directly from their ancestral home in Africa or more likely by way of one of the many plantation islands in the sun-drenched Caribbean. The survivors of the horrid middle passage were stripped, poked, prodded, and humiliated in a slave market in New Orleans, Charleston, or maybe Washington D.C. The lucky ones would end up with a paternalistic master who felt obligated to them; the less fortunate would end up being whipped, rapped, mutilated, or even murdered. After the demise of slavery, they spent the next several generations as second-class Americans. Some achieved success; but most got the leftover jobs, poor housing, few educational opportunities, and a constant reminder that not everything American would be available to them. I shall make no attempt to trivialize nor justify their experience in Southern society nor in American society. Most blacks accepted their lot in life, but that does not mean that they liked it or that they were happy with it.

So why do I insist on focusing on blacks? Simply because they are an integral part of the South. I have always liked the egg analogy.

The egg has a yolk, which is surrounded by the white part. Each is easily identifiable, yet as a whole, they make up an egg. Traditionally, Southern history has become synonymous with white Southern history. Meanwhile, one studies African-American history if they are interested in blacks. The fact is that more than a third of the Southern population has been black, and most black Americans have Southern roots (although this is changing with the recent increase in immigration from Latin America and the Caribbean). We cannot understand the egg without understanding both parts and, most importantly, understanding how it is the two together which make an egg.

Though some blacks have understandably rejected an identity with the South, many have not. The famous African-American historian John Hope Franklin claimed, "The South, as a place, is as attractive to blacks as it is to whites." He added, "Blacks even when they left the South didn't stop having affection for it. They just couldn't make it there." He understood that living in the North did not solve all their problems and that in many ways the South was better. "It's more congenial, the pace is better, the races get along better. It's a sense of place. It's home. In rare moments, it's something that blacks and whites have shared."[4] Franklin's opinion was supported by a recent survey in *Southern Cultures*. When asked if they had identification as a Southerner, blacks responded more positively than whites with 78 percent responding in the affirmative compared to 75 percent of the whites.[5] I hope to demonstrate that black Southerners are part of the South and that the Southern heritage is theirs too.

My hope in achieving this task is that white Southerners not only can better appreciate the black perspective, but that also the blacks can better understand the white point of view. I know that at this point, I am being somewhat repetitive, but this is a critical issue. I assume that blacks were not reduced to slavery and second-class citizenship because they are inferior. I also assume that the actions of Southern whites were not due to inferior morality. It has been common throughout history for one culture to feel superior to another. It is not a matter of

---

4   Peter Applebome, *Dixie Rising: How the South is Shaping American Values, Politics, and Culture* (New York, 1996), 341.
5   Larry J. Griffin, "The American South and the Self," *Southern Cultures* (Fall 2006): 13.

right or wrong but just the way people are. Europeans have been in the process of global conquest since 1492, if not before, and for the most part were successful. This only served to justify such feelings, at least in their minds. It is amusing that while so many Americans have rejected Darwin's ideas of natural selection in animals, they have embraced them as an explanation of white American superiority. Social Darwinism not only infected Americans but also Europeans. The sad thing is that many blacks also accepted this kind of thinking. They often preformed below their abilities because they conformed to the expectations of the whites.

It is not a matter of morality, no matter how wrong we may think it is today. It was not morality that caused men to believe the earth to be the center of the universe; that is just the way people see themselves. The white mind saw their success as proof of their superiority. As science replaced God, Darwin explained our expansionist skills—survival of the fittest.

I will not try to show that white Southerners were right any more than I will try to show that black Southerners were inferior. My main belief is that even though the war between the North and South was caused by slavery, it was not a morality play. Before abolition, after the war, during Reconstruction, and up until the civil rights movement, racism was an American thing, not simply a Southern thing. At first, few people, North or South, believed slavery to be wrong. As time passed, the Northern states did away with it, and the Southern states became dependent on it. This was due more to a matter of profitability than morality. There were some who believed it to be wrong, and as time passed, more and more agreed. Americans became convinced of this. There were also people in the South who believed it to be wrong. This was a trend throughout the world and is usually the case when we change our morality—some were convinced sooner than others.

It was not morality that caused the Northerners to invade the South; kill hundreds of thousands of Americans; rape their women; burn their cities; loot their property; destroy their farms; and deny them their right to self-determination. Rather, it was a power struggle, and as such, the United States tried to justify their actions on the grounds of morality and democracy. This has been a practice used before 1861, and it is still used today. Ironically many Southerners have accepted this as part of the American foreign policy today.

The revisionist liberal historians of today seem to be even more merciless in putting the blame on Southerners. It is rather amusing that while they cry about American racism; identify American imperialism; and are critical of the American patriotic interpretation of their history, they seem all too eager to accept the theory that from 1861 to 1877, the North was simply conducting a crusade against one of the great evils in the American past. They believe that Abraham Lincoln was not a self-absorbed politician as so many other American politicians have been, and thus, he is the United States president most admired by Librevs. He ended slavery the only way it could be done. They ignore the fact that 75 percent of the Southern population never owned a slave. They trivialize the fact that the United States was the only major power that had to kill many of their own people to end slavery. They still rave about the Emancipation Proclamation even though they know that it did not free a single slave at the time it was issued. They ignore the political and economic reasons the North had to conquer the South even though they claim that this has been the reason for other American wars. Simply put, the Librevs praise the North for their moral crusade against the evil South.

Blacks in the South were clearly second-class citizens between 1877 to about 1970 or 1980. I will not attempt to deny or justify this fact, but rather simply point out that this too was an American issue. There are still many parts of the North today that have few blacks. When blacks did begin to go North in large numbers after World War I, they were restricted access to certain neighborhoods, schools, transportation, recreational facilities, and certainly from touching white women. The main reason there were more problems in the South is that there were more blacks, just as the West had more problem with Indians than those in the East. There have been numerous race riots and racial tension in the urban areas of the North, which did have large black populations. Anytime one group of people try to dominate over another, there will be more problems where the dominated are larger in numbers.

I will point out many positive contributions of black Southerners, not as an attempt to deny the negative but rather to point out the positive. I love the South. I love Southern culture. The blacks have contributed much to creating the culture I love. I am hoping that by knowing the truth, black and white Southerners will have a better understanding of each other and thus become more tolerant and respectful of each other. I have a dream that someday most blacks will understand that Confederate icons are just part of our past. I believe that most of the protest against Confederate icons has been led by the politically motivated, who have turned the destruction of our heritage into a racial issue.

Despite the fact that blacks were slaves and then second-class citizens, there is still a bond between blacks and whites in the South. I am not trying to say that they were happy with the way things were but simply that there was some acceptance and some bonding between the two groups. They lived together; they grew up together; they knew each other's families; and they shared each other's grief. More importantly, from the historical perspective, is that they shared the same culture. The large black population is one of the main reasons that the South is so much different from the North. They have influenced our language, our lifestyle, our food, our music, our storytelling, and even our religion and philosophy. Whites need to recognize how much blacks have influenced us, and I am hoping that blacks will realize how much the history of the South is their history too. This was summed up very well by Ann Moody

Ann, who worked with Martin Luther King, Jr., since the earliest days of the civil rights movement, wrote an autobiography. In recalling the time she marched in a parade as her seventh-grade class queen, she wrote, "When the band reached the center of Main Street, they stopped marching and began playing. As they hit the first notes of 'Dixie,' I thought I would die, especially when I saw some of the familiar white faces bellowing out the lyrics." She found one fat man especially amusing, but she also observed "'Dixie' seemed to have made everyone happy, Negroes and whites." Then the band played "Swanee River." "There was something about 'Swanee River' that touched most of those old whites singing along with the band. There was also something that made the old Negroes even sadder." She added, "I got a feeling that there existed some kind of sympathetic relationship between the older Negroes and the whites that we younger people didn't quite get or understand."[6]

---

6   Anne Moody, *Coming of Age in Mississippi* (New York: Dell Books, 1968), 108–9.

There are still some blacks who understand this feeling; I have met them at the Sons of Confederate Veterans reunions. They are not large in numbers. They are called "Uncle Tom" by some other blacks, but they are very popular with the white SCV members. There is one man, H. K. Edgerton, who has attracted considerable national attention marching across the South for the Confederate soldiers. H. K. was at one time president of the NAACP chapter in Asheville, North Carolina. Today he works closely with the Southern Legal Resources Center, which defends Southerners who are discriminated against for displaying pride in their heritage. He had problems at his mother's funeral in February of 2005 because they wanted to display the Confederate flag; the Hill Street Baptist church cancelled the services. "The cemetery was packed. The Sons of Confederate Veterans and the ladies of the Order of the Confederate Rose, and the ladies in mourning from the Society of the Black Rose, mixed in with my Mom's friends and relatives," H. K. said. "It was a dream. She wouldn't have had it any other way." H. K. later said, "It was a special day. I was proud [to] accompany my Mom to the cemetery, carrying the flag. It is our flag, the flag of our Southern heritage."[7]

There are few blacks who have the feelings that H. K. has, and many will not be able to accept the statement about the old people which Ann Moody referred to. However, I hope that there will be more. I hope that some will read my book and realize that H. K. was right when he said, "it is the flag of our Southern heritage." We need not deny the negative side of our shared past; however, I believe we will all be better off if we as Southerners accept this as the truth about the way things used to be, and we are glad that it is better now. Meanwhile, let us focus on the positive and work for a better future. I hope that black Southerners understand that if the whites are forced to bury their past and spit on the graves of their ancestors, it is natural to expect resentment.

The Plan

In chapter 1, I will cover the colonial era up to the French and Indian War. Prior to 1763, there were many communities throughout the colonies. Unity did not begin until after the French and Indian War ended in 1763. Between 1607 and 1763, slavery became more common

---

7   *The Asheville Tribune*, January 27–February 2, 2005.

in the South and less common in the North so that by the time of independence, there was a growing regional difference. More important and somewhat related was the difference in economy. Northern economy became increasingly diverse while most in the South tended to depend on agriculture. I believe the preference for slavery in the South was based on economic opportunity and not any sort of inferior morality. Before 1776, slavery was a dividing issue between the regions, at least for some, but it did not prevent them from creating the United States.

Chapter 2 will be about the creation of the central government. This covers the years 1754 to 1789. The war ended in 1781, and the British accepted United States independence two years later, but it was not until the ratification of the Constitution that the country that we know today was created. Of course, the power of the central government would continue to be an issue and is still not completely settled. Since 1776, there has been a trend toward a stronger central government at the expense of states' rights.

Chapter 3 will cover the early days of the United States. Between 1789 and 1848, the economic gap continued to widen, which manifested itself in economic issues. The South continued to depend on slavery while the North cultivated alternative sources of cheap labor. The manufacturers of the North favored protective tariffs while the predominantly consumer Southerners opposed tariffs. The North developed internal improvements, and even though many were state funded, the Southerners tended to see the federal government as an agent for internal improvements in the North. Though there was some conflict between North and South, this time period could be better described as a time when community competed against community, not necessarily based on any split between North and South.

Chapter 4 covers the period between the end of the Mexican War and the election of 1860. Some of the Librevs claim that this was when Southern identity developed, though most of them insist that it was not until after the war. This is the time when the struggle over the spread of slavery into the new territories became the major dividing issue. It is also the time when more and more Northerners began to hate Southerners. The existing political parties divided between North and South as the general population did. The Librevs are correct in identifying this period as crucial in determining the cause of the war. What is ironic is that after recognizing that the main problem was the spread of slavery in the territories, they then seem to ignore that fact as they give their admiration to Abraham Lincoln as the man who freed the slaves.

Chapter 5 will cover the War for Southern Independence. This is the period in American history that is most critical in the issues relating to the Confederate flag controversy. It was also after this that the country emerged with a much stronger central government. I will cover the diversity of those who fought for the Confederate cause with some discussion of why they fought. The modern liberals like to think that it was a race question, but I will show that there were plenty of other races who supported the Southern whites. I repeat for emphasis that our people were racist but no more so than those of the North.

Chapter 6 will be about Reconstruction, from the end of the war up to the Compromise of 1877. This has become a major battleground for the Librevs in their campaign against traditional interpretations of Southern history. They are right about some, but I feel that they have gone too far.

Chapter 7 will cover a period of reconciliation. Between 1877 and the end of World War II, the South was left pretty much to itself. Many saw this as a time to forgive and forget. As the Civil War veterans died, it became easier to do. Northerners saw those in the South as simple-minded, but colorful. Southerners were racist, but most Americans were. White Southerners initially refused to celebrate July 4, but in time, they began to accept defeat and progressed toward becoming Americans once again. By the end of the Second World War, Southerners were at least as patriotic about being American as those in the North, and by the time we got through the sixties, they were even more so.

In chapter 8, I will talk about the struggle for black equality. Since World War II, the rise of the civil rights movement emphasized the differences between North and South. Race riots and violence occurred in Northern cities and schools, but it was more intense in the South. We have ourselves to blame for some of the antagonism toward the Confederate flag as many of our people embraced it as a symbol of states' rights, which at the time also meant anti–civil rights. Stereotypes of the South became more negative, such as the movie *Deliverance, Smokey and the Bandit,* and the television show *The Dukes of Hazzard. The Dukes of Hazzard* may have been more benign, but those loveable hillbillies were still stereotyped as ignorant and backwards. I will also cover what is known as the Southern Diaspora, when millions of our people left their native land.

Chapter 9 will take us up to the present. Since about 1980, resistance to the rights of blacks and other minorities does not seem to be any worse in the South than it is in the North. The invention of air-conditioning has made the Southern sun more appealing to Northerners. They had to change the name since it seemed easier to accept a move to the Sun Belt rather than a move to the South. For many Northerners, the Southern image is still negative but in a different way. The more recent image has been that of the Bush supporters and the American theocracy. These people are not the ones I am speaking to; they are more concerned with their political agenda and look to the Republican Party as their Messiah. They are willingly sacrificing their Confederate heritage to get support from the Republican Party. They see our Confederate past as a small price to pay if we can stop flag burning, gay marriages, or bring Jesus back into the schools. Their compliance in our cultural genocide has made it much more difficult to preserve our heritage.

CHAPTER ONE

Colonial South

Introduction

The colonial period has become an important battleground for true Southern history. The Librevs claim that the South did not really have a regional identity until shortly before the war and, in fact, was not really all that strong until Reconstruction. They call this the "lost cause myth." They consider the Sons of Confederate Veterans and United Daughters of the Confederacy to be defenders of this myth. I am like most unreconstructed Southerners in that I have no doubt that our people are different and that the difference is too deep-seated to be the result of the Civil War. Grady McWhiney has been the chief defender of the view that has become popular among the unreconstructed. I must clarify that I am not claiming that McWhiney was one of the unreconstructed but simply that his work is popular among us. McWhiney said that not only were Southerners different but that difference dates back to the British Isles. It is part of the Celtic fringe theory. The idea is that the colonists of New England were Anglo-Saxons who came from the Southeast of England. The dominant culture in the South was Scottish, Irish, Welsh, and those from the west and north of England. I will not attempt to add to McWhiney's efforts but simply point out that my history of the South is based on the assumption that he was right. Most of the liberal revisionists do not like his thesis and they do not accept it, but they have not proven him wrong.

I personally do not accept the main part of the Celtic fringe theory, which is that because of the Celtic background of Southerners, they are more warlike. I do not believe that among the Germanic northern

European population that one is any more or less warlike than the others. McWhiney argues that the Scottish are this way because of the many generations of warfare between them and the English. Many people around the world have traditions of rivalry with neighboring cultures; the Scottish are not unique in this. Nonetheless, I do believe the idea that the Celtic population was different from the Anglo-Saxon and that this culture has had more influence on the South. Even the Librevs do not dispute the homogeneity and Anglo-Saxon ancestry of the New England colonies nor the large number of Scots in the South. For me, the main point is that they were different from the beginning and became more so once in America. This is opposite of the Librev theory of the "lost cause myth," which is widely accepted among the liberal academic historians.

I can only guess as to why they think this is such an important issue, but I believe they use it to justify their siding with those who favor the banning of our Confederate heritage. I accuse them of bias on this topic. They have accepted the fact that most of us do not see the Confederate icons as symbols of racism, and they have heard our cries of "heritage not hate." Now they argue that these are not really symbols of our heritage. This way they can use history to justify the cultural genocide that is aimed at our Confederate heritage.

I recall seeing a concert of the Highwaymen recorded in Aberdeen, Scotland. At one point, Kris Kristopherson said, "We are in our country," he went on, "the three best countries to play in—Ireland, Scotland, and Wales." I doubt that Kristopherson is familiar with the Celtic fringe theory, only that he connected with these people compared to those in other nations where they have played. Most Southerners sense a connection with Celtic culture, and I can think of no better example of the cultural connection than the music of the South. When dealing with history, we should depend on what is provable. However, sometimes we just know inside that something is true. This is one of those cases. Historians debate the merits of McWhiney's view, but we Southerners know we are not the same race as those to the north.

European Background

There is some background information that we need if we are going to understand the English colonies in America. I do not believe that the conflict between North and South was over any morality issue such as slavery. I believe that the war was the result of economic and political competition. For this reason, it is important to understand the development of economic interest in America. The age of exploration and resulting colonization in the Americas came about because of the development of world markets. The world markets came about because of the transition from the agricultural feudal economy to the merchant economy of the modern age. This change did not occur overnight. The foundations were laid a long time before 1500. The transition was not complete by the founding of the colonies. In fact, we still have remnants of European feudalism in our culture today. I do not agree with those who have viewed the South as the last defenders of the dying feudal society. However, there are some aspects of this transition that are relevant.

Perhaps the greatest influence of feudalism on America was the lust for land. Though the modern Englishman led the way in the development of capitalism, they still attached a great deal of status in the ownership of land. Many of the nouveau-riche English merchants purchased a country estate as soon as they could afford one, and many even bought a title if they could. Most of those who came to the colonies came in search of land. Some were the younger sons of the aristocracy but most were the rising "middling sort." This included those in the Northern and central colonies too, but the love of land is greatest in the South. Whereas the man who strikes it rich in the North looks for a penthouse in Manhattan, the Southerner still wants acreage with a big house, white rail fences, and grazing horses. Of course I am speaking in generalizations to which there are many exceptions, but any Southerner will see the truth in what I say.

The lust for land caused Southerners to be more expansionist in the years before the Civil War. They needed the land for their plantations. Even though Europeans understood the principle of crop rotation, they evaluated the cheapness of the land compared to the high profits from planting the same crops year after year. They established the habit of growing one crop until the land could not produce any more; then they would abandon their old place and moved west. The demand for land also came from the growing population, most of which was due to natural population growth. By the early twentieth century, the American people paid for the abuse of the land with massive erosion problems throughout the West and South. The most famous example of this is the Dust Bowl.

The Growth of the World Markets

Markets existed in feudal society, but they were not as important as in modern society. This can best be demonstrated by the growth of cities. Cities equal market economy; that is the reason for their existence. During the Middle Ages, the city of London never had more than ten thousand people. By the seventeenth century, it had hundreds of thousands.

The first world markets were the Italian city states, such as Florence, Rome (the Papal States), Milan, or Genoa. Of course, theirs was not a true world market but rather the world as they knew it. The merchants prospered and purchased art and culture with their profits. Though Spain got a great head start with "discovery" of the New World, the first true world market leadership soon passed to Antwerp. Because of their conflict with Spain, the center of world commerce shifted to Amsterdam. By the eighteenth century, England captured the title and retained it until the twentieth century. The colonists who went to America were part of the British Empire and thus key players in the world-market economy.

Nationalism

Nationalism came with the rise of the world markets. Whereas the feudal peasant or knight could turn to the local lord for protection, the globe-trotting merchant needed something more all encompassing. At first he turned to the king. It was during the modern age that kings found "absolute" power as reflected in palaces such as Versailles. The greater the power of their king, the more protection the merchant might expect and find in the world. When the English achieved domination of the world markets, they did so with the rise of the English navy. The English still label their navy as "His or Her Majesty's Ships." When the English and the French established their colonies in America, they were still second-rate powers struggling for their share of the world-market economy.

This struggle for national identity was as much a part of what was happening in the nineteenth century as anything. Though the Great Britain that we all know and love today was established with the unification Act of 1707, it took several more generations before the average Englishman achieved the level of national patriotism that we see today. There was still no unified Germany until the mid-nineteenth century. Neither was there a unified Italy. When we speak of Robert E. Lee as a man who was a Virginian first and an American second, we are not talking about someone clinging to the vestiges of feudalism. We are talking about a man going through the same experience that many other Europeans went through. The struggle for national identity was neither unique to the United States nor an example of Southern backwardness. Some people are still reluctant to surrender their local identity for the sake of the nation. Southerners should understand this better than other Americans.

The Development of Ideas

Increased literacy came with the rise of the merchant economy. The merchants and their families had a need to keep up with their business transactions, and thus, they had to learn to read and write. As more people became literate, they read the Bible, which of course led to the Reformation. Soon after came the scientific revolution, and people began to turn to the laws of nature as an explanation for the events around them. After defining the laws of nature, we next learned to harness them. This led to many technological advances that climaxed with the Industrial Revolution.

As the foundations of feudal society crumbled to the advances in literacy and learning, men began to question the nature and order of their societies. This is called the Enlightenment. This period gave us many things that we associate with the modern age, such as novels, encyclopedias, dictionaries, newspapers, and coffee houses for debating intellectuals. It also gave us economics, democracy, and the notion of government by contract. It is also at this time that we find a significant number of people questioning the institution of slavery.

The rise of new ideas did not occur everywhere at the same time. Some become convinced before others. This is also true regarding the abolition of slavery. In the early modern period, slavery existed in many parts of the world. Today few people would condone it. As of 1861, more people in the North were convinced that it was wrong. However, most Americans, North or South, still believed in the superiority of the white race. No doubt the profitability of slavery contributed to Southern thinking. It is always difficult to prove what people thought in the past, but it makes sense that those who clung to slavery the longest were those who profited the most. It does not mean that they lacked morality or that they were inferior to the ones who could find profits without slavery. A major flaw with capitalism is that it fosters selfishness. Adam Smith called it self-interest. This means that people do what is best for them and quite often it is to the point of being selfish.

The Concept of Class

I believe that the moves for independence in 1776 and 1861 were primarily about economic competition. I also believe that the economic interest varied by class. Therefore it is important to reject the belief so many Americans have that ours is a classless society. The concept of class is considerably more complicated in the modern world. Feudal society had commoners, clergy, and aristocracy. Each of those had their well-defined layers. Everyone knew where they fit and what their roles were. Class in the modern world has often been ignored as the old aristocracy declined and the rising merchants ascended. Some old families are still wealthy today, largely because of the lands they have controlled since the Middle Ages. However, most of the wealthiest and most powerful of the modern age have come from below and were catapulted to new social and class levels by their business enterprises.

America has stood for capitalism since its founding; the aristocratic medieval titles were never transferred to the colonies. This, combined with the American self-image of exceptionalism has led many to deny that class distinctions are as great here. We have all heard it claimed many times that America is a classless society. I have always tried to understand which part is classless—Beverly Hills or Watts? Since the first colonies there has been a demand for cheap labor and those who did the labor have been looked down on by those who used their labor.

Capitalism, like feudalism before it, continued to have people who labored for others. After the merchant class turned to manufacturing they found a need for labor. The cheaper the labor, the greater the profits. This has put the owners in competition with the poor or working classes. This is why socialism and communism came into existence. In the colonial days of America, manufacturing was limited. Those who did this kind of business could meet their labor needs with their own families. Many were cottage industries. The few that expanded their business first used the labor of young ladies between adolescence and marriage. This source for labor shifted to immigrants. At first, the Irish, and later it would include other immigrant groups all the way up to the illegal aliens of today.

The greatest profits accrued to those who exploited the labor of others. In the South, they turned to slavery. I will discuss the reasons for this in greater depth later. John C. Calhoun made a defense of slavery on the grounds that the Southern slave was better off than the Northern working class. In the days of Calhoun, there was a lot of truth in this. Of course we cannot ignore the value of freedom, even if it was only in theory. The reality is that workers depended on their meager incomes, and it was not always easy to quit a job. The main point I want to make at this time is that in both cases, there were those who profited off the labor of others. The Southern planter inherited a system that had been around since the first American colonies; the Northern manufacturer adopted a system that came into being after the Enlightenment. As stated earlier, the Enlightenment was an age when intellectual discussion had turned against slavery, especially the slave trade. This did not mean that the Northern manufacturer did not exploit workers. Karl Marx certainly did not see the virtues of the system utilized by the Northern manufacturers. If a man exploits the labor of another, is one system really morally superior to another? In slavery, one does not have the freedom to choose. In the early nineteenth century, how much freedom did the working classes really have? Even today how many working people toil at a job they hate because they have a family to feed. They had the freedom to starve to death if the factory they worked for cut production. They would often end up maimed or crippled by the machines they worked with. The planter was motivated to care for his workers since he had capital tied up in them. Was the early industrialist morally superior to the planter?

The Northern preference for immigrant labor may have been nothing more than an economic decision. They did not need a capital outlay that one needs when buying a slave. They did not have to feed or shelter the immigrant when production was down. Enlightenment thinking was leading the Europeans away from slave labor, but those who followed also found economic advantages. My purpose is not to defend slavery but rather to point out that the Northern choice of immigrant labor was not necessarily the product of moral superiority.

Growth of Democracy

We quite often equate democracy with the concept of equality. American exceptionalism revolves around the notion that our nation produced modern democracy and thus has been the leader in a world campaign to show that "all men are created equal." For this reason, we have often thought of ourselves as morally superior to other nations. Northerners have seen themselves as the leaders in this. Intellectually they realize that men such as George Washington, Thomas Jefferson, and Patrick Henry came from the South, but they seem to think this fact has been negated by slavery. If we realize that democracy and related ideas did not come from America to begin with then we must reject the notion that Northerners are leaders of the American crusade for equality. If we understand this then it is more difficult to accept the Northern assumption that their invasion and conquest of the South was part of this noble effort to assure the equality of black Americans.

We like to think that we invented such great American institutions as the jury system, democracy, and the two-party system. This is not the case. The jury system that we use has been part of Anglo-Saxon culture since the Early Middle Ages. The bicameral legislature that we established with the Constitution is modeled after Parliament. And the two-party system also came from England, where Whigs and Tories have been around since the seventeenth century. What made our country unique is that Americans got a chance to try out Enlightenment ideas that others in Europe had only discussed. They also had the opportunity to create a society without much of the baggage that came with a hereditary aristocracy.

The British see democracy as their innovation, which historians call the Whig interpretation. According to them, it has roots in the democratic election of Anglo-Saxon chiefs which occurred before they went to England from Germany. The Middle Ages produced the Magna Carta, which legally limited the power of the king. It also produced Parliament, though its powers were initially limited to taxation. The king called Parliament into session if he needed tax money, and he could end the session at will. The Glorious Revolution of 1688 increased the power of the legislature with the passage of a law that called Parliament into session at regular intervals regardless of the will of the king.

The main point I want to make at this time is that the notions of democracy, government by contract, jury system, equality of citizens, and such things came from England to the northern, central, and southern colonies. That idea of equality that we have today was still in the formation stages. The rise of democracy began in England and was brought to America by the colonists or in the books that came to the colonies. The Enlightenment talked of equality and rights. However, the definition of a citizen in those days was not the same as it is now. It was limited to males over the age of twenty-one, who owned property and paid taxes. When they talked of rights, there was little thought about women, the landless working class, or slaves. There is no stone tablet that defines equality. There is no set truth like one would find in math and science. Ideas of right and wrong are not human nature but are part of a culture. In the case of European culture, such things are in an ever-changing flux. We consider our morality of today to be superior that is why we changed. However, it does not seem right to condemn those of the past because their view of morality is not up to our standards. It does not mean that we should abandon our ancestors because they lived by a different code of morality.

Our Southern ancestors were not morally inferior to other Englishmen or to Northerners. The concept of equality and rights that we have today is not the same as what they had at the time that the constitution was drafted. It was not the same in 1861. The fact that Americans were still debating the limits of equality does not prove that Southerners, not even slave owners such as Thomas Jefferson, were morally bankrupt. As the times have changed, morality has changed. We should not judge those of the past by the standards or rules that we live by today.

This is a very important concept in our stand to preserve our Southern heritage. Those who condemn the Confederate flag and other symbols of our past make the assumption that these things represent part of the American past that was evil. To us, they are part of our heritage. The Sons of Confederate Veterans has passed numerous resolutions condemning those who use the flag of our ancestors to promote racism.

Our ancestors were racist. There have been times when the flag was used as a symbol of this racism. Most Americans in the past were racist. Most Europeans in the past were racist. We cannot deny this, and we cannot change the past. The liberals tell us that people who make a mistake are not necessarily bad people. I agree with them. I know that I have done things in my life I would not repeat if I had it to do over. I hope that I can be forgiven for my mistakes and not condemned for eternity. I especially hope that I will not be condemned for breaking rules that will exist in the future. I will extend the same courtesy to my ancestors, especially since their concepts of right and wrong were based on a different code than we live by today.

Some Background on Slavery

When the age of exploration began, Europeans did not have slavery. There had been slavery in the past. The Romans and Greeks had it. The Germanic tribes had some after the fall of the Roman Empire. From the eleventh century *Doomsday Book*, we know that England had about 10 percent slaves at the time of William the Conqueror. Shortly after that, the Pope decreed that slavery was wrong so that by the fifteenth century, there were very few slaves in Europe.

When the Portuguese and Spanish increased trade with Africans, they did accept some slaves. Generally there was a low demand for labor in Spain or Portugal so the slave trade was rather limited. By the early sixteenth century, the Spanish looked for other sources of revenue in the New World other than simply sacking Indian cities or looking for gold. They discovered that the islands of the Caribbean were good for the growth of sugar. With the encomienda system, the new-world Spanish lords sought labor to cultivate the sugar, as well as other crops. At first they tried to use Indians. There have been various explanations as to why the Indian population did not meet their demands for labor, though the one I find most believable is that they simply died too quickly. There are those who like to think of the white man as the source of all evil and therefore call the rapid decline of Indians genocide. I believe that the main cause was simply their lack of resistance to new diseases. For thousands of years, Europeans, Africans, and Asians had the opportunity to share goods and illnesses. They had some resistance, even though plagues could still produce devastating results to these populations. The Indians had virtually no resistance so that entire communities or even civilizations became extinct in a very short time after the arrival of the Europeans.

Capitalism is successful when one finds solutions to problems. When the Indians died, the enterprising planters concluded that African slaves could be purchased and taken to the New World. Africans had traded in slaves for many generations before the age of exploration. The Librevs realize this as true, but they claim that it was never done to the same degree by Africans or those of the Middle East. I will concede that this is true. However, everything that Europeans did in the modern age was done on a larger scale than it had ever been done before. They built faster ships, greater cities, and technological innovations exploded. This is why they shifted from the mediaeval agricultural economy to the modern merchant economy. This is why they were successful in conquering the world.

The slave plantation system was well-established by the time the English began their colonies in America. However England was a land of laws even at that time. In 1607, when Jamestown was established, slavery was not part of the English civilization. They had only begun to dabble in slavery in some of their colonies. As will be seen later, the first arrivals to Virginia did not anticipate slaves as a source of labor. They began the colony with indentured servants.

Life in America Before the English Colonies

With the age of Columbus, Europeans began a process of world conquest. Europeans rationalized the taking of other lands and enslavement of the natives because they considered them savages. To this day, I see American textbooks that talk of how the colonists conquered a wilderness. They did not conquer a wilderness, they conquered Indians. The most important point to understand in accepting this fact is that when we talk of the participation of Indians in white man's wars, we are talking about a third party. Their decision to participate on one side or the other was based on what they thought to be best for them. When they sided with the French during the French and Indian War, they knew that it was the English who took their lands. When they sided with the British in the Revolution, they knew it was the colonists who took their lands. Likewise, when we later look at the decision of the Indians who joined the Confederacy, they made their choice based on what they believed to be the best for them.

We also have a tendency to overlook the non-British colonies in America. We have been taught about how the pilgrims settled in Massachusetts with the implication that they were the first. Since the South lost the war, American schoolchildren have been brought up with the impression that our nation began in Plymouth rather than Jamestown. However, St. Augustine, Florida, was founded before Jamestown. Another Spanish settlement, Santa Fe, New Mexico, predates the Mayflower as well.

Today we think of the North as being more diverse. However, in the days before the Civil War, there was more diversity in the South. The Indians of New England that were not exterminated were pushed beyond their borders. Though later Indians would be removed from the South, not only did many remain but numerous Southerners also boasted of their mixed bloodlines. Those Spanish colonies absorbed into the South produced many Confederate soldiers with Spanish surnames. The South had slaves, but that does not necessarily mean they were more racist than the Northern capitalist. We can at least say that they were more diverse than those in New England. Those who condemn our ancestors for their racism should realize that in some ways, they were less prejudiced that those in the North.

Tobacco Colonies

The first permanent English colony in America was established at Jamestown, Virginia, in 1607. It was purely a business venture conducted by the Virginia Company. No one went for religious or any other kind of freedom. In the first years, there were numerous trials. Captain John Smith had problems with the gentry who felt that manual labor was below them. Smith finally had to make a rule that anyone who wanted to eat would work. As a result, some felt that Smith was too much of a tyrant. The colony underwent radical changes following the great massacre of 1622, in which many were killed by Indian attack.

The massacre brought revisions, and the colony began to stabilize as a tobacco plantation colony. In the years between 1623 and 1676, the two main issues involved finding the labor to work the plantations and dealing with the Indians. It was the laborers who created conflict with the Indians. A solution appeared shortly after Bacon's Rebellion.

The first to arrive in Virginia fit into three main social classes. First, the gentry who sought large tracts of land. Second, the rising middle classes who wanted a plantation which could be worked by the family although I am sure that some dreamed of becoming large planters themselves someday. The third group were poor laborers. The gentry could acquire land easily but they needed someone to work it. The middle classes could labor on their own land, but they would find it increasingly difficult to compete with the large planters. The poor could not afford to pay their own passage so they became indentured servants. The gentry covered their passage and the poor paid them back with their labor.

I, like many historians, lump Virginia and Maryland together and call them the tobacco colonies or Chesapeake colonies. Maryland began as a refuge for Catholics under the leadership of Lord Baltimore. However, like the elder and larger colony, the economy was founded on tobacco and the plantation slave system became the method by which they produced the product. The status of the charter changed through the years from the Calvert family to a royal charter, and then back to the Calverts. Likewise, the "Catholicness" of the colony changed over time. The Toleration Act of 1649 sanctioned nondiscriminatory practices related to religion. However, in 1691, the colony became Anglican, and Catholics were denied the right to hold office or hold religious services outside of their homes. By the time the charter went back to the Calverts, Lord Baltimore had become Protestant. The main reason I have put discussion of Maryland in with Virginia is because of the similarities in the economy.

One of the sad facts of capitalism is that the very wealthy usually get that way off the sweat of others. A man can make money off of his labors. When his family works too, they can make more. When a man uses the labor of others, he can become very wealthy. This has been true in all times and in all cultures. History is full of conflict because of this. A good capitalist will tend to view the situation as one man offering a job and another accepting or refusing the job. This is seldom the reality. Let us not forget the basic assumption of Adam Smith; people operate on the principle of self-interest. The employer will try to get the labor as cheap as possible, and the employee will try to get as much as possible. On the surface, this seems like an objective situation. The reality is that the employee is quite often dependent on a job for survival whereas the employer is simply trying to accumulate surplus wealth. Thus, the wealthy employer has an advantage. This is how societies end up with slavery or some other form of exploited working classes. The worker who appears to have a choice is not necessarily better off than a slave. This is why Karl Marx came along.

Three-fourths of all new arrivals to Chesapeake between 1630 and 1680 came as indentured servants. There were numerous attempts by the landowner to take advantage of the indentured. However, since England was a land of laws, the laborer did have rights that enabled him to prevail at times. Many died from overwork or harsh conditions, but others served out their terms and became property owners themselves. The planters received fifty acres for every man they brought with them into the colony thus giving the well-to-do more motivation to bring in the poor. By 1675, the population of Virginia exceeded forty thousand, many of them former servants who wanted land. The landless poor became a source of problems.

The Dutch brought the first boat of slaves to arrive at Jamestown in 1619. They needed supplies, and that is all that they had to trade with. English law did not recognize slavery, and so these first Africans were servants. Most Europeans of the time believed black Africans to be savages and inferior to white people. Even though at first they were not slaves in the traditional sense, they lingered in a gray area of English law and custom. Some acquired land and servants of their own while others lived a life that would approximate our traditional view of slavery.

Bacon's Rebellion probably had an impact on the shift from indentured servitude to slavery. By the later part of the century, the wealthy land owners became more concerned about maintaining peace with the Indians than in the further acquisition of land. Meanwhile, the population of freed indentured servants increased. Under the leadership of Nathaniel Bacon, who had his own motives, the poor of the colony rebelled. They burned numerous plantation houses and made it clear that they wanted land. The governor wanted them to leave the Indians alone but the rebels insisted in taking Indian land. With the death of Bacon, because of dysentery, the rebellion fizzled. The leaders of the colony realized that such problems would exist as long as they depended on poor whites for labor. The use of slaves would solve that problem. By 1660, slavery was legally part of colonial law. There is always an element of speculation in trying to understand why people did what they did. The fact is that in 1670, there were no more than two thousand slaves in Virginia; by 1700, the number increased to ten thousand, and in the next century, the South had 390,000 slaves. After Bacon's Rebellion, the planters preferred slaves to indentured servants. Most historians today accept the idea that one caused the other.

The Carolinas

South Carolina was a restoration colony. After Charles II became king, he rewarded some of his supporters with charters for colonies in the New World. Carolina was named after the king from the Latin form for Charles—Carolus. The eight recipients of the charter planned to use The Fundamental Constitutions, which was an experimental plan for government written mainly by John Locke. It guaranteed religious freedom but authorized the establishment of the Church of England. It also created an aristocratic ruling class. The theory never became reality.

By 1680, a colony settled in the present site of Charleston. Some settlers came from New England but more came from Barbados. They brought the slave plantation system with them. Rather than tobacco, they grew rice and indigo. They still required a lot of cheap labor. They settled on slavery. Some French Huguenots added to the population. They quickly assimilated to the ways of the English planters. Some drifted down from Virginia and Maryland, and a number of the Scotch-Irish would find their way to South Carolina as they flowed down the Appalachian valleys.

North Carolina was initially included in the same charter but it became clear that this older settlement had already started in a different direction. The first English colony of Roanoke had been established in the North, though it had disappeared long before the settlement of Jamestown. Other settlements dated back to 1650 in a colony first known as Albemarle. By 1691, they officially took the name of North Carolina with the founding of permanent colonies by those who moved down from Virginia. The Fundamental Constitutions worked about as well there, and in 1719, the Lords Proprietors formally surrendered their charter, and North Carolina became an independent royal colony. They too had a slave labor based plantation system in the tidewater areas. Many of what historians call the yeomen farmers moved to the Piedmont and even the mountainous regions. Generally speaking, North Carolina had some planters but was more back-country middle and lower class while South Carolina had some back-country settlements but was dominated by the tidewater planters. The poor were drawn to the frontier regions where they had hopes of acquiring their own land, or at least squatting on the land that belonged to speculators or Indians.

Georgia

Georgia was founded for the purpose of providing a buffer between Carolina and Spanish Florida and as a depository for the increasing London poor created by the Industrial Revolution. Despite earlier attempts, it was not until 1732 that the crown approved a charter granting the Board of Trustees a twenty-one-year lease. The next year 115 settlers led by James Oglethorpe laid out the town of Savannah. The first settlers consisted of artisans, tradespeople, and some of the poor. They were supplemented by Scottish and German settlers. The trustees tried to prevent Georgia from duplicating the tobacco colonies or the Carolinas by restricting exotic crops and slavery. With the expiration of the original charter, the new royal charter relaxed these restrictions. The colonists believed this necessary to compete with Carolina, and the prosperity that followed the changes suggests they were right. The population increased from five thousand in 1750 to twenty-three thousand in 1770. By the eighteenth century, an increasing number of Enlightenment-era Europeans questioned the morality of slavery. However, it was clearly profitable for the British capitalists in the colonies.

Non-English Colonies

Florida had become part of the British Empire after the French and Indian War but would be returned to Spain with the acceptance of the independence of the other colonies. Though St. Augustine was the oldest European city in the present United States, it remained a small settlement. The tourist appeal of South Florida would not dawn until the twentieth century, so the alligators and gars would continue to rule until then. Attempts to expand the colony failed. They never proved a threat to the English in Georgia, much less the Carolinas.

The Spanish took control of Louisiana after the French and Indian War and thus added their influence to what is one of America's favorite cities today. When the Spanish took command, New Orleans had only 9,500 people, and the majority of them were slaves. The warm climate spurred the growth of profitable exotic crops, and like the rest of such colonies in the New World, the French and Spanish turned to slaves to fill the demand for cheap labor. Slavery in Louisiana did have a slightly different flavor than in those colonies founded by the English. Those who love to hate the Anglo-Saxons seem to feel that the Spanish and French system was more humane. It is clear that there were more opportunities for free blacks, and the large Creole population indicates that they had a more relaxed attitude toward the mixing of the races. However, I should point out that the term "Creole" in Louisiana does not have the same mixed blood implications that it does in other American colonies, such as the Caribbean.

The far western limits of the South were part of Spain and stayed that way until the independence of Mexico in 1822. New Spain did not rely on slave labor as much as other American colonies, though there was a small black population. The new country of Mexico never did have slavery. When the territory became part of the United States, the only ones that could be found in Texas had been introduced by the Americans. Of course, their heavier economic dependence on cattle instead of crops such as sugar, rice, or tobacco did not make slavery as appealing. New Mexico and Texas had some white settlers, but most of the Northern parts of New Spain were still occupied by the native population. Slaves were mainly in the coastal regions or dribbled over the border near Arkansas or Louisiana.

"Public Square, St. Augustine, Florida." One of many cities throughout
the South that was of Spanish origin. (Courtesy National Archives)

"La Ciudad de Santa Fe." Though founded as Spanish, the colonies in
New Mexico and Texas would become part of the South. They varied
considerably from those in Florida. (Courtesy National Archives)

Some Eighteenth-century Developments

By 1700, most of the colonies had been well-established, and most of the Southern colonies had grown to depend on slave labor. By 1763, the planters controlled the tidewater and the middle class or small farmers dominated in the Piedmont regions. The Scotch-Irish, Germans, and assortment of others moved into the Appalachian valleys and even began to overflow into the interior. That, in fact, is what sparked the French and Indian War. On one hand, the class barriers were clear; but on the other hand, mobility was quite possible. Many of the Scotch-Irish became middle-class farmers also known as yeoman farmers. A few of these yeoman farmers even became wealthy planters, such as the families of John C. Calhoun and Andrew Jackson.

Americans like to think that our predecessors came here for freedom. The reality is that the majority of them came for land or other economic opportunity. By 1700, they had learned the greatest profits could be made in planting, and like other capitalists, the most could be made off the sweat of others. They settled on slave labor, and the system escalated in the eighteenth century. As stated earlier, only ten thousand slaves had been brought in by 1700, but the number would increase to 390,000 by the next century. Those colonies which formed the United States were only 5.4 percent of the total number of slaves taken from Africa to the Americas.

Few have failed to see a contradiction in the fact that Thomas Jefferson wrote "all men are created equal" while slaves worked his fields. Edmond S. Morgan saw the growth of slavery as an explanation for the growth of democracy in the Southern colonies. In eighteenth century England, the ownership of property was one of the requirements to participate in the running of the society. The theory was that only those who owned an economic interest in the society could or should make decisions on the governing of that society. Since so many came to America to get land, they earned with it the right to participate in the selection of their leaders. This was true in the Northern and Southern colonies. However, there was still a significant number of landless poor. In the North, these people made up the lower rungs of the social ladder, whereas in the South, they had slaves to fill the lower ranks. Even the poor whites had a greater confidence in their place in society so that they felt that they were as good as any other white man. That is the theory anyway. When historians talk of democracy in America, we talk of Jeffersonian democracy or Jacksonian democracy. These men who became adjectives for American democracy were not only Southerners but Southern slave owners. Morgan's explanation for the contradiction does seem to make the most sense and is generally accepted by the Librevs.

By 1763, the colonies, both North and South, had firmly established councils which they used to govern themselves. The British government left them to their own devices except for the brief period when they tried to create the Dominion of New England. That collapsed with the Glorious Revolution of 1688. The mercantilist economic theory that they operated under viewed the colonies as a source of raw materials. London seemed more interested in keeping the raw materials flowing than in dominating the colonies. William and Mary pushed patriotism as a way to keep the colonists performing their function in the empire. It would not be until after 1763 that the British would again attempt to subjugate the colonists.

The Great Awakening of the eighteenth century was a religious revival that greatly impacted the common man. The preachers came from their ranks and not from the universities or clerical establishment. More protestant sects came into being or increased in size as people drifted from the ranks of the more established and institutional churches. They even began the process of making the slaves Christians. This no doubt had a long-term affect on the attitude toward slavery. As the white men accepted the blacks into Christianity, it is only natural for more and more people to see them as children of God. It would be a logical step to think it wrong to enslave one's brothers and sisters in Christ.

There were some other side effects of the Great Awakening that helped to lay the foundation for the movement toward independence. The first is that as the preachers traveled up and down the colonies, as well as to England, and thus they established more communication with each other. This would be important as the subject of discussion changed from religion to politics. Another side effect of the Great Awakening is that the people began to show less deference to their superiors. It began with the religious leaders, and in time, it spread to political leaders or aristocracy. More and more of the common people refused to accept other men as their superior just because of their birth or greater wealth. Some would believe it when Thomas Jefferson declared all men equal.

As the population grew and the colonists traveled North and South throughout the colonies, they began to feel a bond with each other that was not felt with their fellow Englishmen. The fact is that in the late colonial and into the early Federalist period, the regional differences did not go from North to South as much as from coastal to back country. The middle-class farmer in Virginia might have more in common with his counterpart in Pennsylvania, whereas the wealthy planter in South Carolina would have more in common with the wealthy merchant in Boston. No doubt the wealthy of all colonies would be more educated and thus more familiar with the Enlightenment ideas that flowed from England, France, and Germany. I have little doubt that the interest of the middle and lower classes revolved more around land or business than ideas. The growth of democratic thinking no doubt helped to inspire them, but I doubt if they cared all that much about the subjects of discussion in the Enlightenment coffee houses. As today, the wealthy have more time to spend on intellectualism while the poor and middle classes expend more of the energy on supporting their families.

Summary of Librev Myths

There are two main issues in the colonial period in which I take exception with the liberal revisionist historians and others who are overly critical of Southerners. I should clarify that there are some of them who would agree with me and that I am speaking in generalizations. The first is that many believe Southern distinctiveness to be a relatively recent development. The second is that the symbols of the South, especially the Confederate battle flag, represent a culture that was morally inferior to the North.

I realize that we have much in common with those in the North and that in fact we still have much in common with those in the old country. However, the colonists in the South, for the most part, came from different regions of the British Isles. Once they arrived here, they had a different purpose. Whereas the Puritans wanted to build a "city on the hill," those in the Southern colonies wanted land. Those in the North had small family farms, those in the South developed a plantation economy. Those in the North were mostly middle class who divided themselves between saints and nonsaints. Those in the South quickly developed class distinctions with the main groups being planters, middle-class farmers, servants, and slaves. They started off different from those in the North, and the gap widened with each passing generation.

When I speak of Northerners above, I am thinking of New England; those in the middle colonies were different even though they were considered the North in 1861. The people in New York, New Jersey, and Pennsylvania did not have the Puritan background of those in New England. Some had plantations but with the exception of a few areas, such as the Hudson Valley, they did not depend on slavery as much as those to the south. Many of the later arrivals such as the Germans, Scottish, and Scotch-Irish moved on down the Appalachian migratory path so that a large number of Southerners have ancestors that first arrived in the middle colonies. Generally speaking, the people in these states would tend to be more sympathetic to the Confederacy, and even those dedicated to the Union would be less intolerant than their fellow countrymen from New England.

Obviously, the main reason liberals believe the Southerners to have lower standards of morality is because of the fact that they owned slaves. I cannot think of anyone that I know who would endorse slavery today. Slavery was something that has existed since the beginning of history in many different parts of the world. With the Enlightenment, more and more Europeans began to condemn slavery so that by the mid-twentieth century, it has been banned throughout the world. The morality that different cultures live under is defined for them by their codes of law or their religion. In the days that our ancestors owned slaves, both law and their religion told them it was right. This is not true today. Those in the North led the way in this change, but it appears to have been as much a matter of economics as morality. They did not have the same demand for cheap labor than those in the South had at a time in world history when slavery was practiced.

Summary of American History Myths in Colonial America

The acceptance of some common myths in American history can get in the way of us defending our culture. I repeat that one of our biggest problems today is the fact that many of our own people are fully reconstructed and therefore patriotic Americans first, and thus defensive of the propaganda interpretations of United States history. The view of so many of our detractors is that the Northern conquest of the South was part of the process of making the United States the greatest country in the world. First, the United States was not started with any great design. Like the rest of history, ours is the result of generations of struggle between those seeking their own self-interest. Our forefathers did not conquer a wilderness, they conquered the land that belonged to Indians. Some came for religious reasons, like the Puritans who wanted to build their "city on a hill," but most came for land. They did not come to build a democracy. Western European democratic theory is something that came out of the Enlightenment. The English colonists brought it with them from Europe or, like their countrymen back in England, kept up with the latest political and economic developments going on at home. There was no grand design and certainly not one that involved the abolition of slavery.

A very important myth is the idea that America developed a classless society. England had classes before the founding of the colonies, and they brought their classes to America with them even though they did not adopt the aristocratic titles. Those of the Northern colonies were no less class conscious than those of the South even though they tended to have a greater percentage of middle class. They even had slaves in the colonial period. The main difference is that they did not develop a plantation economy that created greater demands for cheap labor.

The colonists came to America because they were part of the British Empire. They worked for the building of that empire and, from their first days, continued to conquer land from the first inhabitants. We will see that the colonies continued to expand until they declared independence from the motherland and that their propensity for territorial expansion did not diminish with the founding of the United States of America.

CHAPTER TWO
Birth of a Nation (1754–1789)

Introduction

There are a number of themes, issues, or assumptions during this time period important to understanding Southern history. First of all is the development of an American identity; none really existed before 1754. Second, we must remember the basic assumption of Adam Smith and the concept of capitalism; people do what they do out of self-interest. Third, we will find that the question of states' rights came with the creation of the United States. In fact, when the colonists declared independence from England, they were taking the same stand as those who believe in states' rights—localism versus centralism. Fourth, we will find that class has played a very important part in our history. We Americans seem to avoid or ignore the question of class, and as a result, we miss some major issues in the development of our nation and of our Southern identity. Fifth is the role of black Southerners which is very much intertwined with the class issue. The biggest difference between North and South is the fact that the South turned to slavery as a source for cheap labor whereas most of the rest of western civilization created a working class out of their own people. The growth of the world-market economy created more rich people, which in turn meant more people who depend on the labor of others to generate that wealth. The sixth issue I will focus on is the rise of Southern identity. The Librevs claim that Southern identity did not really exist until after the Civil War. Even if this is true, the origins of Southern culture predate American culture even though it is not called that. I am of course referring to the Celtic fringe theory of Grady McWhiney. The seventh issue that I feel is important to clarify is that the rise of democracy was not an American thing. It started in Europe, developed with the Enlightenment, and did not truly exist until the twentieth century. The reason it is important to understand this is that we Americans have often justified what we do on the grounds that it is all in the name of democracy and the American way. This has included the Yankee conquest of the South. The Yankees have justified their conquest of our native land on the grounds that it is they who were the torch bearers of democracy and the American way. The Librevs seem to have taken up the torch and added diversity to the battle cry. They assume that the North had to conduct their war and conquer the South so that we can have the racial equality we have today.

The State of Great Britain in 1754

Between 1754 and 1789, the people who had been part of the British Empire created a new nation and with it a new identity—Americans. Most of those living in the colonies, at least most of those who had a say in the colonies, had come from the British Isles. However, by the mid-eighteenth century, it had been several generations since they or their ancestors had left. During that time, things had changed in both Europe and America. The United States today, despite the population that has different ancestral origins, is still predominately a European culture. We use the term "western" to include countries like America, which are basically European even though we are not on that continent. We must remember that when we speak of modernization, we are talking specifically about progress in western civilization. This is especially important when we are talking about those who are not of European origin. We tend to think of these people accepting modernization when in fact we are talking about their accepting western civilization. Many of the more important aspects of modernization arose between 1607 and 1754. In other words, they came about or were rapidly expanded at the same time the colonies were becoming established. This includes nationalism, world-market economy, and many new ideas associated with what we call the Enlightenment. The Enlightenment ideas include capitalism, the development of economics, and the origins of democracy. Our belief in American exceptionalism has often led us to look at things as being American when in fact they are European. They developed in Europe and continued to do so on a more or less parallel path.

In the mid-eighteenth century, England had become the dominant power in the world-market economy. Like France, they trailed behind the Spanish and Portuguese in the beginning of the first true world market. After a series of world wars, they came out on top. This climaxed with the French and Indian war, also called the Seven Years' War in Europe. In this last contest not only did the British come out on top over the French, but the cost of empire also led to the conflict between London and the colonies.

The Rise of Nationalism

States' rights is the same thing as localism, which is the opposite of centralism. Centralism is a belief in a strong central government, which gives rise to nationalism. It is important for us to understand the development of nationalism if we want to intelligently discuss states' rights. Prior to the creation of nations, we had a world where most people identified with their local community. People living in the British Isles thought of themselves as being from York or Chester or Devonshire rather than being English. Do not forget that Great Britain included the Irish, Scottish, and Welsh as well as the English. The common people looked to the local gentry to solve their problems and had little concern for global issues. This is localism. The increase in the world-market economy produced a class of people who needed protection for their business activities, both within Great Britain and in other parts of the world. This resulted in a demand for the growth of the central government and of the militaristic capability to protect the merchants. The success of the British Empire hinged on their ability to create a powerful navy, which protected British merchants and built the British Empire.

This has helped to create a major conflict that has existed between not only the countrymen that the merchants wanted to dominate but also those in other cultures who became the victims of British imperialism. This is also known as centralism versus localism. Business benefits from a strong central government so that those who want to maximize profits are the supporters of centralism. The price of this strong central government is individual and community freedom. Common sense dictates that the larger the group, the greater the diversity. The greater the diversity, the less likely we will agree with each other. We are forced to make compromise for the sake of unity. We are forced to surrender our local identity for the sake of a national identity.

This conflict can appear on many levels. When the white men first arrived, the Indians profited from the exchange of goods and ideas. Some Indians favored getting along with the white men. Others realized that they were losing their culture. These were the ones more likely to fight the Europeans. This has been the case since the beginning of European expansion and conquest. It has been true in the Americas, Africa, and Asia. It is as true today as it was in 1492. European civilization still tries to dominate as much of the globe as possible. The need to dominate is motivated by the desire for greater profits. Some of the conquered want to participate in the profits while others are more interested in preserving their way of life.

The tricky part for us Southerners comes when we realize that this is true for the population within the South. The issues that separated North and South also divided the Southern population. In the beginning, the division between those who supported a strong central government and those who opposed it was more between the wealthy coastal dwellers and the common people found mainly on the frontiers. As I approach discussion of the War for Southern Independence and the period of Reconstruction and the concept of the New South as well as Southern populism, we will see that the conflict is between those who have money and those who don't. After the Civil War and before World War II, most Americans with money were Yankees. Those Southerners with money have often been willing to sacrifice our history and heritage for a license to participate in American capitalism and the American empire. The most successful strategy the politically correct have used to get Confederate symbols removed is to point out that their display could be bad for business.

It is important to understand that when the North won the war, it was a big step toward centralism. Since it is the North that won, it is the Southern culture that has been sacrificed for the sake of unity. Today there are those who want to suppress what is left of our Southern identity so that we might have a stronger American identity. Unfortunately many of our Southern people are contributing to the destruction of our culture as they swell with American pride and patriotism.

The Rise of Democracy

Many Americans foster the myth that democracy came with the birth and development of the United States. This has become the justification we have used for territorial expansion. Today this type of thinking is probably even more popular in the South than the nation as a whole. This is the main reason that I say that the biggest problem we have in preserving our Southern heritage is that many of our Southern people have become American again and are willing to sacrifice our past for the sake of American unity. What the liberals have done is taken this myth of American democracy and made the Civil War an important part of the progression. It was the United States and Abraham Lincoln who freed the slaves by defeating the rebels. They have also linked this war to the end of slavery and the ideal of America of diversity. The Northerners view themselves as the defenders of nonwhite Americans and continue to be such today. The neoconservative Southern Republicans of today feel a twinge when they hear this but offer much less resistance than the Southerners of the past. Unlike our ancestors in 1861, they are American first and Southerners second. Those of us who are unreconstructed continue to be Southerners first.

The truth of the matter is that democracy grew out of the Enlightenment, which means that it began in Europe, not America. By 1754, Britain had gone through their own civil war in the mid-seventeenth century as well as the Glorious Revolution of 1688. Since the days of the first colonies, the people of England had beheaded a king, created the New Model Army, diminished the power of the Church of England, and expanded the power of Parliament. Not only did they talk about government by contract, but some even pushed for redistribution of wealth.

The English Civil War ended with the restoration of the monarchy but not without establishing that the king ruled with their consent. It also demonstrated why some claim that the rise of democracy is directly connected with the protestant reformation. At first, the Church of England differed little from the Catholic Church. Henry VIII just wanted to divorce his wife and, in fact, had previously written a book defending the Catholic Church. The Puritans, who took over England during the Civil War, wanted to eliminate the Catholicism that remained, especially the hierarchy. Bishops remain in the Anglican Church today. However, as time passed, more of the British chose alternative churches. Rejection of the church hierarchy made it easier to reject the governmental hierarchy.

The Glorious Revolution not only ended with a more powerful Parliament but produced the two-party system. The two-party system did not begin in America. As it became obvious that Charles II would be succeeded by his brother James, the members of Parliament became more concerned with the fact that James was a Catholic. The Whigs were those who favored exclusion of James from the throne while the Tories defended James. The issue came to a head with the birth of James's son. They feared the establishment of a Catholic dynasty. With the removal of James and the seating of William and Mary on the throne, Parliament also passed a law that prevented the king from dissolving their sessions at will. Prior to the Revolution of 1688, the only real power Parliament had was the power of taxation. The king did not have to call them into session if he could do without increased taxes. Now Parliament became a branch of the government that the king could not dissolve at will.

This was still not democracy since Parliament represented the merchants. Voting was restricted to property owners, and of course, women could not vote. Nonetheless many of the advances we associated with modernization began during the colonial period. The scientific revolution followed by the Enlightenment led to industrialization, capitalism, democracy, and later, even socialism. Of course, we must not lose sight of the fact that these are all developments in European civilization.

The important thing to remember relating to Southern history is that these advances came about prior to 1776. The Americans became part of the movement, and the new thinking helped to bring about the move for independence, but they began in England and were brought to America. This means that they were no more Northern than Southern, and in fact, Southerners had just as much to do with the creation of the United States and the later rise of democracy as Northerners. It could even be argued that they had more of an influence. This would mean that the idea that the United States had to defeat the Confederate States for the sake of the ideals we believe in today could not be true. These ideals would be better described as Enlightenment ideals rather than either American or British, much less Northern or Southern.

Population Growth

Perhaps the most important variable related to the changes in America in the eighteenth century is the fact that the population continued to grow. Much of it was natural population growth. Even in those days, people practiced birth control, although it was based on economic factors rather than any concept of planned parenthood. The western part of Europe had a nuclear family culture even in the Middle Ages. This created the economic need to be able to provide a home and sustenance before one could establish and expand their family. Most of the colonists had gone to America for the prospect of getting land. This not only would provide a home but, since many were still farmers, it would also be the way they would provide for their families. The colonists had land, they had hope, and they were optimistic about the future. They popped out kids like Pez dispensers. One of the reasons Samuel Johnson did not like Americans is that he calculated that the way the population was growing in the colonies, they would soon exceed the population back in Great Britain.

Immigration into the colonies also continued at a good pace. The majority of them did not have enough money to buy the higher-priced lands along the coast, either North or South, and so would tend to head west in search of more affordable lands. This included the Scots-Irish, an American term to describe those of Scottish ancestry who had lived in Northern Ireland for one or more generations. Because of rebellion in Scotland, many came directly from Scotland. It is hard for historians to determine the exact numbers of each since the main way we have of telling their influence on American population growth is the Scottish surnames. The Germans continued to pour in too and likewise headed west and then south.

Most of the immigrants landed in Philadelphia, the main port of entry in the eighteenth century, and then moved into western Pennsylvania.

As that land filled up, they migrated down the Appalachian valleys to the South all the way to Georgia. This helps to give credence to the Cracker Culture thesis of McWhiney who claimed that the South was primarily a Celtic culture. The South picked up a large number of these Scottish, as well as German and some others, but this meant that the frontier culture of America was also heavily influenced by the Celtic culture.

The slave population also had a significant natural population growth. This was a major difference in the slave system in British North America as compared to other colonies. Most of the Sugar Islands of the Caribbean, whether French, Spanish, or Dutch, had a tendency to buy slaves with the idea that they would work for five to ten years and then die. This, combined with the importation of few women, limited the natural population growth in those colonies. This meant that they had to depend on the continued importation of additional slaves. As the slave trade and eventually slavery itself became abolished in America, all the colonies and future independent countries would eventually depend on natural population growth. In British North America, this had started by the eighteenth century and would become truer after the United States abolished the slave trade in 1808.

This continued population growth in the colonies meant that there would be more and more pressure for territorial expansion. This would mean a growing invasion of Indian lands. After 1763, the British government tried to limit this, but once the British were eliminated in 1783, the days of the Indians in America became limited. Think about it: up to 1783, most of the British colonists were restricted to lands east of the Appalachians. By 1850, a mere sixty-seven years, California was admitted as a state.

Don't Forget the Non-Anglos

There are significant portions of the South that existed before the establishment of the United States, which became incorporated into the South with American expansion. Not only are these areas an example of Southern diversity but also a reason why some Southerners would have been resistant to domination of the central government. Remember what I said earlier: the more diversity, the more we have to sacrifice for unity. The stronger the central government, the more we have to sacrifice for unity. A less centralized government would allow for the preservation of diverse cultures including the non-Anglo cultures. In other words, states' rights actually fostered diversity.

The least populated of the non Anglo South was Florida. In 1760, they had about three thousand settlers, mostly Hispanic but some African. As early as 1740, Governor Oglethorpe of Georgia tried to evict the Spanish from Florida. Though not successful, most of the Spanish, as well as their slaves and some Christian Indians left Florida with the end of the French and Indian War when Spain turned the land over the Britain.

In 1760, Texas had about 1,200 Spaniards and New Mexico had another 9,000. They would continue to be part of New Spain but eventually be absorbed into the South. Louisiana had the largest population with four thousand whites, mostly French, and another five thousand Africans. They were turned over to Spain in 1763 and would be absorbed by the United States, along with some of the Spanish that came with the 1803 Louisiana Purchase. These numbers seem small, but remember, at the same time, South Carolina and Georgia had only forty-five thousand whites and fifty thousand blacks.

The Myth of Why They Came

As a historian, one of the most irksome things I hear is when people claim that America was established by those seeking religious freedom, equality, democracy, or other such patriotic rhetoric. Some people came to America for other reasons, but the vast majority came to make their fortune. This is an important point since I believe that the subjugation of the Southern people was not over a morality issue but rather economic and political power. If we are going to understand the motivation they had for what they did after they got here, then we need to accept the motivation they had for coming in the first place. Land was still highly prized. Most of the land in England belonged to the gentry. Land is what the colonies had plenty of. This is what allowed them to participate in the running of the government. Some of the younger sons of the gentry acquired large grants and thus became aristocracy in the New World. The "middling" sort acquired more land than they could back in England. The poor had little hope of becoming property owners in England. They had at least some hope of getting their own land in America. Though many failed to achieve this goal, in the colonies, some were successful. One of the main reasons that we have this myth of democracy as something American is that more people were able to vote in the colonies because more people became property owners. The increased opportunity to own land meant an increase in those who could participate in governing the land since the owning or property was a prerequisite for voting.

As they settled the land, the wealthy acquired the prime real estate near the coastal ports while the middle class and poor were forced to move west. This of course fueled the expansion of the colonies, and later the United States, as the white people took more and more land from the Indians. This was the driving force in American expansion. The way it was done also created a class division, which was also a regional division. Those in the coastal areas tended to be wealthier than those on the frontier.

The Rise of the Common Man

Much of the conflict that took place in England and the colonies was between the gentry and the common people. With the expansion of enlightenment thinking, the commoners seemed to be more and more confident in demanding more say. In the colonies, much of this appears to be a conflict between the frontier and the coastal areas since it was mostly the commoners on the frontier. Some of these conflicts arose before the start of the Revolution. With the war, some felt that their interest lay with the planters fighting against the king, but others believed that the colonial aristocrats were their enemy. Many of those who did not see it as a class struggle in 1776 would realize it after 1783. The most famous examples of this in the pre-Revolution South is what we call today the regulator movements. Historians have not always agreed on what degree of these conflicts was class related, but it is clear that the commoners and/or frontiersmen demanded concessions from the aristocracy.

In North Carolina, six thousand western farmers demanded confirmation of land titles and an end to the speculators' monopoly of the best land. Remember, their main objective was to get land. The movement began in 1766 and climaxed in 1771, when the government sent the eastern militia. They were met at Alamance Creek by two thousand Regulators who were dispersed. Nine were killed on each side, many wounded, and six Regulators were hanged for treason. In addition to their concerns about land, they had demanded a secret ballot so as to end the influence of the rich. They wanted adequate representation and wanted the government to provide more protection from the outlaws that ravaged the frontier settlements. They also complained about the high taxes collected by the local sheriffs who had been appointed by the colonial governor.

The South Carolina Regulators were somewhat different. However, they too wanted more fair representation for the country folk and protection from frontier robbers. In 1768, the assembly did give the back country more representation and permitted the crown to dictate the terms of judicial appointments. Despite the class differences when the Revolution came, the former Regulators supported the local gentry against the English rulers. This suggests that they saw their fellow Americans as having more of the same interest even if they were rich.

The main point I wish to make is that not only was it clear that three distinct classes existed in the South, but that at times this also resulted in violence. The rich ruled and generally showed little interest in the welfare of the common people. The middle class were property owners. Some would struggle to become rich themselves while others simply wanted to have the independence to support their families. The poor were the outcast and some of them ravaged the countryside in both North and South Carolina. They would steal horses and cattle; destroy property; and sometimes torture and kill their victims. They were mostly "propertyless" whites and some free blacks and escaped slaves. The Regulators were mostly the middle class whites who resorted to vigilante justice when the government failed to protect them. They wanted to enforce morality as well as the law. They captured and whipped suspected felons; took some to jail; and evicted others from the colony. In other words, the middle class despised the tyranny of the wealthy and the lawlessness of the poor.

The French and Indian War

The French and Indian War, the fourth in a series of world wars, became a turning point in colonial history. Before 1754, no one seriously considered the possibility of independence from England. They were Englishmen, and many fostered patriotic feelings of being part of the empire. The changes that came about because of the war led to the declaration of independence.

The first three world wars began in Europe; this one started in the colonies. This also demonstrates how the colonists were part of empire and that they depended on London for protection. It is also an example of the importance of the colonialist greed for land. The Ohio Company of Virginia made plans to sell land near the present site of Pittsburgh in 1749. The French constructed forts to stop the incursion of the Anglo-American traders and Virginia land speculators. In 1754, the governor of Virginia sent a militia officer, George Washington, to construct forts to defend their interest. The 160 colonists under Washington's command lost to the French and their Indian allies. This sparked the fighting which, in 1756, escalated into the Seven Years' War.

There is evidence that, in the beginning, the colonists had no interest in being independent though they jealously defended their local interest. In 1754, seven of the colonies sent delegates to Albany, New York. They were able to negotiate an alliance with the Iroquois when most of the other Indians saw a greater advantage in backing the French. It was then that Benjamin Franklin came up with his plan for a unified defense. His proposal was not at all anti-British. It did call for an intracolonial government empowered to tax, pass laws, and supervise military defense. Even though the delegates supported the plan, not one of the colonial assemblies passed it. It is clear that as of 1754, most of the colonists did not want to abandon their individual colonial rights, a principle the Southerners would continue to defend in the name of states' rights.

It is also clear that they depended on London for protection from the French as well as the Indians. By 1756, the French had penetrated into New England and dominated in the West. The tide changed after the British statesman William Pitt took command of the war effort. He poured British money and men into America, though he did expect support from the colonial legislatures. Success was achieved in 1763, with the French being forced out of North America.

There are three significant aspect of the war that would lead to conflict between the colonists and London, and which would end with the creation of the United States. First, the four world wars of the late seventeenth and early eighteenth centuries left the British the most powerful empire in the world. However, they began to feel the financial burden of empire. They would turn to the colonies to help pay the tab. Second, with the French gone, the colonists did not feel the need for protection of the British Army and Navy. They still hungered for the Indian lands to the west, but the British army ended up becoming the ones who prevented them from taking what they wanted. The third thing is something a little less obvious and also more difficult to document. The colonists had a greater exposure to their cousins from Europe, and this helped them to realize how much they had grown apart. The informal colonial militia fought with the professional British infantry. It was about this time that the British established the first regular army, something that did not exist at the time colonists first sailed for the New World. The colonial militias saw the British regulars as immoral, profane men who needed to be controlled with brutal discipline. The colonists had developed an identity distinctive from their cousins back in the old country.

George Washington receiving French Generals at Mount Vernon.
Virginia aristocrats such as Washington played an important role in
the First War for Independence. (Courtesy National Archives)

Taxation without Representation

Historians still debate the nature and causes of the American Revolution. Many Europeans even laugh at the idea of calling it a revolution; it was in fact a war for colonial independence. The wealthy gentry who dominated the colonies in 1763 continued to dominate in the new United States. Where is the revolution? However, there are historians who still defend the idea that it was a social revolution in the long run. If we have any hope of understanding what happened, we need to recognize that the American history version of what happened has been based on what started out as radical rhetoric by those who promoted the idea of independence. It is true that the tax question is what upset many of the colonists. However, what the tax issue did is create a constitutional crisis which left many of the colonists feeling that the only solution would be independence. Some pushed for it from the start, but as things escalated, more and more went to the cause of independence.

The fact is that many people were involved, and they had varying reasons for becoming so; I have divided them into three main groups. We must remember that not everyone favored the movement, and those who eventually went to the side of the Whigs did so at differing stages. John Adams said one-third favored it, one-third opposed it, and one-third sat on the fence of indifference. The wealthy were the vanguard of the activities; they are the ones who paid the most taxes, and they were the ones more familiar with the enlightenment thinking that they used to justify their actions. The middle class had a lesser concern about the tax issues but had other economic concerns, specifically the acquisition of land. The poor also wanted land, and the red coats kept them from getting what they wanted.

A Constitutional Crisis

After the war, the British decided that the colonists should pay part of the cost of the empire. After all, this last of the four world wars began in America as the colonists attempted to expand into French and Indian territory. They tried various ways to raise the revenues, and we have all heard about the dreaded Sugar Act, Stamp Act, and Townsend Revenue Act. Most of us were raised on the radical interpretation that the king was a tyrant and that the colonists should not have taxation without representation. The fact is that the colonists averaged only one shilling per person in taxes while their countrymen back in England averaged twenty-six shillings per person. With the Stamp Act Greenville projected, the revenues would be about sixty thousand to one hundred thousand pounds, which would only be 20 percent of the expected military expense to protect the colonies. As to the tyrannical government of London, they reacted by repealing the taxes.

The crux of the constitutional crisis revolves around the issue of representation and role of the colonial assemblies. The colonists claimed that their various assemblies were their parliament and that only their parliament could tax them. They said they did not have any representation in the Parliament in London. The British said they had "virtual representation." They did not have direct representation like the United States Congress of today, but rather each member of Parliament represented every British subject, including the colonists. They understood that the colonists had to pay taxes to support their colonial governments, and no doubt, this is the main reason London never taxed them at the same rate they did those back in England. The British government clearly attempted to keep the colonists happy. However, when they repealed the Stamp Act, they also passed the Declaratory Act which affirmed the power of Parliament over the colonies. Ultimately, the attempts to avoid a constitutional crisis failed.

The Proclamation Line of 1763

I firmly believe that most historians underestimate the significance of the Proclamation Line of 1763 as a reason that many of the middle class and poor joined the cause for independence. My view is based on the assumption that the majority of those who came to the colonies came for the opportunity to get land. Many Librevs like to think that all the world's problems were caused by rich white males. When it comes to the conflict between white people and Indians, most of the problems were caused by the poor or middle-class white males. The rich had their plantations in the tidewater regions, and their struggles for personal empire ended well before the eighteenth century. By the time of the French and Indian War, most of the land in the thirteen colonies had been distributed or was still occupied by Indians. As the white population grew, the demand for new lands grew with it.

This is why most of the Indians sided with the French during the Seven Years' War. The French had a fur trading empire that did not require the white men to take possession of the land that the Indians had lived on for many generations. Many of the Frenchmen even took Indian wives. The English colonists were farmers and family men, and they valued the ownership of the land they lived on.

As the settlers flooded the Ohio Valley, many of the Delaware, Shawnees, and Iroquois rallied behind the Delaware prophet, Neolin. Neolin preached that the Indians must reject Christianity and European goods, particularly rum, and that they needed to revive their own Indian cultures. An Ottawa follower of Neolin led what has become known as Pontiac's War. The Indians ran low on ammunition and succumbed to smallpox. However, the British realized that further attempt to take Indian lands would lead to continued warfare. This is why they created the Proclamation Line of 1763, which forbid any of the English colonists to go west of the line that more or less followed the crest of the Appalachians. So now, not only did the common people not need protection from the French who were no longer there, but they began to see the redcoats as the ones prohibiting them from getting the plentiful western lands.

This problem affected those in the North as well as the South. In late 1763, a band of western Scots-Irish in Pennsylvania used violence to force the Quaker-dominated assembly to provide military protection. They murdered a number of Christian Indians at Conestoga then marched on to Philadelphia. By the time they arrived, the legislature passed a bill to raise a thousand troops to protect the West. Those in Pennsylvania realized they were underrepresented in the government, just as those in North and South Carolina did in the Regulator movements. The conflict developing in the colonies was a war between the frontiersmen and the coastal dwellers. This was also a class war as I explained above.

The South had the Cherokee War. Even though they suffered encroachments and abuses, the Cherokee remained allies of the British. In 1759, before the Proclamation Line, some Cherokee warriors returning home may have stolen some horses belonging to the white men. The colonists attacked and killed some of the Indians. The Indians knew what the white men wanted; when the Cherokee captured Fort Loudoun in eastern Tennessee, one of the conquering Cherokee stuffed the commander's mouth full of dirt and said, "Dog, since you are so hungry for land, eat your fill."

The fact is that the white settlers, North or South, wanted land and had no problem with killing the Indians to get it. It is also clear that the British government realized that this fostered conflict with the Indians which led to war, which in turn cost money to conduct. The government tried to stop them from taking land, and thus, the colonists began to see the British Army as a barrier, not as protectors.

The Poor and the Seeds of Democracy

We Americans like to think that the greatest thing about our country is that it has been a place where the common man could prosper alongside the aristocrat. Of course, many of our people deny that America had an aristocracy. This could not be further from the truth. Whether we are looking at the Boston merchants or the Virginia planters, the people with money ruled the land. The Enlightenment planted seeds of change, and the success of the Revolution fertilized these seeds. The rhetoric used to justify the move toward independence was taken to be reality by the people.

At first, the wealthy, even those descended from English aristocracy, did not posses great wealth. As the colonies grew and prospered, their wealth grew too. Many had come from the rising "middling sort" of the seventeenth and eighteenth century, but they soon realized that their self-interest now resided with the aristocracy. Rather than a demise of aristocracy, there was merely a change. The reality of capitalism is that the really wealthy are those who can benefit and profit from the labor of others. More and more Northerners began to criticize the Southern slave owners, but they too needed labor in their mills and factories. As of the late seventeenth century, the Northern demand for cheap labor was not as great as that of the planters. After the Civil War, their need for cheap labor would increase. They would find another way to meet the demand.

In this period between the end of the French and Indian War and the end of the Revolution, there is considerable evidence of a change among the common people, especially the poor. I have already discussed the rise of the common man; in this period, deference continued to decline, and the concept of democracy continued to be more inclusive. The growing middle class tended to see themselves as the successful people of the future; the poor saw themselves as those being denied the promise of the colonies. The belief in equality expanded. This included the growing working class of the Northern and middle colonies, the landless and poor whites of the South and frontier, as well as the slaves. This is why some historians have seen this as a true revolution.

In 1766, in Charleston, 1,400 seamen and a group of black slaves threatened serious disorder. The sailors had problems getting released because their ships had not paid for the stamp tax. Some slaves followed their example of disorder and marched through the streets shouting, "Liberty!" The city prepared itself for slave revolt and had enough concern that they restricted slave imports for three years.

On October 4, 1779, armed members of the Philadelphia militia met at Burn's Tavern, planning to capture and exile from the city four suspected Tories. All four of the accused Tories were wealthy, and rumors spread that the militia planned to arrest others, about thirty "gentlemen." The so-called "Fort Wilson Incident" worried Whigs too because the lower class patriots had directed armed force against the Whig elite as well as the accused Tories. Henry Laurens of South Carolina stated, "We are at this moment on a precipice, and what I have long dreaded and often intimated to my friends, seems to be breaking forth—a convulsion among the people."

This growing rejection of deference to the wealthy continued throughout most of the states of the United States after the Revolution. The South Carolina incident between William Thompson, a tavern keeper, and former governor John Rutledge serves as an example of how the wealthy considered themselves above others and, at the same time, demonstrates the increasing rejection of deference among the common people. Thompson claimed that Rutledge "conceived me his inferior." Thompson was a former officer of the Revolutionary Army and asked for no more that the respect he deserved. He called himself "a wretch of no higher rank in the Commonwealth than that of Common-Citizen."

Not only did Thompson fail to act deferentially, but he also assaulted the citadel of deferential government. The common man took the revolutionary rhetoric as reality. After the war, the number of wealthy men in the Virginia Assembly declined by half. The same happened in Maryland and South Carolina. With the end of the Anglican Church in America, the aristocracy lost a valuable crutch. Democracy and the rise of the common man were on the way.

Terrorism and the Beginning of the War

The situation began to spin out of control as the colonists turned more toward terrorist tactics. In the Boston Massacre, an unruly mob was fired on, and five men were killed. The radicals such as John Hancock and Paul Revere exploited the situation as much as possible, even though the British government launched an investigation and put the soldiers on trial. Two were convicted of manslaughter and the rest acquitted with the help of their attorney, John Adams. It seems that a true tyrant would not have had an investigation and trial.

In the Boston Tea Party, the colonists destroyed a shipment of tea. The British government, like the United States government of today, could not tolerate such an act of destruction. They passed a series of Coercive Acts, mainly aimed at the city of Boston, trying to get them to pay for the damage. The colonists responded by forming the First Continental Congress to find a course of action to what they labeled the "Intolerable Acts."

In April of 1775, the British Army landed in Boston Harbor and marched toward the villages of Lexington and Concord in search of arms that they suspected would be used against the forces of law and order. The shot heard around the world was fired at Lexington on April 19, and by time they went to Concord and returned to Boston, the insurgents left seventy-three dead and two hundred wounded or missing, and the colonists counted forty-nine dead and forty-three wounded or missing.

The Second Continental Congress met in Philadelphia on May 10, 1775, but it would be more than a year before they would take the step of declaring independence on July 4, 1776. The British objective was to restore control over the colonies while not yielding to acts of violence and rebellion. The colonists increasingly felt they were being invaded, and as things progressed, no doubt more and more moved toward the cause of independence. In other words, more and more moved toward the cause of localism over centralism.

The War

At first, the British efforts were centered on the North. After all, that is where the trouble started. They invaded and occupied New York and Philadelphia. When George Washington was picked as their general in May of 1775, the Virginian commanded an army that was basically made up of New Englanders. There were victories on both sides, but the British could not put down the rebellion. In February of 1778, the Americans forged an alliance with France, and most historians agree that this was a major turning point toward success in their bid for independence.

The Indians played an important part on the frontier from New York to Georgia. Though some sided with the Americans and others remained neutral, most supported the British. For the Indians, it was not a matter of which side was right; it was a question of what outcome would be most beneficial to the future of the Indians. Just as they recognized the British colonists as more invasive than French, they realized that the British government was a force to prevent the colonists from taking more of their land. For various reasons, the neutral and Whig Indians suffered almost as much as those who had supported the British, such as the Mahicans of western Massachusetts who had supported the American army. When they returned home, they found that whites had taken over their land.

The British turned their strategy to the South in 1778, having become convinced that there were many more loyalists there. So many had suffered because of the Indians and outlaws that some petitioned the king for protection with a promise of loyalty. The British captured Savannah and Augusta, Georgia, in 1778 and by 1780 controlled the coast up to Charleston, South Carolina. The invasion helped to turn more of the Southerners to the Whig cause. The British army was stretched so thin they could not protect the loyalists. The Tories aggravated the situation as they turned to plunder and revenge. Banastre

Tarleton's Tory Legion executed prisoners of war and destroyed houses and fields, leaving many homeless. By the time that the British moved on the interior in 1780, the Americans were able to achieve victory at King's Mountain and Cowpens. Even though the British General Cornwallis won the Battle of Guildford Courthouse on March 15, 1781, his supplies were so low that he had to reach supply lines on the coast. He then turned north, and the fighting stopped after being defeated by Washington at Yorktown in October of 1781.

Colonel William Augustine Washington at the Battle of Cowpens.
The success on the Southern front paved the way for recognition of
independence by the British. (Courtesy National Archives)

African-Americans in the War

It is amusing that the Librevs most often reject the idea that blacks would have supported the Confederacy, yet they go out of their way to show how many had fought for the American cause during the Revolution. No doubt this is due to political correctness. On one hand, they don't want to show any support for the Confederacy while on the other hand, they want to talk about the contributions made by black Americans. The fact is that the British promised the slaves freedom for those who supported the king. The Union in 1861 did not even let blacks join their all-white army, much less promise them freedom.

In 1775, blacks made up 20 percent of the 2.5 million people living in the colonies. Most were Southern slaves, but free blacks lived in the North and the South. Lord Dunmore, royal governor of Virginia, declared "all indented servants, Negroes, or others" who would support the king would be free. The American planters considered this foul play and assumed that the objective was to generate slave rebellion. Many of the blacks took advantage of the offer, and no doubt, their knowledge of the countryside gave the British some assistance. The rumors spread among the slave population and many began to "believe that their freedom depended on the success of the king's troops."

In contrast, black support for the Revolution received little welcome. Boston excluded slaves or even free blacks from participating. As it became more difficult to achieve their recruiting quotas, many Northerners accepted blacks. In Virginia, some masters sent their slaves as substitutes. An estimated five thousand blacks served in the Continental Army and state militias or at sea on American ships. At the end of their service, many of the slaves who fought received their freedom.

When talking about the Indians or African-Americans, we must remember the principle of self-interest. The Indians were not motivated by the same issues as either the British or the colonists. They tried to determine which would benefit them the most. Likewise, the blacks, free or slave, had to decide which would be best for them. Of course, don't forget the element of risk. What happens if the side they choose loses? Don't forget the element of opportunity. How many of the slaves really had a choice? How much did they know about what was happening, and could they really do much? This no doubt explains why most did not fight for either the Whigs or the Tories. The bottom line is that it is not logical that so many Librevs can promote the idea that blacks fought for the American side in 1776 but refuse to accept that some freely chose to fight for the side of the Confederacy in 1861. The planters and slave owners of 1861 were Americans in 1776.

The surrender of Cornwallis in Virginia marked the end of hostilities with the British, though it would take some time before the final treaty was worked out. (Courtesy National Archives)

The Articles of Confederation

States' rights would be a continuing issue dividing the population because of the fact that the new government of the United States was very weak. The name tells us a lot about the situation—our nation does not really have a name like most others. It is simply called the United States of America. This is the root of the issue that was not resolved until 1865 and lingered to a lesser degree after that. Does this new government have power over the individual states of America that had united to fight for a common cause—independence from London and the king?

In the beginning, it was not a matter of North versus South but the general question of centralism versus localism that existed among the modern western peoples. Remember, nationalism came about with the rise of capitalism as the best way to protect modern business in the European quest to dominate the world markets. The wealthy merchant who had interest in business activities beyond his local community would have more of an interest in seeing a central government which could protect him. The common man had few concerns outside his local market. This is why the Federalist Alexander Hamilton did not want to see political power in the hands of the common man.

In many ways, Alexander Hamilton was the founding father of the modern United States. He was the major spokesman for those who wanted the see the new nation industrialize and become an active competitor in the world markets. He accurately understood that to be successful, they would need a strong central government. Since he believed the common man could never comprehend this, the aristocrats should be the movers and shakers. Not only did he become the spokesman for a strong central government, but he also became the leading opponent to democracy. As the North became more industrialized, they would have a greater interest in the world markets and thus more of an interest in a strong central government.

Thomas Jefferson represented the other side. In many ways, the main controversy among the founders of the United States could be summed up by the conflict between these two men. Jefferson did represent an element of modernization but not the business side that Hamilton seemed most obsessed with. Jefferson was concerned about the Enlightenment ideals of human rights, democracy, and personal freedoms. He pictured an idyllic nation of farmers armed with certain rights. He believed that the best government was that which governed least. He became the defender of states' rights as well as personal rights.

The Constitution

There were two main variables that convinced many of the new nation that the central government needed to be stronger. The first and most important was undoubtedly economics. This not only meant the capability of the government to pay its bills but also to create the best opportunity for Americans to compete in the world markets. The second is related to the first—the ability for Americans to protect themselves. For the wealthy, this included protection abroad. The first American military engagement outside of the United States was the attack against the North African pirates who had made a living out of demanding ransoms from European ships. No farmer in Tennessee could have much of an interest in this. The common American, especially those in the South and West, would want protection from the Indians as they encroached deeper into Indian lands. They had little concern about something across the ocean. The wealthy merchant involved in the world markets would be the most concerned about something like the barberry pirates of North Africa. There has been recent research that did claim that the common American did want to do something about the abduction of their fellow countrymen, and thus supported the war.

Once it was determined that they would create a new document of guidance rather than simply revise the Articles of Confederation, the biggest issue was how to see that all states had fair representation in the central government. For those with large populations such as New York or Virginia, this meant that representation should be based on population. Smaller states had feelings of equality regardless of how many people they had. This was resolved with the Great Compromise. In the upper house and the Senate, all would be equal. In the lower house representation would be based on population.

After finding resolution to this, as well as a number of lesser problems, such as how the slave population should be counted for representation purposes, the Constitution was ratified and went into effect in 1789 with George Washington elected as first president. Let us not forget that consent was not unanimous among the people. The split was not so much along regional lines as it was along the frontier versus the coastal areas. The fact that the South ratified the Constitution means that they accepted the sacrifice of states' rights which came with its adoption. Keep in mind that those along the coastal counties from Boston to Charleston were dominated by the older wealthier families. Those on the frontier were the poor and middle classes who, for the most part, had not yet made their fortunes. Obviously, the wealthy coastal dwellers would be more interested in the world markets and would thus benefit the most from a strong central government. To understand the South as well as the North, it is necessary to recognize the class differences in America.

Please note that this document did not create a democratic nation. Alexander Hamilton, one of the Northern Federalist most responsible for the Constitution, said "It has been observed that a pure democracy, if it were practicable, would be the most perfect government. Experience has proved that no position is more false than this." He added, "The ancient democracies in which the people themselves deliberated never possessed one good feature of government. Their very character was tyranny: their figure deformity." He made this speech on June 21, 1788, to endorse the Constitution. He obviously did not see this document as one that made the United States a democracy. I see this as an important point because of the fact that the Librevs like to see the War of Southern Independence as something created by the planters and that the common Southerner was not so much in favor of it. I will discuss this issue in more detail later. The point I wish to make now is that in 1789, it was still the aristocracy, North and South, which ran the country. I have already discussed the conflict between the rich and common men, and as I proceed, I will talk of the rise of democracy. These are trends in the entire United States, not just in the South. In fact, the Librevs seem to accept the idea that democracy rose in the South.

Unresolved Issues

There were a number of issues that remained unresolved, some because they seemed insignificant and others simply a classic case of agreeing to disagree. First would be the amount and type of taxation. The poor rebelled when their lands were confiscated for taxes or when they had to pay too much for whiskey tax. Chronic problems arose related to tariffs. The North had more manufacturers who wanted American industry to be protected by tariffs. The South had more consumers who wanted limited tariffs.

A matter of little concern in 1787 which would increase over time is the question of internal improvements. This would include turnpikes, canals, and later, railroads. Of most concern would be those passing through two or more states. What would the role of the central government be in the development of these important links of trade? Southerners tended to view internal improvements as something that benefitted the Northern states.

The most serious problem would become even greater over time and would be the most important variable that would lead to the division between the states. How would the new territories be administered? From the beginning, the new country had this problem to deal with since the British had recognized that land north of the Ohio River and south of the Great Lakes as part of the United States. Under the

Articles of Confederation, the land ordinances of 1785 and 1787 had extinguished claims to this land by the various states and set up the system by which it would be surveyed, distributed, and determined how they could become new states. Nonetheless, controversy would grow as the regional differences over slavery grew so that it was not slavery but rather the status of slavery in the territories that would lead to the formation of the Republican Party after the Mexican War. For the Northwest Territory, this question was resolved by the prohibition of slavery in any of the territory. However, future expansion would revive this issue.

African-Americans

The most obvious contradictions to the principles that we boast of in our pride to be American is that Thomas Jefferson, the man who immortalized the words "All people are created equal," was able to spend time philosophizing because he had slaves doing his work at home. It seems logical to conclude from this fact that he did not consider the slaves people. When the patriots and founders of America spoke of equality and rights, they were speaking of propertied white males. These are the only ones who could vote, the theory being that these are the people who owned an interest in the society. They were like stockholders. This is the main reason I have pointed out that our country was not founded on any principle of democracy. The nation was founded by propertied men, and it was designed to be ran by such men. They ignored women, Indians, poor whites, and the slaves. This also shows how our nation had classes. The founders, Northern or Southern, did not think in terms of the all-inclusive, nondiscriminatory democracy that we have today, or at least strive to have.

There are those who expanded the Enlightenment thinking, along with some of the basic philosophy of Christianity, and began to see some inconsistencies in the spirit of this new democratic thinking and the reality by which it was being applied. Jesus did not make distinctions between people based on class, race, or the color of their skin. This no doubt was the logic behind the eleventh-century papal decision which had eliminated slavery in Europe in the first place. By the eighteenth century, more and more people began to condemn the slave trade and eventually slavery. I have little doubt that the reason more did not join in the antislavery campaign is that too much money was being made in what was an effective solution to a major economic problem for capitalist to this day, a good source for cheap labor. I have no doubt that the planters who participated in the founding of America had their morality clouded by profits.

The nonslave owning Americans, which was the majority of the population, were largely influenced by racism. Most Europeans of the time assumed that white people were superior to people of color. They were more intelligent and were believers in the true God. This included those in the North and back in Europe as well as Southerners. That is simply the way things were in those days. There were a few exceptions, such as the Quakers, but most believed in white superiority.

The Quakers were the first to take steps toward doing something about it. They began by condemning the owning of slaves among their own members, but even then, it took some time to convince all of them. In 1780, Pennsylvania passed laws to eliminate slavery in that colony. Massachusetts followed in 1783, Connecticut and Rhode Island in 1784, and later Vermont and New Hampshire. New York did not introduce a gradual abolition until 1799 and New Jersey in 1804.

Southerners profited most directly from slavery since they owned the plantations worked by the slaves. Nonetheless, there were many Southerners of the day who questioned the morality of slavery. Patrick Henry wrote, "Would anyone believe that I am Master of Slaves of my own purchase! I am drawn along by ye general inconvenience of living without them, I will not, I cannot justify it." He admitted that he depended on the profit even though he cannot justify it. He also pointed out that he inherited the system. Thomas Jefferson blamed the king in an earlier draft of the Declaration of Independence. There are numerous examples of Southerners who freed their slaves so that by 1860 about 10 percent of the black population was free, half of those in the South.

What about the African-Americans themselves? Is there anyone who would prefer slavery over freedom? Then there is no reason to believe that the black men and women on the plantations of America would have or that they were happy with their lot in life. I have read numerous accounts of their experience by those who were slaves. I have seen those who admitted that, in some ways, it was better times since they did not have to worry about having a home or food on the table. But few of us would be willing to sacrifice our freedom for security. Any choice about whether to fight for the Whigs or the Tories during the Revolution was no doubt based on what they believed offered the best opportunity for them to gain their freedom. They had other variables to consider, but I have no doubt that this was the number one factor.

On one hand, I see that it is necessary for us to put aside the notion that the slaves were happy in their servitude. To insist on this is to jeopardize our credibility. On the other hand, I do not believe that the Southerners should be singled out for their racism since most people were racist at that time. Rational people do not think that way today, however, Southerners did not create this attitude. They were victims of their age. They profited the most from slavery because fate had given them a plantation economy that demanded a cheap labor force. It was whites of an earlier age that chose to meet that demand with slavery. The quotes are numerous from Southerners who felt that their inheritance was more of a curse than a blessing. I firmly believe that in time they would have condemned the institution, as those before them and after them did.

Conclusions

The period between 1754 and 1789 was a time of great change, but my focus is on those which had the greatest impact on Southern history. The most important is the rise of American identity. After the French and Indian War, the British government tried to raise taxes, which led to the events that produced a constitutional crisis. The colonists of the eighteenth century did not live in a dictatorship, they lived in a land of laws. They also lived at a time when the Enlightenment thinking generated beliefs in equality and democracy. The move toward independence started because of taxes but was fueled by the principle of self-interest. The colonists increasingly felt that their interest could be better served if they were on their own. There were also feelings of being different from their kinsmen back in England. The wealthy merchant may have been concerned about the taxes. However, the poor and middle class simply resented the fact that the king would not allow him to take the Indian's land.

The Librevs like to point out that Southern identity is something new, and in some ways, they are right. If American identity did not exist before the Revolution, it is logical to think that Southern identity also increased during their struggle for independence. However, there were cultural roots that went back to before the founding of the colonies. Grady McWhiney pointed out the Celtic influences in the South and that thus the differences between Anglo-Saxon and Celtic Britons were carried across the Atlantic to the colonies. They started out different, and after arriving in the colonies, the gap only widened. Perhaps the greatest contribution to the difference between North and South in this period is that Thomas Jefferson became the spokesman for the concept of states' rights, and over time, Southerners would increasingly be associated with this belief even though there are numerous examples of Northerners defending localism.

At first, states' rights were more of a class issue than a regional one. States' rights is another way to say localism. In the early days of the United States, localism was supported more by the common people, who were most often people on the frontier. When we look at the breakdown of the way the voting went on ratification of the Constitution, we see more of a split between the frontier and the coastal areas than between North and South. I will later show that over time, states' rights became more Southern, and many Southerners tended to look at Thomas Jefferson as the most important of the founding fathers. With growing industrialization, those in the North became more and more in agreement with the principles of Alexander Hamilton or a strong central government, mainly for the sake of their business enterprises.

African-Americans were Southerners too. They were dominated and controlled by white Southern society, so there is no reason to doubt the statement that Southern culture influenced them. There is no doubt in my mind that they had influence on Southern culture. We must not be tempted to fall into the old trap of thinking that they were happy being slaves. The Librevs like to recognize the contributions blacks as well as other non-Anglos have made to American culture, and this is a good thing. But we must not go to the other extreme of thinking that Southerners were evil and that this justifies the extermination of their culture. It is true that the Northern states passed laws against slavery before Southern states did. This does not mean they were culturally or morally superior. They did not profit from slavery as directly, and so the condemnation of slavery was easier to do. We will see in future chapters that most Northerners did not want to abolish slavery, and many of those who did wanted to send them back to Africa. They were racist too and did not want the freed slaves living in their communities. We will find that they did not vote for Lincoln and the Republicans to abolish slavery, but rather to stop the spread of slavery into the territories.

CHAPTER THREE

Early Constitutional United States (1789–1848)

Introduction

Nationalism was only beginning during the early days of the United States. The fact is that a national identity of any kind was vague at best. Apparently, many did not have a strong British identity, which is why they could sever their ties. Most had the greatest bonds with their respective states. There are some quotes from the founders of the United States that do indicate some similarities existed among the Southern states. However, when we look at the split over the ratification of the Constitution, we see more of a class divide than regional. Obviously, the North and South found that they had enough in common that they joined together to declare independence from England and to form a new nation. It is equally obvious that the main reason for joining together was for the sake of a military alliance; it was the only chance that they had for success. It would also be logical to assume that they had more in common with each other than either region did with the mother country. We must remember that the persistent issue of localism versus centralism revolves around individual perception. Unification occurs when those unifying have perceptions of commonality. Disunion occurs when the individuals see some of their fellow citizens as foreigners. During the period between 1789 and 1845, the gap between North and South widened so that by 1845, it became obvious to some that the South would have a difficult time maintaining equality in the newly created nation. This chapter deals with some of the changes.

The United States grew economically, geographically, and in population. Economic opportunity abounded for people in all regions of the rapidly growing country. After a brief period of Federalist rule, Thomas Jefferson and his Republicans, predominantly Southerners, seized control, and it appeared that their dream of America would be the way of the future. The Federalist Party faded away. However, those who wanted the United States to be a nation of business that would actively compete in the world markets did not go away. During the period covered by this chapter, most of them found a new voice with the Whig Party. In the next chapter, we will see that the Northern businessmen, or Northern Whigs, will band together in the Republican Party. What happened to the Southerners who had ambition to find economic success in the world markets?

On the eve of the Mexican War, the sun would be setting on Southern domination of the central government. The Librevs have identified slavery as the catalyst for disunion. On this, they are correct; I will discuss this subject further in the next chapter. Meanwhile, it was clear that even before the war began that the North was growing in population and as a result would be able to seize control of the federal government. Those of the South, especially the planter class, would begin to realize that such trends had all but solidified. During the war, both Union and Confederates would claim that it was "a rich man's war and a poor man's fight." They were both correct. The growing gap between North and South began with the upper classes. Do not be misled into thinking that all rich white Southerners supported the Whigs. Only those who comprehended their role in the world market embraced the Whig philosophy. Some planters remained with the Democrats. As long as the Southern businessmen saw future economic success with the Union, they were Whigs. As the perception of Northern aggression increased, Southerners rejected the Whig Party, which contributed to its collapse. The Northern businessmen turned to the Republicans. This left Southerners with the Democratic Party—the party which had been founded for the common man.

Federalist

The support for the Constitution came from those who expected to benefit the most from the world markets. They were called Federalist. Ironically, the common man is just as much a part of the world markets as the successful businessman, whether they understand this or not. Those who wanted the central government comprehended that they would be in a better position to compete in the world market if their government was stronger. Some of the Jeffersonian purists may have understood this too, but they feared the loss of personal liberty as part of the price tag for economic success. This is what separated Yankees from Southerners. The historical fact is that Alexander Hamilton and his Federalists supported the Constitution. Thomas Jefferson and the anti-Federalist opposed the Constitution. A myth has grown around the belief that the Federalists were Northern and the anti-Federalist were Southern. A more accurate distribution would be that the centralist businessmen supported the Constitution, and the localist and those most interested in protecting their rights opposed it. Many of the common people, North or South, also opposed it. Like today, many fear and despise being dominated by rich guys. In other words, the common people tended to be localist. This is what Hamilton did not like about them.

Though both sides talked about the preservation of liberty, it is clear by the programs proposed by Hamilton that the real issues were economic. The first step in his plan would be the federal assumption of state debts. Economic strength lies in good credit, which can only be achieved if all the states enjoy good credit. A national bank would be necessary to maintain economic strength. This would produce a major political issue as the Americans debated the Bank of the United States. Hamilton saw the future in manufacturing. Only by joining the Industrial Revolution could American business compete in the world market. Tariffs would not only provide a source for national revenue but would be beneficial in the protection of domestic manufacturing. More merchants, shippers, financiers, and manufacturers came from the North; and thus, there would be more support for the Constitution from that region.

The fact that the South ratified the Constitution tells us that support for a strong central government was not restricted to the North. George Washington did much to lend support to the notion of a stronger central government. The fact is that the planters had ruled the Southern colonies and that, for many years to come, they would dominate in the Southern states. The early nineteenth century would see a growth in the power of the common man, what historians would call Jacksonian democracy. However, the planters would retain power and influence that far outstripped their meager numbers. Washington was one of this class. Most of these men were educated and had at the least a basic understanding of the growing field of economics. Adam Smith published his *Wealth of Nations* in the same year that the United States began. The capitalism that Smith wrote about is the only thing that has been a part of this country since its founding. The planters were just as much a part of American business and the world market as the Northern manufacturer. The South remained predominantly agricultural until the twentieth century. However, the planters were agricultural in the same way as the million-acre farms of California are agricultural today. Their contribution to the world economy was the growing of products for the market; products such as tobacco, rice, indigo, sugar, and later, cotton.

Thomas Jefferson and his Republicans have become regarded as the founders of Southern states' rights and the opponents of centralism. His dream for America, at least the South, would be a nation of farmers. He had seen the Industrial Revolution of Paris and London and had no desire for manufacturing to come to his country. Jefferson loved to putter around Monticello and develop his plans on how to improve productivity. He also loved to philosophize on things like the rights of man, government by contract, and other Enlightenment ideas that stood against the forces of tyranny. Jefferson and his Republicans lived in fear that the Federalists were the enemy of his ideal America.

The great contradiction is that these Southern idealists would end up cultivating American democracy while supporting themselves with American slavery. I have already mentioned the book by Edmond S. Morgan, *American Slavery, American Freedom*. Almost every school child has noticed and wondered about the contradiction. One of the founding fathers wrote "All men are created equal," but he and many of the others were slave owners. This did not prevent them from absorbing the patriotic rhetoric fed to them by their teachers.

Just as there were those in the South who favored a strong central government, the North also had a class of people who defended localism, though they did not often refer to is as states' rights the way Southerners would. Anytime they believed their Northern values were threatened, they too spoke of nullification and even of secession. The first such talk came from New Englanders who resented Southern domination.

Another theme I will cover throughout this book is the conflict between rich and poor. I am writing about Southern history, but this division exists in the North too. The New Englander maintained a more homogeneous population because of the common puritan background. Whenever I talk of New England, I am usually speaking of the puritan elite, not the working-class immigrants or others who happen to live in New England. In the North, it is the small farmer, Puritan or not, or the beginnings of a working class who more often opposed a strong central government.

The George Washington Years

George Washington was a Southern planter and a believer in the principles of the Constitution and thus became a great unifier for the new nation. If any other man had become the first president, perhaps the nation would not have survived the difficult first decade. Southerners have always been proud to claim Washington as one of their own, but the fact is they do not or never have looked to him as the defender of states' rights the way they have regarded Jefferson.

Washington was a military hero and was "first in the hearts of his countrymen." He was well aware of the party differences around him; and in fact, when he left office, he warned Americans of the dangers of political parties. He apparently felt that some difference existed between North and South as he kept a balance between the two regions in his cabinet. Most historians would agree that he had Federalist sympathies, but he made an effort to appear nonpartisan.

Progress was made during the Washington administration for both the Federalists and the Republicans. Hamilton got his financial plan of funding and assumption of debt. However, in return, a site in the South was chosen for the national capital. Hamilton got his Bank of the United States, and Jefferson got his Bill of Rights.

The Federalist Blow It in the First Round

The election of 1796 reflected a pattern that can still be seen in elections today. The Federalists represented the forces of centralism, and their support came primarily from New England and the North.

The Republicans represented the forces of localism, and most of their support came from the South and the West. Nonetheless, the Federalist made some advances in the South in the election of 1798 and 1799, even in Virginia. In 1799, the old dominion state sent eight Federalists and eleven Republicans to Congress. Adams appealed to the Southern Federalists when he avoided being drawn into war with France. However, he blew it when he attempted to stifle descent.

In 1798, Congress pushed through the Naturalization Act, Alien Act, and Sedition Act. The Federalists wanted to limit immigration because of a fear that they helped the Republicans more in election time. The Sedition Act made it a crime to attack government officials. This was no mere bluff. Government lawyers prosecuted Republicans, especially newspapermen, and Federalist judges sent them to jail. In the process, Jefferson and James Madison established another precedent for Southern politicians; they advocated the notion of nullification. Madison wrote resolutions to the Virginia state legislature proclaiming the Alien and Sedition Acts unconstitutional and stressing states' rights. Jefferson took a similar position for the state of Kentucky, thus making the states' rights issue a Western thing as well as a Southern thing. They both took the position that the states could nullify laws passed by the federal government that were deemed to be unconstitutional by the states. This helped to solidify Jefferson's association with the issue of states' rights.

The South Takes Command

Southern Federalist did not disappear with the election of 1800. However, the Republicans won fifty-three of the region's sixty-three electoral votes. Nationally, Jefferson, the Republican presidential candidate, won by only eight votes since New England remained solid Federalists. The Republicans gained some support from the central states with New York giving Jefferson all twelve of their votes, and Pennsylvania contributed eight of its fifteen electoral votes. There would be many times in American history that Southerners would find some support from the central states. The greatest conflict between North and South would be focused in the differences between New England and the Deep South.

The South, the West, and Nationalism

All three regions in the original thirteen states would contribute to western expansion. However, Southern influence would prove to be greater. No doubt the plantation economy increased the Southern demand for land which would send more people from that region over the mountains. This helped to cement a bond between the South and the West. Historians tend to overlook a powerful variable that every genealogist is well aware of—the familial bond. Those from New England had the greatest influence on the Northern tier of new states and territories while those from the Southern states pushed westward in the southern tier, preferring those lands with a long growing season. Those from the central states could go either direction.

The Land Ordinance of 1787 kept slavery out of the Northwest Territory. However, this did not bother Southerners much since most of this land had limited growing seasons. Slave owners found new land in Kentucky and Tennessee and later in Mississippi and Alabama. Thomas Jefferson gave them more territory with the acquisition of the Louisiana in 1803. It would be the Mexican War that would generate the final point of contention in the contest for regional expansion.

The Republican success in the elections of the early nineteenth century, along with the Louisiana Purchase, helped to instill in Southerners a sense of nationalism. They began to become more and more aggressive in the territorial ambitions and, in fact, had dreams that never materialized such as the acquisition of Cuba, Mexico, and other Latin American and such Sunbelt locations. In the early nineteenth century, the drive for territorial expansion of the United States came from the South. The North was critical of expansion and the militarism that was part of it.

Southern Factions

Three distinct groups developed among the Southern ruling class. The most conservative called themselves the tertium quids. They felt that Jefferson did not live up to the principles of the Kentucky and Virginia resolves. They were led by John Randolph of Roanoke and

Nathaniel Macon of North Carolina. They called on Republicans to never desert the principles that had given birth to their party: local power, small government, and a just fear of the executive. They became symbolic of those Southern planters that lacked the more pragmatic American philosophy. No doubt they would be like those romantic planters that viewed themselves as the vestiges of Southern aristocracy. A step above everyone else, they saw themselves as the defenders of honor and nobility.

Henry Clay would be typical of those Southerners who wanted to see their region participate in the Hamiltonian dream of American leadership in the world markets. Clay began his life in Virginia but moved to the West at an early age. He married into a prominent family and became a planter and slave owner. He was one of those men who tried to become president on many occasions but never succeeded. Though he did not remain with the Whig Party, he was typical of those who facilitated American business regardless of the region they came from.

John C. Calhoun was with a Scotch-Irish background. However, his family became wealthy planters. He is evidence that refutes the view of the planter as the defender of an aristocratic past. He had risen in social class and ran his plantation more like modern agribusiness. He was also one of those rare people who could see into the future by using logic rather that any clairvoyant ability. He seemed to be motivated by regional economic competition rather than romanticized defense of feudalism. He never lived to see Southern independence. However, he realized that the North was growing, and even though the South dominated the federal government most of his lifetime, he knew that her days of glory would be limited.

The Situation in France, England, etc.

Americans could not find complete isolation. The European affairs continued to impact their own in two main ways. First, European powers maintained colonial interest in America, which would put them in direct conflict. Second, the wars that resulted from the French Revolution and subsequent European expansion would interfere with the American desire to conduct free trade. The French Revolution added a philosophical tint to the situation.

The Federalists tended to support the French loyalists on the idea that it is they who had helped the colonies to achieve independence; the Republicans defended the Enlightenment principles of the revolutionaries. Both parties tried to prevent the United States from the entanglement in European alliances, which Jefferson warned us of. In 1798, the Adams administration conducted a quasi war with the French while Jefferson resorted to peaceful persuasion with his Embargo Act.

Despite American isolationism, the European wars threatened the new nation. Napoleon was no doubt motivated to sell Louisiana to Americans to keep it out of the hands of the English or other European rivals. Even though the French were gone, other European powers remained in America. Spain would be a potential threat from either Florida or the West. The British continued to occupy Canada and the Pacific Northwest.

The War of 1812 and Northern Resistance

In 1860, Northerners would be willing to kill Southerners rather than allow them to go their own way in peace; they seem to have forgotten that the first serious discussions of secession came from the New England states. These days, we often think of war protestors as unpatriotic; the fact is that for every war this country fought, a significant segment of the population objected to it. There would be times when those of the North disagreed with the war path, other times Southerner's would not agree. Despite claiming that they represented states' rights in the early nineteenth century, it is the South that led the way in American nationalism. They wanted to see the country expand and therefore supported the wars of the time. It is primarily opposition to American expansion that led the Northern states to threaten secession.

The first bid came following the Louisiana Purchase of 1803. New England Federalists feared that the addition of new western states would diminish the power of the Federalists since westerners seemed to have a preference for the Jeffersonian philosophy. The plan known as the Essex Junto began in Massachusetts. A group of the most extreme Federalists concluded that the only hope for New England would be to form a Northern Confederacy. They believed that it could succeed only if joined by New York and New Jersey. They turned to Alexander Hamilton for leadership who condemned "dismemberment of our empire." He went on to say that it would be "a clear sacrifice of great positive advantages without any counterbalancing good, administering no relief from our real disease, which is democracy." After that, the group turned to Aaron Burr, who ran for governor of New York. Hamilton, like many others, believed Burr supported the move for independence. It was Hamilton's accusations of treason which led to the famous duel between the two men. Burr fled to the West, where he got involved in another plot to carve a new nation out of United States territory; meanwhile the New England movement faded into the pages of history. This would be forgotten by the New Englanders who labeled Southerners "rebels" and "traitors" in the 1860s.

A second movement began again in Massachusetts and again sought New England independence; this time it would come about because of disagreements over the War of 1812. The governor of Massachusetts secretly contracted separate peace with the British. In late 1814, a group of Federalist organized the Hartford Convention and issued a report supporting the right of states to declare federal laws "unconstitutional." This was the same states' rights position laid down by Jefferson and Madison in the Virginia and Kentucky resolves. The list of demands made by this convention gives us a clear picture of the main disagreements developing between the North and South as of 1814. The only reference to slavery as a problem is the three-fifths rule, which counted the slave population in the distribution of congressmen. Other items on the list included a two-thirds majority in Congress to declare war and admit new states, a one-term limit on the president, and a ban on residents from the same state succeeding one another in the office. They also prohibited naturalized citizens from federal positions since most were Republicans. In fact, it would appear that their problems did not come from slavery but rather the fact that the South was dominating the federal government. This is a prime example of why I believe that the main cause for the Civil War and the bloodshed that came with Reconstruction is that the North seized control of the United States government, which had previously been in the hands of Southerners. The South preferred independence over submitting to Yankee domination. More on that to come.

Southern Power and Western Expansion and the Real Issue

Southerners needed land for their plantation economy, which led to territorial expansion and a trend toward Southern domination of the West. Clarification: the South would be more populous in the West. However, it is not until 1920 that more Americans lived in urban areas than rural areas. Industrialization and thus urbanization grew more rapidly in the North. However, in the early nineteenth century, the American dream for most still revolved around the family farm. In fact, it is the Northern desire for farmland that caused them to compete against Southerners for western domination.

Ironically, in the years after the War of 1812, Southerners seemed to abandon their desire for small government; no doubt this came about because of the fact that the South was gaining control of the central government. It seems that some Southerners did not object to nationalism and centralism as long as they were in control. Keep in mind too that just as some Northerners yearned for land, some Southerners recognized the benefits and the economic advantages of a strong central government. Southerners in the House voted in favor of the national bank at a two to one margin. The Quidlike objections based on doctrinal purity held little sway. Southerners did oppose tariffs and internal improvements, but it is clear that those in the South did not all adhere to the Jeffersonian ideal of remaining an agricultural nation.

The Southern resistance to the new nationalism was centered in Virginia, though not all Virginians shared their sentiments. They no longer went by the name of Quids. Thomas Ritchie, editor of the *Richmond Enquirer*, spoke for the new group known as the Richmond Junto. He warned his readers that the nationalist cause undermined the hallowed truths of the 1790s.

Jeffersonian traditionalists lost out in the South to the vigor of nationalism under Southern leadership of such men as Henry Clay and John C. Calhoun. These younger men had not been around for the debates in the 1790s, and the prosperity that came with western expansion strengthened Southern control of the central government. It became increasingly clear that the philosophical questions addressed by the traditionalists played second fiddle to regional economic competition. The reality is that most questions of war and peace, whether talking of the War of 1812 or of the Civil War, revolved around economic competition, and ideology was reduced to a propaganda tool. The South dominated in the early nineteenth century, and the growing strength led to the decline of Jeffersonian values. The regional conflict between 1789 and 1848 had much to do with economic competition and little to do with slavery.

"View of Main Street, Louisville, in 1846." Kentucky and Tennessee were only the beginning of Southern expansion in the West. From there, the Southern people would move into Missouri, Texas, Arkansas as well as points further west. (Courtesy National Archives)

Western Expansion and Slavery

The most important issue that separates those who condemn Southern and Confederate symbols from those who claim that they are merely part of our heritage is the assumption that the Confederate symbols represent a nation that was based on the defense of slavery. They then assume that slavery is morally wrong and that Southern icons represent something that should be condemned. Northern liberals, blacks blinded by NAACP rhetoric, and now Southern scallywags claim that the war was fought to free the slaves while Southerners have always claimed that the war was fought over states' rights. Part of the reason for this disagreement is failure to understand that the issue of slavery is what sparked the crises over states' rights. This led to Southern secession, which caused the Northerners to invade the South, determined to preserve Union economic control. Neither Republicans nor Abraham Lincoln spoke of abolishing slavery until the war had dragged on for many months, and it became increasingly clear that the war would not end until the entire nation abolished slavery. The issue that began the war was not the abolishment of slavery but rather the spread of slavery into the territories. What's more, the concern about the spread of slavery was based more on economic competition rather than morality.

I have never met a member of the Sons of Confederate Veterans or the United Daughters of the Confederacy who has endorsed the institution of slavery. People that idiotic have been restricted to the Jerry Springer Show and have entertainment value only. We need to be careful if we do not want to be dismissed as kooks. We must recognize that slavery did play a role in the Civil War. This is not the same thing as saying we accept the lie that Lincoln and the North invaded the South in order to end slavery and that thus all the murder and destruction of homes and other property was justified.

There were some who objected to slavery on moral grounds. However, I believe that most had objected to the spread of slavery into the territories for two other reasons. First, economic competition. They feared that they could not compete with the planter and his slave labor, and therefore if the planter went into the new lands, the small independent farmer would be shut out. Second, for racist reasons they preferred to keep black people out of the new lands, for the same reason they passed laws not allowing blacks to settle in parts of the North.

The first serious debate over the expansion of slavery in the territories came with the admission of Missouri as a state. The two regions had achieved peace by keeping a balance between the slave states and free states. This is itself an example of the power struggle between the North and the South. The admission of the new state as a slave state would jeopardize this balance. The question was resolved by the admission of Maine as a free state. However, before that, a congressman from New York named James Tallmadge proposed an amendment to the statehood bill. His proposal had two parts. First, no more slaves would be allowed to enter Missouri. Second, all slave children born after statehood would become free at age twenty-five. Like I said, the whole issue became mute with the Missouri Compromise of 1820 but not without beginning a national debate that would escalate after the Mexican War.

The Tallmadge Amendment sparked concern among Southern slave owners. First, they began a tradition of objecting to outside interference with slavery. Second, they did not want to see any barriers to the expansion of slavery. They knew that their domination in the federal government came with their growing strength in the West. Third, supporters of the amendment denounced slavery as an aberration in the United States or any nation dedicated to freedom and liberty. Their conclusion would be that the slave owners were immoral.

A curse that came with the Missouri Compromise was the restriction of slavery to South of 36°30'. This would be a major part of the debates that would rage after the Mexican War. We will see later that this issue of the expansion of slavery into the territories is what sparked the war.

The Jackson Era Conflicts

The years 1824 to 1840 reveal a conflict within Southern society. The period brought Jacksonian democracy, the Democratic Party, and the rise of the Whigs. Remember, Jackson was not only a Southerner but also a planter and a slave owner. I will discuss the various classes, ethnic diversity, the Indians, and slavery in separate sections; for now I will talk only about the political changes.

Jackson had more votes than any other candidate in the election of 1824, but too many candidates and political bargaining put John Quincy Adams in the White House. All the other candidates were Southerners, which only serves to support my previous claim that the period was fraught with conflict within the region. William Crawford was from Georgia but represented the Virginia dynasty. Henry Clay represented the West. John C. Calhoun, though he would later be associated with nullification, believed in a stronger central government. The only Northerner, Adams, wanted a stronger national government and supported internal improvements and a tariff to protect American industry. These other candidates and their supporters believed Jackson a potential military despot. Jackson won the election of 1828 with support from parts of New York, Pennsylvania, and parts of the former Northwest Territory. His support in the South was nothing less than impressive. He won in Alabama by more than eight to one, in Tennessee by twenty to one, and in Georgia he got 100 percent. Southerners believed that Jackson would deliver them from the evils of a strong central government, though they would later find that may have been an invalid assumption. New England was not totally Adams but did distinguish itself from the rest of the nation by offering him the greatest support. Remember this election when I later speak of the division between the rich and poor Southerners.

The biggest contest during the Jackson administration was the battle between him and South Carolinian Calhoun. The latter served as vice president during Jackson's first administration. However, some personal issues and the nullification crisis led to the selection of Martin Van Buren for the second term. Jackson sided with Peggy Eaton when the ladies of Washington rejected her while Mrs. Calhoun led the attacks. Jackson also found out that Calhoun had tried to get Jackson punished for his military aggressiveness in Florida following the Battle of New Orleans. These personal conflicts just fueled the main issue which centered on tariffs.

Jackson inherited the situation but was determined to enforce the tariff voted in before the presidential election of 1828. Calhoun became the leader of the South Carolinians who turned to the Virginia and Kentucky resolves for support in their nullification of the tariffs. Calhoun argued that the states had created the Union, and as creators, they were sovereign. He also said that the states gave the federal government only the particular powers specified in the Constitution and nothing more. Jackson took the same position that another Southerner, Abraham Lincoln, did in 1861; he threatened to use the United States military to enforce federal law. Calhoun and the South Carolinians backed down under this threat, but the question of states' rights would not go away.

Whigs, Southerners, and Economics

The support of economic growth is the connection between the Whig Party and the later Republican Party. The main support for the party came from those men who believed in American business and that a strong central government was necessary. What separated the two so that Southern Whigs could not support the party of Lincoln, is that fact that the Whigs catered to the planters and thus the slave owners as well as Northern businessmen. The common man in the South continued to look to the Democratic Party of their hero, Jackson. About three quarters of those in the South never owned a slave and so they would not have the same concerns as the planters. So why did many relate to the interest of the planter? Perhaps they hoped to become slave owners themselves someday. More likely, they might have feared the economic competition that would come with millions of freed black men.

When the Southern Whigs arrived at the national convention in Harrisburg, Pennsylvania, in December 1839, they supported the candidacy of Henry Clay. Clay had dumped his American system, which supported economic nationalism, and he advocated states' rights and condemned abolitionists. When Clay lost out to William Henry Harrison, the Southerners had no major problem. Harrison had become associated with Indiana. However, he was a native Virginian, and his father had been a signer of the Declaration of Independence. As a congressman, he supported the South during the Missouri crisis, and he too denounced abolition. His running mate was another states' rights Virginian, John Tyler. Harrison carried seven of the slave states and won more than half of the popular vote in the region.

Harrison died after the first month in office, and the first vice president turned president, John Tyler, took his place. Tyler seemed in many ways to carry on the conservative states' rights philosophy of Jefferson and the Quids. Soon, Whigs, including Southerners, did not consider him one of their own and especially after he opposed a national bank as unconstitutional. Southern Whigs broke with others from their region by adopting a policy of economic nationalism. They turned to Clay for leadership since this was the basic idea of his American System.

The Revisionists have been right in identifying the growing significance of slavery in the nineteenth century politics. Both the Democrats and the Whigs knew that they needed the support of Southerners if they hoped to win national elections. Calhoun was among the first to realize that if the population in the North continued to grow at a greater rate, it would be just a matter of time until a party might threaten slavery and win with Northern support only. Every revisionist is also well aware of the fact that the Republican Party did not rise by threatening the existence of slavery. Nonetheless, they still seem to admire Lincoln as the great emancipator. I will discuss this in more detail later; for now I wish only to make the point that the Whigs were not perceived to be a threat to slavery whereas the Republicans would be.

It is not easy to distinguish Southern Democrats from Southern Whigs. Both parties had a large number of planters and slave owners among their ranks. The Democrats tried to present their party as the one which advocated "equal suffrage." The Whigs responded by claiming that the Democrats kept the voters "laboring under tyranny and oppression." The best explanation for the regional divide is that the Whigs were more commercially oriented and lived in more commercially oriented towns and counties.

Ethnic Diversity and Regionalism

Part of the stereotype that justifies those who attack the South today as a bastion of racism is the fact that the region is less ethnically and racially diverse than the North. This is true today. However, at the time of the Civil War, this was not the case. The South was especially more diverse than the bastion of Northern righteousness, New England. In the first census of 1790, the country as a whole was 47.9 percent English. In New England, the percentage was eighty-two, and in the South, they were only 35.7 percent, less than the population with African ancestry. The Librevs like to refer to the central colonies as more diverse, but the Anglo-Saxon population in the mid-Atlantic region was slightly more than in the South with 36.9 percent. The central states had only 5.3 percent African population.

This is based on the 1790 census; by 1860, there was even greater diversity in the South compared to New England. Both regions removed Indians, one way or the other. However, many of those in the South married Indians. I have seen nothing to contradict that common claim of Indian blood for many with Southern ancestry. The records on the removals of Indians to present-day Oklahoma indicate a considerable number of mixed bloods. Significant areas of the South had an existing Hispanic population, which became absorbed into the future Confederate states including Florida, Alabama, Louisiana, and Texas. Let us not forget the French population of Louisiana as well as the number of Huguenots who immigrated into the South. Only one-third of the American Jewish population lived in the South, but I feel confident in claiming that the majority of the Northern Jews were not in New England. As to Southern bigotry, it is interesting to note that half of the Jews who held congressional seats came from the South. Please make note of the fact that the numbers are too small to have any statistical significance, but from the small sampling we have, the indication is that Jewish politicians found a greater acceptance among Southerners. It apparently was not a fluke that the first Jew to hold a cabinet post in America was with the Confederate States of America.

We are often misled by the popular boasting of America as the land of immigrants and diversity. The fact is that prior to 1830, there was very little immigration into the United States. Immigration increased between 1830 and 1860, but we are talking about virtually an all-European population. The English only accounted for 18 percent of the new Americans, but the rest also came from Northern Europe. This included 27 percent German, 43 percent Irish, and the remaining 12 percent from the rest of Northern Europe. With increased immigration, the North became more diverse, including New England.

The Celtic population was British, and so in some ways, it could be argued that those of Irish, Scottish, or Welsh backgrounds are not part of American diversity. Nonetheless, the Celtic population of New England in 1790 was only 11.9 percent compared to 21.8 percent of the South. The Central states had the highest with 24.6 percent, less than 3 percent more than the South. However, the common immigration pattern for the Scottish in the late seventeenth and early nineteenth century was to land at the port of Philadelphia, move west in search of affordable land, and as that filled up, they moved South through the Appalachian valleys in the direction of Georgia. From there they migrated west along with the older population. The Celtic fringe theory claims that the Celts were the dominant population in the South. These statistics suggest that they were not necessarily more numerous that the Anglo-Saxon. However, they may have been. The key word in the theory is "fringe." This means that many of those of English background came from the north or west of England and not the predominantly Anglo-Saxon southeast. Most of the New England puritans came from the southeastern parts of England.

The Northern Economy and Cheap Labor

The main defense of my Southern heritage is not based on denial of the fact that my ancestors were racist but rather that they were not any more racist than other Americans, or even other white people of the time. The condemnation of all things Southern, and especially Confederate, is based on the assumption that this region had slavery and that the Confederate nation existed for the preservation of slavery. The North, on the other hand, did not have slavery and even harbored the majority of the abolitionists who wanted to rid America of the evil institution. The conclusion of those at the vanguard of eradicating our Southern heritage do so on the assumption that the Northern way of life was morally superior and that they were right to kill our ancestors; burn their cities; destroy their crops; and leave millions dead, crippled, or homeless.

It is difficult to prove, as is usually the case when speaking of motivation; however, I firmly believe that the Northern choice for nonslave labor was more of an economic decision rather than an example of the moral superiority of the Northern people. In the colonial days, New England was a land of family farms, whereas the South began to develop a slave plantation economy. This was not due to any moral depravity of those settling in the South but rather that the climate of the Southern colonies was more comparable to the warm climate of the Caribbean islands, where the plantation slave economy thrived in other English colonies. The children of the prolific puritans met most of the labor demands of that population. New England had some slaves; they just did not need as many.

By 1840, New England businessmen began to construct manufacturing facilities, and naturally, the demand for labor increased. At first, their needs were satisfied by their own female population. Even back in the Middle Ages, young women had a time where they sought employment outside the family, often as domestic servants in the homes of the wealthy. They started when they were old enough to make a significant contribution and quit when they married and went off into their own family unit. Like most nuclear family cultures, they married at an older age, which means that they worked for several years. The first manufacturing plants in New England, such as the facility in Lowell, Massachusetts, were idyllic communities which were more humanely ran than those found in most European industrialized cities.

Between 1840 and 1860, manufacturing increased dramatically and with it the demand for cheap labor. By that time, the Northern businessmen found a source far superior to the slave labor of the wealthy Southern planters—the rapidly increasing immigrant population. There is no doubt it is the manufacturers who wanted to allow the increased immigration while the majority of the older American population wanted to stop them from coming in. They even formed a political party, the Know Nothing Party, whose main political platform was to put an end to the great influx of immigration. Whereas the manufacturer saw a source for labor, the rest of the population saw a threat to their way of life. On the lower end of the socioeconomic ladder, they thought of the Irish or Germans as competition for jobs and housing. For the more middle class, they saw a growing voting population that could steal elections. In the larger cities, the immigrants outnumbered the native population, and they even became a significant number in the state and national elections.

The Librevs helped us here because they will be the first to point out that the wealthy controlled America in the colonial period and continued to do so after the formation of the United States. This is why the immigrants continued to come in despite the objections of the more numerous lower and middle-class population. In 1840, manufactured goods in America stood at $483 million; by 1850, it was over $1 billion, and in 1860, it doubled again to $2 billion. In 1860, seventy-four thousand of the factories were in the Northeast, and they accounted for two-thirds of the output. Of the 1,311,000 American factory workers, 938,000 were employed in the mills and factories of New England and the mid-Atlantic states.

The growth in the immigrant labor force created a system in which the Southern planters could argue that their slaves were better off than the Northern workers. This was not just a rationalization of their labor system. Remember, Charles Dickens and Karl Marx made a living writing about the deplorable conditions of the nineteenth-century working class. It has been claimed that the American working class was better off than their counterpart in Europe, but nonetheless, most lived in flimsy shanties, in grim conditions that were hazardous to their health and that of their families. The slave owner offered healthcare for their slaves; the manufacturer just replaced a sick worker with a healthy one. The slave owner provided food and housing for their slaves even in the off season, whereas the factory owner left the workers to fend for themselves when the factory shut down production. No one can put a price on freedom. However, when it comes to the physical comforts, there was much to say for the argument that the slaves were better off than the Northern working class.

In the North as in the South, the wealthy ruled, and with industrialization, the situation worsened. Even at the time of the Revolution, 45 percent of the wealth was in the hands of 10 percent of the population. By the mid-nineteenth century, the concentration was more pronounced, at least as much if not more so in the North. In Boston, in 1845, 4 percent were estimated to own 65 percent of the wealth. In 1860 Philadelphia, 1 percent possessed more than half the wealth. Overall, according to some Librev scholars, 5 percent of the families in America owned more than 50 percent of the nation's wealth. The Librevs generally accept these statistics and are also quick to point out the influence of the planters in the South, but they seem to overlook the wealthy Northerners and their influence in that society. They do not seem to be as critical of the Northern ruling class. I agree that the planters ruled in the South; I also believe the rich ruled in the North.

The bottom line here is that the situation does not seem to imply that the Northerners, especially the wealthy manufacturers and businessmen, were morally superior to the Southerners, but rather that they developed a different system for meeting their demands for cheap labor. There is every indication that those in the North were just as racist as those in the South. The free black worker was at the bottom of the social totem pole so that even the other white workers despised them. The Southerner inherited a system that dated back to the early days in the New World, whereas the Northern businessman did not have the same needs for labor until after European philosophy questioned the morality of slavery. More importantly, those in early America had to force the workers to go to the colonies, whereas by the nineteenth century, the immigrants not only wanted to go but the price of transporting them across the ocean also had decreased to the point that the poor could afford to pay their own passage. There is no evidence to accept the difference between the two cultures as being the result of anything other than an economic decision, not superior morality.

The Southern Economy

The main myth I need to focus on when dealing with the antebellum Southern economy is the idea that the South was the last bastion of feudalism. This is as much of a problem when dealing with Southerners as it is the liberal South haters. There are plenty of neo-Confederates who love the Confederate balls where they can play like they're in a scene from *Gone with the Wind*. This is nothing new. Sir Walter Scott was very popular in the antebellum South, and many of the planter class fancied themselves as the last cavaliers defending their way of life from the Northern Roundheads. Reality is that the South too was in the process of industrialization, and even though they were predominantly agricultural, they were going in the direction of modern agribusiness.

There was an internal conflict as Sothrons struggled to modernize their plantation economy so that they could compete in the world-market economy. Total Southern textile manufactures in 1860 was $4.5 million, a threefold increase compared to twenty years before. This was still only 2 percent of the raw cotton exported that year. However, the key here is that we are comparing to the production of cotton. Cotton production increased dramatically during the same twenty-year period I discussed above—from 1,347,640 bales in 1840 to 3,841,416 bales in 1860. Remember, cotton is produced to supply raw materials for the textile industry. Not only was cotton a major product in the Southern economy, but it was also a major product in the American economy. The Northerners depended on the production of Southern cotton for their textile mills. One major error Confederates made in their decision-making process was that the Europeans, especially the British, would intercede on their behalf because their textile industry would not be able to survive without Southern cotton. The fact is that the British had already begun to find other supplies of cotton in places like Egypt and India.

For two reasons, the Librevs do not like to talk about the fact that the Northern textile industry depended on slave-grown Southern cotton. First of all, this means that the Northerners who condemned slaves depended on slave labor as much as Southerners did. Second, this dependence on Southern cotton could explain why the North was determined to keep the Southern states in the Union. They like to think that the Northern states invaded the South to free the slaves. Even the preservation of the Union would seem like a noble cause to kill and die for. The reality may be that the Northern businessmen and politicians were well aware of the consequences of losing Southern resources. I have already explained how the rise of nationalism is the result of the growth of the world-market economy and the need for protection of businessmen. In the modern world-market economy, and in fact in most other times and places, most wars have been fought for the benefit of businessmen. They are the ones who cover the expenses, and they are the ones who reap the profit. When they quit fighting it is most often because they are the ones who realize the cost will exceed the expected return.

The relationship of the Southern economy to slavery is more complex than it appears. Prior to the nineteenth-century increase in cotton production, many Southerners questioned the benefits of slavery. This is when they first created the colony of Liberia and entertained the idea of returning the slaves to where they came from. The plan never worked, mainly because of the high price tag, and in fact, the number of slaves continued to increase at a much higher rate than the exodus.

As the planters increased cotton production, the dependence on slave labor increased. In 1840, there were 2,487,213 slaves, and the number increased to 3,957,760 in 1860. What we will never know is how slavery would have ended if the Northern hordes had not invaded and killed hundreds of thousands of the Southern people. There is no doubt that by now slavery would be gone; the question is when and how it would have ended. I can never accept the idea that it was necessary to kill hundreds of thousands of Americans to end slavery. This did not happen in any other country. Many countries had slavery at one time, and none of them have it today, and in no other case did they kill hundreds of thousands of their own people to achieve abolition.

I have always thought of Maryland as an example of how modernization took its toll on the institution of slavery. Slavery still existed there in 1860. However, they had the highest population of freedmen. One reason for this is that there were a significant number of Quakers who lived in Maryland at the time that the church urged manumission. There was also a greater dependence on manufacturing in Maryland, especially in Baltimore. Another trend in Maryland was toward the production of specialty crops. This industry did not lend itself to slavery as easily as tobacco, rice, cotton, or sugar. Virginia also had a large number of freedmen. They were not that far behind Maryland on the path to industrialization. Louisiana also had a large free population. Historical differences are probably the main explanation for this. Slavery had been different under the French and Spanish. However, New Orleans was also a large city of commercial significance.

When we look at these various locations, we can see the possibility that slavery would have died a natural death. Another possibility is that as the Northern businessmen capitalized on the cheap labor of immigrants that the Southerners might have realized the economic advantage of this system. As we will see when we get to discussing the postwar South, the sharecropping system offered advantages over slavery. First of all, they increased the labor supply by taking in a number of poor whites in addition to the African population. Second, numerous expenses went away, such as providing housing, food, clothing, and medical care. The wages paid should cover these expenses. However, the greatest advantage comes when it is necessary to cut production because of a declining economy. Slave owners had to take care of their slaves or dispose of them when production was cut, compared to the sharecroppers of the twentieth century who simply lost their jobs and homes and were cast out upon the highways of America to fend for themselves.

I am sure it would be possible to write a book on this subject alone. We will never know for certain what might have happened if the circumstances had not forced abolition as they did. I will repeat; we know that by now slavery would have ended. Only the most radical South hater would insist otherwise.

Southern Classes

Most Southerners were farmers of one kind or another. The main plantation crops varied depending on the place and time. The main ones were tobacco, rice, sugar cane, and cotton but also included hemp, corn, wheat, swine, and cattle. The 1860 class structure had not changed much since 1776. The planters are the ones who grew most of the plantation crops, though any middle-class farmer would and could grow a patch of cotton. Historians like to call these middle-class farmers "yeomen." The term is no doubt based on the English class of peasants who owned their own lands and at times were even wealthy and could rise into the aristocracy. There was a smaller white population who did not own slaves and often did not even own their own land. The modern historians like to call these people pine-barrens folk, though through the years, they have been known by other names, such as poor white trash, rednecks, peckerwoods, hillbillies, and in recent times, trailer trash. The region also had an assortment of professional men, such as lawyers, doctors, teachers, clergymen, merchants, and even bankers although banking is one area in which the South was exceptionally deficient.

The relationship between these various classes has been confusing and complicated at times. I have already discussed Edmond S. Morgan's thesis that democracy developed in the South because all these free white men grew to have a confidence in social equality despite economic differences. However, any Southerner will admit that a certain antagonism has and continues to exist between the upper and lower classes. It is the wealthy Southerners who first used the derogatory term of "redneck." The lower classes of the region have always distrusted the rich so that the South was the center of populism, and it should not be a surprise that the region had a large number of socialists over the years. Oklahoma had more socialists elected to public office than any other state, and their most famous poet, Woody Guthrie, has been labeled a "commie" by many.

The Librevs especially like to think that these various classes banded together to defend slavery in 1861. I, for one, find it difficult to believe that the average Southerner would have been willing to fight simply so that the rich guy could keep his slaves. I will talk about this more later.

There is probably some truth in the Librev speculation that even though 75 percent of the Southern white population did not own any slaves in 1860, they could have defended the system on the idea that they might someday rise to the ranks of the planter class. I can see today that many poor people defend capitalism, no doubt with the idea that if we do away with the system, there will be no hope of economic improvement.

Racism also played a role in the defense of slavery. However, this was as true in the North as in the South. The nonslave owner might fear economic competition if the black man entered the free labor market. Many feared what the society would be like if bands of free blacks roamed the countryside unrestrained by the slave owner. This is also true for the working and middle classes of the North. They imagined large numbers of blacks would head to the North looking for jobs and housing. They did not like the idea of black people living among them as can be seen by the laws passed in several Northern states that prohibited free blacks from settling within their borders.

The Slaves

This is not a book of slavery. However, I feel that I must give a brief overview of the institution during this period. My main objective will be to clarify the assumptions relevant to the issue of Southern heritage. We Southerners must avoid the common defense used by our predecessors who would point out that they treated their slaves kindly and that the blacks liked them. There actually is some truth to this, which I will get into later. However, this is an immediate turn off when discussing these topics with blacks or liberals. Every Librev historian is aware of the fact that the slave population in the United States grew mainly because of natural population growth. Why is this important? It is rare for any human population to grow when they live in deplorable conditions. The fact is that even though only 5.4 percent of the slaves brought to the New World ended up in the area now called the United States, by 1860 the slave population in the country accounted for 60 percent of the slaves in the Americas. Remember, in 1808 the United States banned the slave trade. Most historians accept the research that claims only about fifty thousand were smuggled in illegally. Therefore most of the population growth was due to natural population growth. I have always found it amusing how the Librevs avoid discussion of these facts; they must know what the implications are.

Who were the slave owners? Only 25 percent of the Southern population owned slaves. Of those, only half owned more than five slaves, and only a quarter owned more than ten slaves. The planter class is defined as those who owned twenty or more slaves. Of the one quarter of Southern whites who owned slaves, only 12 percent fit in the class called planters. Only 1 percent of the 25 percent owned more than one hundred slaves. Remember, this means that 75 percent of Southern whites did not own a single slave.

Slave Management

The "our family treated their slaves well" defense which I just said we must avoid is recognized by the Librev historians; they call it paternalism. They freely accept that many of the planters had this attitude. However, we must also all realize that there were planters who had the opposite attitude. There are men today who abuse their wives and kids; there is no reason to doubt the fact that some slave owners abused their slaves. Paternalism was part of Anglo-Saxon culture. Even in the Middle Ages, the wealthy considered their servants as members of the household. The philosophy of noblesse oblige (nobility obligates) made it good manners to treat your servants well. This tradition carried over to the planter class in the colonies.

As Americans became more businesslike, they learned the principles of good management just as the Northern factory owners did. A common expression which has been around a long times is "you get more flies with sugar than with vinegar." Fear can be a management tool, but it is much more limited than treating people with some respect and allowing them some dignity. There is no doubt that most used some combination of the "carrot and stick approach." Even today managers use this, even if the stick is nothing more than dismissal or lack of promotional opportunity.

Looking at the situation from the slaves' perspective, this means that even though most slave owners owned less than ten slaves, most slaves came from large plantations. Most were field hands; the lucky ones worked in the big house. On many large plantations, the headhouse servants had positions of considerable responsibility and respect. The larger plantations would have more skilled workers also, such as carpenters or black smiths.

The significance of owning twenty or more slaves is that this is considered to be the point at which the slave owner would need management help. The first level would be the overseer. This was most often a white man, but on some plantations, a trusted slave might have the job. The overseer was often not respected by either the slaves or the owners. They were usually from the lower classes. The overseer handled discipline, including whipping. In *Gone With the Wind*, the overseer was the one who became a scalawag and tried to steal Tara from Scarlet by merely paying back taxes. This was an accurate reflection of the image that many whites had of these men. The overseer might need foremen, which they called drivers. The drivers were usually slaves. The wise master or overseer who could find the right man would pick one who had the respect of his fellow slaves. The driver usually received preferential treatment, perhaps the best cabin or a few more rations.

The Daily Life of the Slaves

To accurately evaluate the life that the slaves lived, we must compare it to the average nineteenth century workman, not a middle-class American of today. I offer here only a brief overview. I will attempt to discuss the conditions of the average slave, but it is understood that the situation varied from plantation to plantation. I should also make it clear that my purpose is not to defend or condemn slavery but rather to give the reader an idea of the life of black Southerners.

The purpose for slavery was to provide cheap labor, so the work is the main part of slave life. Most were field hands. They worked in either the task or gang system. The former was prevalent in the rice-growing areas where they worked at a specific task. The slave had to finish the task assigned to them, which might take up all the daylight hours. The gang system was more popular among the cotton growers. This was simply slave gangs supervised by drivers and overseers.

The foundation of the slave diet consisted of pork and corn. They could get more variety, and the lucky ones would be allowed to have a patch of ground where they could grow their vegetables of choice.

Like the average white farmer, they might get an occasional chicken, and in fact, the slave diet was not generally much different from that of whites. Like the white population, some slaves supplemented their diet with fish or wild game. Hunting was a sport liked by all Southerners, and many times master and slave hunted together. We can see to this day that Southerners have pretty much the same taste in food regardless of race. There are some exceptions. Black Southerners eat some foods such as chitlins, which are avoided by most whites. I assume this is a tradition which comes from their slave ancestors who were given the cheaper foods that the whites did not want. In the early recording industry, they talked of the "chitlin circuit," meaning the black fans. Malnutrition was rare, and most masters realized that the well-fed slave would be the best worker.

Clothing was pretty basic with typically two allotments a year. They received a set of lightweight clothes for the long summer months and something a little heavier in the wintertime. In either season, it would be coarse and plain. Children often went naked while some wore a cotton shirt that covered them similar to a dress. They often received hand-me-downs from the whites. Many of the slaves tried to design their own clothes, introducing more color and variety.

Housing varied from substantial brick structures to barely adequate shacks. Most lived in a small wooden cabin with a fireplace. They were usually grouped together in a small village. By 1860, many slave owners understood the importance of housing.

Much of the research today focuses on the cultural life of the slaves, which of course includes the family life. In the 1960s, many sociologists blamed the high divorce rate among black Americans as a byproduct of slavery. They assumed that the family unit suffered under slavery. Recent research indicates that the antebellum family unit was stronger back then than it is today despite the tragedy that came when masters would break up families by selling wives away from husbands or children away from mothers. There is no justification for a system that would depend on such cruelty. However, it struck most plantations regardless of how much priority a master gave to avoiding such things. Even a well-intentioned master would eventually die, and the heirs might sell the slaves in order to divide the estate. Many, if not most slave owners, tried to keep family units together. However, the division of families was the worst part of slavery and no doubt the greatest source of pain and suffering among the slave population.

The year I lived in Africa has given me considerable insight in understanding the influences of African culture on Americans today. The cultures of East and West Africa are as different from each other as the cultures of east and west Europe. I can see from living in West Africa that this is where virtually all the ancestors of black Americans came from. Researchers have traced the influences on American music, dance, architecture, diet, and overall lifestyle. We have always understood the obvious cultural impact of the European masters on their slaves, but few understand how much the African slave population influenced the white Southerners. I repeat, I am a firm believer in the Celtic fringe theory, which claims that Southerners and Northerners were different from the very start. I also believe that the differences increased over time. Much of the reason for this is that Southern culture and lifestyle borrowed considerably from the black Southerners.

I have always looked at the music as the best example. The world listens to Southern music, including blues, jazz, gospel, country, bluegrass, and rock. This music is a blending of African melodies and rhythms combined with the folk music of England, Scotland, Wales, and Ireland. Though the British have imitated it since World War II, it is still distinctly an American music which cannot be found in either Europe or Africa. It is the combination of the two. I believe this to be true about the rest of Southern culture. This is why not only are Southerners different from Northerners, but also from Englishmen, Australians, or other British colonial cultures. Southern culture is a melding of Anglo-Saxon, Celtic, and African culture with a trace of French, Spanish, American Indian, and other influences.

Free Blacks

In 1860, the black population of America was about 4.5 million. Of these, about a half million were free. Of the free blacks, about half of those lived in the North and half in the South. North or South, the free blacks were considered second-class citizens, a status that would continue in both regions until after World War II.

The free population grew with time. We have few accurate statistics from the colonial or Federalist period. Maryland had 1,817 free blacks, and as late as 1780, Virginia had even fewer. By 1790, Maryland had 8,043, and Virginia had 12,766. Much of the increase came with the revolutionary rhetoric of liberty, but some also came because of the Quaker population in these two states who freed their slaves with the encouragement of the church. The French and Spanish influences accounted for much of the free population in the Southwest. Regardless of where they lived, they were rarely considered equal to free whites. They were often bared from trades; had restricted access to theaters or railroads; and their legal status in things such as serving on juries or voting was usually limited.

Some slave owners were black. This is a select group of Americans, but it does mean that there is a possibility that some of those who want to ban our heritage may be condemning their own ancestors. The best guess is that we are talking about three thousand six hundred black slave owners in 1850. Seventy percent of South Carolina's black masters lived in Charleston. They were also in the elite group of slave owners who used slave labor in manufacturing.

One of the latest Librev trends is to point out that by 1860 some Southern states did take steps to rid themselves of free blacks. Arkansas passed a law that they must all leave the state by January 1, 1860. They had a choice—choose a master or be sold into slavery. Florida passed a similar law, and Mississippi was on the verge of it. This does not justify or condemn the attacks on our Southern culture. The North also made it clear that they did not consider blacks to be of full citizenship status, and some prohibited free blacks to live in their states too. I repeat, one of my main defenses of our heritage: I do not deny that our ancestors were racist, only that they were any more racist than Americans from the Northern states. Few of the Northern freedmen owned property or businesses; most worked at menial low-paying jobs. In most parts of the North, blacks could not vote; could not attend public schools; or use any of the public services available to the white population. Whereas some Southern states had passed laws against free blacks, so did some Northern states. Many of the abolitionists wanted to end slavery coupled with the idea of returning them to Africa. This is called the colonization plan, which I discussed earlier. Mr. Lincoln was a firm believer and advocate for this plan.

Abolitionists

I have often challenged my students to provide a biblical scripture that condemned slavery. So far I have not received an answer. The fact is that there has not been any literature from the Roman Empire that morally condemned slavery. In those days, it was accepted as a way of life. In the eleventh century, the Pope spoke out against slavery, and because of the position of the church, European societies ended the institution. As I have already stated, it was reintroduced in the early days of the Age of Exploration. With the Enlightenment, more and more people began to consider the institution morally wrong. Some spoke out at the time of the Constitution, but they clearly did not garner enough support to condemn the institution. In 1804, New Jersey became the last Northern state to outlaw slavery.

With the failure of the colonization movement, abolitionism began to decline by 1830. With the efforts of William Lloyd Garrison, who established the abolitionist newspaper the *Liberator* in 1831, the movement began to grow. By 1835, there were more than 400 chapters and, by 1838, 1,350 chapters with more than 250,000 members. Though growing, there were numerous riots that began in Northern cities by those who did not support abolition. Many had fears of hordes of freedmen moving north. The growing immigrant population feared the competition for jobs and housing. The reality is that many Northerners were racist, even some of the abolitionists. They were still a minority, and the Republican Party knew that an abolitionist would not have a chance of getting elected to the White House, even in the North. The Librev historians have often stated that the abolitionists were less than 5 percent of the population.

Southern Justification of Slavery

As the attacks escalated against slavery, Southerners became more creative in their defense. Their defensive arguments fall into five categories: historical, racial inferiority, equality of whites, comparison to the conditions of the white working class, and religious. We must also keep in mind that there were Southern abolitionists. Since colonial times, there are many examples of Southerners who freed their slaves because they believed it to be wrong to keep them. This was the main source for the free blacks living in the South. Many even worked in the underground railroad. Levi Coffin, so-called "President of the Underground Railroad," came from North Carolina. Even after he moved to Indiana, he still defended Southerners to his Northern friends and like most Quakers, did not hate the slave owner. Logic would tell us that the origins and most dangerous aspect of these activities had to be in the South; this is where the slaves were.

Slavery defenders who used historical arguments pointed out that slavery had been an integral and legitimate part of western history. It was around in the Greek and Roman civilizations. They emphasized the high civilizations of these cultures and tried to relate slavery to being a symbol of civilization.

Belief in racial inferiority justified the reintroduction of slavery to Europeans after the papal ban of the eleventh century. In the early days of exploration and colonization, such attitudes were based on the fact that the Africans were not Christian. In the nineteenth century, Southerners as well as others of European ancestry used science to prove the inferiority of Africans as well as the other dark-skinned peoples of the world. The field of ethnology looked at the physical differences between the races and claimed these to be proof of racial inferiority. Such Southern scholars as Dr. Josiah Nott of Mobile, Alabama, and George Gliddon of Philadelphia contributed to the scholarship of ethnology.

Southerners of the time made equality arguments similar to the thesis proposed by Edmond S. Morgan in his *American Slavery, American Freedom*. They pointed out that all civilizations had class differences, and this, of course, meant that someone had to occupy the bottom rung of the social ladder. Southern whites had a political democracy unmatched anywhere else in the civilized world. Southerners argued, "the poor white laborer at the North is at the bottom of the social ladder, whilst his brother here has ascended several steps and can look down upon those who are beneath him, at an infinite remove."

John C. Calhoun defended slavery on the grounds that the slaves of the South lived in better conditions than the working class of the North, which I have discussed to some degree above. There was some truth to this; Karl Marx and Charles Dickens became famous for pointing out the deplorable conditions of the working class of the Industrial Revolution. Neither wage worker nor slave lived in fancy houses nor wore fine clothes, but I have little doubt that the slave was much more of a stranger to hunger. An injured or sick wage earner would most likely be unemployed, whereas the slave owner had money invested in his slaves and like any other property must make do as best he can. He will see that the slave gets medical attention, if for no other reason than to restore his productivity. A factory owner will lay off a worker in idle times, whereas the master must maintain his slaves even at times when there is little work for them to do. I have noticed many examples in the slave narratives recorded during the depression years in which the interviewee admitted that he longed for the economic security he had in his earlier life. However, most denied any desire to return to slavery despite physical comforts. We must realize that few men would prefer a life of comfortable servitude over a more stressful freedom.

Disputes about the morality of slavery caused splits among the Methodist and Baptist and threatened such a split for the Presbyterians. There may be no direct condemnation of slavery in the Bible, but some clergymen used the golden rule or other such scriptures to support their point of view. The Southern preachers not only gave the slave owners religious sanctification but became a source of consolation for the slaves. The preachers would emphasize the importance of the afterlife over any burdens that we might have to bare in this world. We all know how Karl Marx referred to religion as the opiate of the masses. Americans prefer to ignore the fact that the patriot Thomas Paine made a similar statement. The stories of Moses and how his people eventually found freedom helped to serve as a source of hope. It could also give a boost to their self-esteem knowing that even God's chosen people had at one time been slaves.

No one today would accept these arguments to justify slavery. However, I point these out to show that the defense of slavery in the early nineteenth century was not due to moral inferiority of the Southerners, not even the slave owners. Most Northerners, and even most Europeans, accepted some aspects of these intellectual defenses. Very few of the abolitionists accepted racial equality; they merely condemned the institution of slavery. I do not see any justification in the scrapping or even condemning our heritage because many or even most of our ancestors believed in things that we do not believe in today.

The Indians

We can use the fact that many of the Indians allied with the Confederacy as evidence that our ancestors were no more racist than Northerners. However, we must be careful to not go too far with this argument. It is true that those in the South sought an Indian alliance, whereas the North did not, probably for racist reasons. However, the bottom line is that white people in both regions were less than kind to the first inhabitants of the land. The actions of the Indians were not unanimous, and even those who did support the South did so because they saw it in their best interest to do so.

In nineteenth century America, most Indians were treated in much the same way as those of foreign nations. However, the fact remained that they lived in the land that whites considered to be part of the United States of America. They wanted to be accepted as sovereign, but the United States government did not do this. Neither did they consider the Indians American citizens, except for any who had assimilated and moved in with the white men and lived like white men. The key is whether or not they paid taxes. The Cherokee learned to write; built schools; and published newspapers, all part of their adoption of western heritage. They did not do these because they wanted to abandon their heritage nor because they believed themselves inferior to the white man. They did so because they realized that the white man was winning, and the best way to defend themselves would be to learn their winning ways. They used their education to write a Constitution so that they could be a nation like the European nations. The reward for their efforts was to be forced from their ancestral homes to a new land in the West. Later these lands would be taken from them too, and their last symbols of sovereignty scrapped. I mention these things because the Indians were Southerners too and because many of them helped to defend the Confederacy despite the treatment they received from white Southerners. They must have been convinced that the Confederate States of America was less racist than the United States of America, and there is every indication this is true even though I think most Librevs would try to deny it.

Some of the Indians continued to exist without even attempting the steps toward recognition that the Cherokee had. By the nineteenth century, it was painfully clear that the white man would never stop until they had possession of all of the Indian lands. Some simply gave up and signed the treaties forced on them. Some did not give up until they made their last desperate stand at defending their homes against the flood of white migration. This would continue in the West after the Civil War. Meanwhile those in the East were either killed, removed, or assimilated. Not so many in the last category.

Andrew Jackson maintained a favorable image among Southern whites when it came to his policy toward the Indians. Sparked by the discovery of gold and the subsequent demand for land in Georgia, he forced the Indians to leave. Like the Southern attitude toward blacks, Jackson took a paternalistic view toward the Indians. He believed that whites were better guardians of the Indians' welfare than the Indians themselves. He did believe that they could survive even if they kept their traditional ways, but they would have to do so in the West. This led to the Indian Removal Act and the subsequent transfer of the Southern Indians to present-day Oklahoma. His theory was based on the assumption that white people would never live west of the Mississippi. This, of course, was the major flaw with his theory. When it came time to decide between going with the Confederacy or remaining with the Union, the Indians realized it was the Southerners who chased them from their ancestral lands and thus did not want to support them. However, some said it was the United States government that did this and thus they did not want to support the Union. Others saw it as an opportunity to make a stand against the divided white men and win their own sovereignty. More on this later.

Conclusions

The period 1789 to 1845 began with a Federalist victory and the ratification of the Constitution but concluded with Southern domination of the United States government. The ironic thing is that the Southerners had become the force for nationalism. This is contrary to the defense of states' rights—what Jefferson had stood for in 1789, and what the South would stand for again in 1861. It would appear that everything was going their way with the victory in the War of 1812—the acquisition of plenty of plantation land and the rapidly expanding cotton industry. Some, such as John C Calhoun, had visions that the Southerners were riding the crest of a wave that was about to break in a big crash. The North was growing faster, and it would be a matter of time until they dominated the House of Representatives and that they would have enough votes to take control of the White House, a predominately Virginian residence on Pennsylvania Avenue. To make matters worse, those in the North did seem to be speaking out against slavery. Many Southern planters began to see them as a threat to the labor system that they had depended on for generations. Ironically, the imperialist territorial expansion fueled by planter greed would eventually lead to the war which they would lose.

CHAPTER FOUR

Northern Hatred of the South and Southerners (1848–1860)

Introduction

During the years after the Mexican War, Northern hatred for the South escalated and gave birth to the Republican Party. The main interest of the Librevs in their studies of this period is to prove that the war was caused by slavery. Their "proof" lies in the argument that regional conflict grew during the post–Mexican War period and climaxed with the secession of South Carolina and that the majority of the issues which generated the conflict revolved around slavery. They look more specifically at the development of the political parties beginning with the 1844 election in which both major parties had supporters from both the North and the South, but by 1860, the Whig Party vanished because of regional division, the Republican Party arose with Northern support alone, and the Democratic Party was divided into Northern and Southern factions, which gave the election to the Republicans. The gravitation to political parties was based on the support or rejection of slavery. Their arguments have merit. If the question is "did slavery cause the war?" then the Librevs would be correct. If we ask the question, "did the North fight the war to free the slaves?" the answer would be no.

Most of the Librevs seem to be possessed by the arrogant and self-righteous assumption that the "lost cause myth" of a war over states' rights has been shattered. Though they still argue among themselves over other topics, most seem to agree that the work such as that by David M. Potter, *The Impending Crises, 1848–1861*, has resolved the issue once and for all. For the Librevs, Potter is a prime example of why it has been necessary for the revisionist Northerners to correct the delusional accounts of their history, which Southerners have accepted as fact for more than a hundred years. The reality is that if the Potter thesis is presented without an obvious contempt for the South and the Southern cause of independence, then I am sure that many, if not most, Southerners would agree. Way back in the 1890s, Major Jed Hotchkiss of Virginia expressed the same theses in his history of Virginia as it appeared in the *Confederate Military History*. These volumes of Southern history as told by the former Confederates are a prime example of what the Librevs have labeled "the lost cause myth." Hotchkiss began, "While the war of 1861-65 between the Union, or Northern and non-slaveholding States, and the Confederate, or Southern and slaveholding was not fought by the South as a whole, and certainly not by Virginia, for the perpetuation of slavery, nor by the North, at least in its inception, for its abolition." Most good Librevs should be frothing by now as they shout "lost cause myth." However, Hotchkiss went on to say, "yet every candid student of the history of the colonies and the States must admit that the slavery question, often under the name of 'State rights' of one kind or another, was a dominant factor making issues that led to the temporary disruption of the Union."[8] I repeat, the war was caused by slavery as Potter and Hotchkiss say. However, it was not fought to free the slaves, and the South did not fight to preserve slavery.

No doubt the Librevs would claim that they are only interested in presenting an accurate history of the United States. I believe it to be much more than that. I see much of what they do as a perpetuation of the Northern rhetoric, which began with the Republican South haters during the period of impending crises covered by this chapter. The supporters of Mr. Lincoln blamed the whole war on the planters of the South, which has become known as the planter conspiracy. I must admit, I too believe that it is the planter class which led the South down the path of secession. However, it is Lincoln and his Republicans who turned it into war. It is they who killed, maimed, and destroyed their fellow Americans. The South haters prior to 1861 had one thing in common with the South haters of today—a feeling of moral superiority based on their despising of slavery. They totally reject the Quaker attitude that it is slavery that is to be hated and not the slave owner. They all

---

8   Maj. Jed Hotchkiss, *Virginia, Confederate Military History* Volume III. (Atlanta: Confederate Publishing Company, 1899), 17.

but ignore the fact that in 1860, 75 percent of the white Southerners did not even own any slaves. The best they can do in this area is try to show that the non-slaveholding Southerners did not truly support the Confederacy. This is a thesis which I do not accept as proven.

The Librevs continually vote for Lincoln as the greatest American president. I do find it ironic that the liberal college and university educators in America today project an image of not only being unpatriotic but have also been called "America haters." The Librevs do not reflect any of this attitude when it comes to talking about the Civil War. They praise Abraham Lincoln as the leader of the United States in what many of them would consider one of the few justified wars in American history, the crusade to abolish slavery. Therefore they endorse the slaughter committed by the United States military as a necessity in ending the institution of slavery. To them, cherishing any symbol of the Confederate cause is to worship slavery and to endorse the racism that the institution was predicated upon.

Three American Myths

At times, I have been accused of being one of those liberal America haters by my students. The fact is that we cannot understand the true story of the South if we continue to accept the patriotic rhetoric which has become so much a part of our history. There are three myths most relevant to the historical era covered by this chapter. I have already discussed all three to some degree but feel I should repeat them again here as I discus how they are related to this period. First is the idea that this country was founded on any principle other than the making of money. Second has become most popular today: the idea that we are a land of immigrants and that as such we stand for "diversity." The third is the denial of the fact that the United States is an empire.

The first myth is that many Americans believe that our nation was founded on some noble principle that makes us all Americans, such as a love of freedom and democracy. The fact is that most people came to this country to make money. There are differences which distinguish Northerners from Southerners. The most obvious of these in early America was the Southern dependence on slavery for a source of cheap labor. We must realize how important the plantation economy was to the Southern way of life and that the system of slavery served no purpose other than economic. No African was brought to this land for freedom. However, another side to this coin is that the North could not easily accept the loss of the Southern states as many Northern cities depended on the Southern resources. Cotton was an American product, not just a Southern one. We must also realize that the political competition reflected in the development of the political parties was based on economic competition. The cities and states of America compete against each other, and any notion of an American economy is dependent on their individual profits. Who in Atlanta would be happy with a prosperous American economy which neglected Atlanta? Or who in Boston would live in poverty so that the rest of the country could prosper? Regardless of region, the average American looks after their personal interest first. Any concept of American prosperity is based on what most benefits the individual who is part of an economic community.

The second myth is that we like to think of America as a land where people of all nations are welcomed. If we accept this then we will never comprehend the rise of the Know-Nothing Party, which was founded on a desire to exclude the growing population of immigrants. It is the morally superior Northerners who led this fight. Southerners may have not liked the foreigners any more, but they did not pose a threat in the South. This is the same principle as to why Southerners have expressed more hatred toward blacks. The African population did not pose much of a threat to most Northern communities. The immigrant population also produced an alternative labor supply for the wealthy Northerners as they developed an increased demand for cheap labor. The fact that this nation has blacks and those descended from immigrants is not due to any brotherhood of freedom lovers. We have a diverse population because of the rich from both the North and the South had a demand for cheap labor.

As we explore the conflict and impending crises of 1848 to 1861, we are talking about a time in American history in which many prospered. Various communities in America found their niche in the increasingly prosperous young nation. They unified when they saw an economic advantage in doing so. By the mid-nineteenth century, it was becoming increasingly obvious that the central government, once dominated by the South, was falling into the hands of Northerners. By 1860, some in the South believed it to be to their advantage to extinguish the alliance that had been known as the United States. The rich of the South led a crusade for secession to protect their economic interest. The rich of the North chose to kill the Southern people to protect their economic interest. The average person in both North and South rightfully called it a rich man's war and a poor man's fight.

The Third Myth: American Imperialism

The reason that I needed to point out that the United States is an empire is that all those points of contention talked about by David Potter and most of the disagreement over slavery related to American expansion, also known as imperialism. The Republican Party did not come into being to abolish slavery but rather to stop the spread of slavery into the territories, and the expansion of empire is what gave us the territories. In the days before the Civil War, it is the South which pushed for territorial expansion. I have already discussed the attempted movement for independence that came in 1814 because of the New England disagreement over the War of 1812. Though the North did not threaten secession, they objected to the Mexican War while the South not only supported it but insisted on it. During the antebellum period, the South abandoned some of the Jeffersonian principles. They fostered nationalism, either ignoring or uncaring about the fact that the larger the nation, the stronger the central government. This is the great irony; they are the ones who pushed to acquire the territory, which would lead to their discontent and subsequent secession.

The journalist John L. O'Sullivan gave us the name for antebellum American nationalism when he wrote a column about Manifest Destiny. This Jacksonian Democrat voiced the attitude of American imperialism that is with us today. His philosophy appealed to Southerners, and the Democratic Party adopted it as a way to woo Southern voters. O'Sullivan created an American myth that is alive and well today. Americans are not like the Europeans, "our national birth was the beginning of a new history, the formation and progress of an untried political system, which separates us from the past and connects us with the future only." We do not conquer for kings "but in defense of humanity, of the oppressed of all nations, of the rights of conscience, the rights of personal enfranchisement." The planters might acquire new lands that would expand the production of cotton, but that is not our objective. The contradiction in what O'Sullivan said is that "we are the nation of progress, of individual freedom, of universal enfranchisement." Like Jefferson, he said, "all men are created equal." This is the philosophy which would make it more and more difficult to justify slavery.

The greatest fallacy in this belief is that the profits from expanding cotton fields did not motivate the antebellum American expansionist any more than oil fields motivate U.S. foreign policy today. Occupation of Canada had been a dream of pre–Civil War Americans. However, it did not prove to offer the same opportunities as those lands that already had slaves and the plantation economy. In 1854, a group of Americans drafted a private document in Ostend, Belgium; and thus, it has become known as the Ostend Manifesto. They made a case for purchasing Cuba from Spain, and if they refused then they advocated seizing the island by force. Americans had the same problems then that we have today; not everyone in the world comprehended the nobility of our mission. Some called it a "buccaneering document" or a "highwayman's plea."

Southern expansionists worked elsewhere. In 1857, William Walker gained control in Nicaragua, and his new government was immediately recognized by President Pierce. Congressional resistance dried up financial support for Walker's enterprise, and by 1857, the American president of Nicaragua was ousted.

The term used to describe the Southern expansionist is filibusters. No doubt the activities had been fueled by the success in Texas and Mexico. Some Northerners also wanted expansion as they took their apples and moved to Oregon. People of all regions rushed to the gold fields of California, Nevada, and other western states beginning in 1849. Some objected as they questioned the morality. However, O'Sullivan offered them a rationalization. Henry Clay was one man who correctly feared that territorial expansion could lead to scraping the scab known as the Missouri Compromise.

I too would like to believe that we Southerners were all good, and the invading Yankees were all bad, but this is not realistic. In order to blame the Yankees for the death and destruction that followed secession, we must accept Southern guilt. Southern profit motive led to secession. Northern profit motive turned it into war.

It's All about Texas

We like to believe that it was not imperialism that motivated the first American settlers in Texas. The Spanish had a tenuous hold on the Northern lands of New Spain, and the new Mexican government found peace with the Apache and Comanche by agreeing to let them keep their traditions if they would stop raiding the white settlements. Hoping to stimulate economic expansion, the Mexicans offered considerable rewards in land to any who would move to the area known today as Texas. Stephen Austin led a band of Southern pioneers who had agreed to become Catholic and give up their slaves in exchange for more land than they hoped to get in the United States.

At first, Austin fought only for self-government within the country of Mexico, but following his imprisonment in Mexico City, the Texicans declared independence. After defeat and annihilation at the Alamo and Goliad, they captured Santa Anna and won their war at San Jacinto in 1836. They immediately sought annexation by the United States. However, the passive Congress feared that it would lead to war with Mexico. Some feared that it would upset the balance between the slave and free states. Then along came John Tyler.

Tyler had been elected vice president with the Whig victory of 1840. However, the sudden death of William Henry Harrison made him the first man to become president because of the death of his predecessor. Some even questioned the line of succession, but Tyler remained in the White House. In many ways, the Virginian Tyler stood for traditional Jeffersonian principles more than the modern business interest promoted by the Whig Party. He had alienated other Whigs, and he accepted the fact that he would not win the nomination of that party in 1844. He fantasized beating out Martin Van Buren for the Democratic nomination. The Northern Democrats feared domination by the Southern slave holders, and many objected to territorial expansion. However, Tyler hoped to win support of the Southern Democrats by pushing for the annexation of Texas.

John C. Calhoun banded together with Tyler in advocating the annexation of Texas, which they assumed would become a slave state. Some advanced the belief that Great Britain had its eyes on the land and that if the British acquired it, there would be no room for the slave owners. The annexation question became a slave issue as well as an expansion question. Van Buren did not support the idea, which led to his political death among the Southern Democrats. Tyler had hoped to win the nomination of that party, but instead, it went to James K. Polk.

As we will see by the end of the chapter, the main argument of the Librevs is that slavery polarized the political parties. However, with the election of 1844, we can see that there are other issues that separated the two regions. With the nomination of Polk, the Democratic Party adopted a platform to annex Texas. Meanwhile, the Whigs nominated Henry Clay, and Southern Whigs feared that the party would lose to the Democrats over the issue of Texas. Clay did not oppose the idea but apparently did not come across too convincing as he won only four states in the South. The Librevs would have us believe that the Texas question was a slave issue. However, there is no way to know the significance of slavery compared to the general imperialism that had become known as Manifest Destiny. Congress passed the annexation of Texas before the election so that the campaign slogan "54° 40' or fight" is what rallied Polk to victory. The lack of Southern support for Clay would have had nothing to do with the acquisition of Oregon. The pressure to acquire Oregon came from Manifest Destiny only and not in any way related to slavery.

The Mexican War

The Mexican War divided North and South, and at first, there is little to suggest that slavery had much to do with the philosophical disagreement. The Southern quickness in answering the call for volunteers demonstrated the regional support for the war. Tennessee was asked to provide three thousand troops, but nearly thirty thousand came forward. Kentucky filled its quota within two weeks after Congress declared war. Baltimore took only thirty-six hours to raise its allotted number. In the first year of the war, forty-five thousand Southerners had joined compared to only twenty-four thousand from the North. Clearly Southerners supported the war for Manifest Destiny or American imperialism.

The Texas question and lack of support for the Mexican War had weakened the Whig Party. The Whigs became critical of Polk and his policies, which alienated many Southern Whigs whose patriotic feelings demanded that they support their country while at war. As stated above, there was more dividing North and South than simply slavery.

The Wilmot Proviso

The Wilmot Proviso is one of the most important, if not the most important, piece of failed legislation in American history. David Wilmot proposed an amendment to an appropriations bill that would forever prohibit slavery in any territory acquired as a result of the Mexican War. This would not only begin a string of crises in American politics that would dramatically change party alignment in the country but would also climax with the election of Abraham Lincoln and the subsequent secession of the Southern states. Southerners would remain united until the War for Southern Independence in their resistance to the Wilmot Proviso. They saw that not only would this proposal limit the freedom for the Southerners to move into new territories, but that it would also suggest that the Southern system was morally tainted. This will be discussed later when I talk about the growth in Northern contempt for Southerners.

This proposed amendment would disrupt the existing political parties as they would divide based on region. The Southern Democrats not only opposed the proviso, but they also made it clear that they would not support any candidate "who does not unconditionally, clearly, and unequivocally declare his opposition to the principles of the provisions of the Wilmot Proviso." The Democrats would straddle the fence as much as possible, until their selection of Stephen Douglas divided them in 1860. The Whigs, however, were on the path toward extinction as they too split by region. The Northern Whigs supported the proviso as adamantly as the Southern Whigs objected to it. After the death of the party, the Southerners would seek a new party elsewhere while the majority of the Northern Whigs would be the foundation for the Republican Party.

The Compromise of 1850

The admission of the state of California would be the next major blow to the Whig Party as well as the next cut in severing the South from the Union. President Taylor surprised and annoyed his Southern supporters by proposing the idea of dividing the entire Mexican acquisition into California and the New Mexico Territory with the idea that both would be admitted to the Union and that both would be free states. Even though Taylor was a slave owner himself, he did not believe in the spread of the institution into the new territories. Then came Henry Clay with one of his compromises.

The Clay proposal called for a number of measures that would appeal to both factions and thus the term compromise. First, California would be admitted as a free state, the obvious choice of those living in the territory at the time. Second, the remaining territory would be divided into Utah and New Mexico and that the residents of those territories would decide for themselves whether to be slave or free. Third, the slave trade would be abolished in the District of Columbia. Fourth, the passage of a new fugitive slave law to enforce the constitutional provision to return those slaves living in another state. It also settled a border dispute between Texas and New Mexico.

Each side found a particular aspect of this compromise that would become a point of contention. The Southerners liked the idea of "popular sovereignty," which they saw as a way to end the restriction of 36°30' that they inherited from Clay's 1820 Compromise. This opened any new territory as a possible place for Southern expansion. All future political aspirants would insist on the adoption of popular sovereignty if they had any hope for Southern support. Many of those in the North, especially the abolitionists, would have a problem with the fugitive slave law. Not only did the nation maintain the institution of slavery, but also anyone, black or white, who helped runaway slaves would become criminals themselves.

The proposed compromise widened a growing regional split in both of the major parties. The Northern Whigs backed Taylor who opposed the idea. The Southern Whigs supported Clay. The Northern Democrats considered it reasonable and backed it while the Southern Democrats followed the lead of Calhoun and said that Clay had sold out the South. The Calhounites cried "never" to the notion of admitting California as a free state. In the Deep South, the parties broke down all together. A minority of Democrats joined a Whig majority and promoted Union parties while minority Whigs joined most Southern Democrats and looked to states' rights parties.

Taylor found an easy way out when he died, and thus, the crisis had passed. Each part of the compromise had been divided into a separate bill; congress passed each part; and the new president, Millard Fillmore, signed them into law. Calhoun was a minority in recognizing that the future for Southern influence in the national government appeared bleak. Most Southerners were still proud to be Americans and were pleased with the outcome.

Kansas

The next battleground was not the newly acquired Mexican lands but rather involved those yet unsettled parts of the Louisiana Purchase, more specifically Kansas and Nebraska. Stephen Douglas was chairman of the Senate Committee on Territories and pushed for the organization. When he began, he assumed that the Compromise of 1820 meant that slavery would not exist there since both were above 36° 30'. However, Southerners rallied around their new platform—popular sovereignty. Douglas accepted their argument. If it was okay in New Mexico and Utah, it should be good in Kansas and Nebraska. Douglas saw an opportunity to unify the Democratic Party as the proposal served to further divide the Whigs. The Northern Whigs to the man opposed the repeal of the Missouri Compromise and made support of Douglas's Kansas–Nebraska a Democrat platform issue only. Instead of unity, Douglas had created a split in his party. He got it through the Senate easily enough. However, the House took ten weeks to settle the debate, which ended up taking a toll on party unity for the Democrats and the Whigs. The passage ended up a Pyrrhic victory for Southerners; it ended the 36° 30' restriction; however, it had aggravated Northern hatred for Southerners which would eventually lead to the formation of the political party that had no interest in the feelings of those Americans in the slave belt.

Shortly after its passage, settlers began to stream into the new territory. Most were motivated by personal interest as they simply hoped to acquire a family farm; instead they became soldiers in the first battles of the war. Some expected Kansas to become a slave state as it was assumed that those who would vote on popular sovereignty would be settlers who had migrated west from the slave state of Missouri. The abolitionists of New England hoped to prove that assumption wrong when they created the Immigrant Aide Society. Through this organization, they helped to finance Northern settlers who would vote for Kansas to become a slave territory and eventually a slave state. This led to a countermove in which Southerners would go into Kansas, even if it was only at election time.

The land of dreams turned into a nightmare in what became known as Bleeding Kansas. Both sides turned to violence in the struggle, which resulted in death and destruction of property. John Brown first attained national attention as he and his sons not only murdered supporters of slavery but also hacked their bodies to pieces with his sword. Though a mere handful acted this way toward Southerners at the time, Brown eventually grew to be a highly admired martyr to many Northerners.

In 1856, the violence spread to Washington. Senator Charles Sumner of Massachusetts made a speech against what he called the "rape" of Kansas. At one point, he made a derogatory reference to a senator from South Carolina, Andrew P. Butler, which angered his cousin Representative Preston Brooks. Brooks proceeded to the Senate where he confronted Sumner with his cane. The beating not only destroyed the cane but also left Sumner incapacitated for a few years. The battle cry of the newly formed Republican Party became "Bleeding Kansas, Bleeding Sumner."

A nearly fatal blow came to the Democratic Party in the form of the Lecompton Constitution of 1857. The slave supporters held an election in which they hoped to make Kansas a slave territory. The free soilers assured its passage when they boycotted the election which they considered illegal to begin with. Douglas and the Democrats had adopted a platform of popular sovereignty. However, they saw the Lecompton Constitution as a bogus document. Douglas led a crusade for the Democratic Party to reject the admission of Kansas with Lecompton, which turned a friend of the South into a man they could not vote for.

Southern Economy

Since the antebellum era, a common thesis has been put forth and widely accepted that the South resisted modernization. Many of the planter class thought of themselves as the descendants of the cavaliers while the Yankees descended from the Puritan Roundheads. This was the origin of the cultural traditions of courtly manners, defending honor, and other behavior which resembled the stereotypical medieval knight. Much of what they learned came from Sir Walter Scott. This is the image that was portrayed in the book and movie *Gone with the Wind*. It is the courtly way of life that had disappeared after Appomattox.

The reality is that the South was as much involved with the modernization process as the rest of America. Like those in the North, their ancestors came to make their fortunes and those who succeeded were those who found a niche in the modern world-market economy. At the time that the South seceded, the Confederate States of America was the fourth wealthiest nation on earth. There are statistics that can make it appear that the South was falling behind in industrialization, but the reality is that they were not entering the new stage of commercial development as rapidly as the North, but they were still on the path of industrial and urban development.

Between 1840 and 1860, the South declined from 20 percent to 16 percent of total manufacturing in the United States thus making it appear that the South was resisting modernization. However, other statistics suggest that this is not the case. Southern manufacturing increased but at a slower rate than in the North and that is why the percentage of total manufacturing declined. Manufacturing below the Mason-Dixon went from $53 million invested capital in 1840 to $93.6 million in 1850 to $163.7 million in 1860. In the 1850s, manufacturing output increased 79 percent to $186.9 million. This was less than other regions but still clearly growing. The per capita manufacturing output in the South was $17.09 compared to $37.33 in the Northwest, $96.28 in the Middle States, and $149.47 in New England. These are per capita statistics, and of course, the population in the North was growing at a more rapid rate. The bottom line is that the South was modernizing, just not at as rapid a rate as the North.

The fact remains that there were those in the South who promoted modernization and sought to profit from the world markets. Railroad millage in the South increased five times in the 1850s. The South lacked the banks that the North had, but they did grow. In 1846, James D. B. De Bow brought out the first issue of his journal *De Bow's Review*, which promoted commercial development in the region. The more popular industries included iron works, tobacco processing, and textiles. The South remained agricultural, but more and more of the crops produced were for the world markets, not eating. The South actually had food shortages during the war because they could not eat tobacco, cotton, hemp, or indigo. The successful planters were those who ran their plantations like a business, such as Jefferson Davis. Most of the men who promoted modernization were Whigs, like their counterparts in the North.

The question of modernization is very relevant in the discussion of slavery. The greatest crime about the abolishing of slavery in America is that hundreds of thousands of lives and countless loss of property became part of the process. Northerners have always self-righteously assumed that this was a necessary price tag, and they were the noble ones who took the needed steps. I, among many, have always believed that slavery was not compatible with the modernization process and that it would have died a natural death. We can never know this for sure, but it is a fact that such wanton death and destruction did not occur in any other country in the world as they evolved from slave labor toward other sources of cheap labor.

There is evidence that suggest my assumption is valid. On one hand, the 1850s was a very profitable time for the planters who used slave labor to produce their cotton. On the other hand, immigrant labor offered economic advantages. One does not need to maintain a hired worker when production declines. Labor becomes a variable cost so that there is lower start-up cost and no payback period to calculate. This makes it easier for the small entrepreneur to become part of the system. Maryland sits before us as a good example of how slavery was becoming replaced by alternative cheap labor sources; in America, the alternative became immigrant labor. Maryland had the greatest number of free blacks since they had so many of their citizens who voluntarily extinguished the system. There were still slaves in Maryland in 1860, but it is clear that the institution of slavery was not as popular in the Southern state that had made the most progress in modernization.

Party Realignment

The Librevs support the notion that the war was fought over slavery. The argument follows the logic set down by David Potter in which he pointed out that all of the issues which created the crises of the 1850s revolved around the question of slavery. More specifically, they see that with each issue the political parties evolved toward becoming regional parties. In the case of the Whigs, the split led to its demise. The Democrats split into two parts thus allowing the new strictly Northern Republican Party to win with less than 40 percent of the vote.

The Whig Party

I begin by defining a Whig. It is tempting to describe the Whig Party as one made up of men with money. This would be wrong; there were rich men who were Democrats. It would be better to look at the Whigs as those who aspired to make money by seizing the opportunities of American participation in the world markets. Whigs would not be the descendants of Jeffersonian Republicans and thus would not represent a dominant view in the South since the formation of the United States. They would instead be those who tended to support a more centralized government since such a government would be more protective of the American businessmen in the world market. Many of the Whigs, including those from the South, would not be directly involved with slave labor. However, those in the South were involved with the moneyed men and would thus have at least an indirect interest in the preservation of the Southern plantation slave economy. Some of the planters were Whigs too. The best way to understand them is to reject any image of them as defenders of aristocracy, but rather as being predecessors of the modern American agribusiness. They did not run their plantations like a feudal lord, but rather as a businessman who produced cotton instead of widgets.

Henry Clay's American System is a good example of what I am talking about. He was a Southern planter, but he was a businessman. This is why at first, Southern Whigs stood behind him in the election of 1844. They supported the economic policies of Clay, but they could not support him after he came out as opposed to the annexation of Texas. The Southern plantation economy was dependent on expansion. He carried only four states in the South as the Democrats adopted a platform of annexing Texas.

The next blow for Southern Whigs came with the Wilmot Proviso. Southern Whigs opposed the Proviso while Northern Whigs just as adamantly supported it. The Party took no official position on the issue, and until it did, the Southerners would not abandon the party. With the Whig nomination of Zachary Taylor, the Party remained alive. Taylor had been a hero of the Southerner who supported Mexican War, and he was a planter and slave owner.

The 1852 nomination of another Mexican War hero, Winfield Scott, delivered the final death blow to the party in the South. Scott was a Southerner. However, unlike Taylor he did not seem to represent planters and Southern interest. In the South, he carried only Tennessee and Kentucky. No Whig presidential nominee had ever done so poorly in the slaves states. Not only that but the Whigs did poorly in the state elections of 1852 and 1853; the only houses they controlled were North Carolina and Tennessee. In the Congressional elections of the same year, only fourteen of the sixty-five representatives were Whigs. Almost all in the South blamed the antislavery Whigs of the North for their demise. By 1854, the party was virtually dead in the South. Some Southern Whigs turned to the Democrats while others hoped to mold the new Know-Nothing Party into a Southern party.

The Democratic Party

The Democratic Party, like the Whigs, began to divide along regional lines, which does support the Librev agreements that slavery generated the growing divide. One could argue that the trouble began with the elections of 1840 and 1844 in which the Southerners led the way in defeating Van Buren in the first election and the selection of James K. Polk as the Democratic candidate in the latter. The dumping of Van Buren for Polk had much to do with the Texas question, which in turn had a lot to do with the expansion of slavery.

The party definitely began to divide after the Wilmot Proviso. Those in the North tended to support it while those in the South rejected it. The main reason that the Democrats did not have the same fate as the Whigs is that they found the policy of popular sovereignty. As the Whigs declined, more and more Southerners turned to the Democratic Party. In the elections of 1852, they picked Northern candidates Franklin Pierce of New Hampshire and James Buchanan of Pennsylvania. The radical abolitionists would have to look elsewhere, but the more moderate Northern voters could support these candidates who gave the Southerners the popular sovereignty they demanded. In 1852, Pierce won his party the most Southern votes since the days of Andrew Jackson.

Even Stephen Douglas yielded to Southern desires when he included popular sovereignty in his 1854 Kansas–Nebraska Act. While the Southern Whigs would continue to shop around elsewhere, most Southerners seemed content with the way the Democrats were going until Douglas took a stand against the Lecompton Constitution. After that, most Southerners refused to back the man that the Northern Democrats insisted on in their 1860 convention.

The Free Soil Party

With the fall of the Whigs and the path taken by the Democratic Party, the Northern abolitionists and anti-Southerners also shopped around. In 1840, the Liberty Party ran a candidate who did not advocate abolition but did preach against the spread of slavery into the territories. When Taylor ran in 1848, the "Conscience" Whigs, some remnants of the old Liberty Party, and a few Northern Democrats formed the Free Soil Party based on the principles of the Wilmot Proviso. Their slogan became, "free soil, free speech, free labor, free men." In the 1848 election, they nominated Van Buren, who won one out of seven of the Northern votes. They did not come anywhere near winning, but they did win ten seats in Congress and demonstrated a growing demand for their way of thinking.

The Know-Nothing Party

Most Northern bigotry was aimed at the ever increasing immigrant population, mainly because they were Catholic. The South had some immigration and certainly had their share of anti-Catholic prejudice, however, the South did not receive as many of the newcomers. Racial and ethnic hatred generally originates from fear; that fear is based on feelings of being threatened. Though almost all of the new Americans came from Northern Europe and did not come even close to the population diversity in the America we know today, the older population feared those who were not like them. This is one of the main points I have been trying to make with this essay. Our Southern ancestors were racist, but no more so than the average Northerner. Many Southerners felt threatened by a large black population, whereas Northerners feared immigrants more; in each case, a matter of numbers, not racism. Those in the Know-Nothing Party sparked many a riot and succeeded in passing legislation barring Catholics from public office and unsuccessfully sought to increase the residency requirement for citizenship from one year to twenty-one years.

Southerners, especially Southern Whigs, looked to the Know-Nothing as a new party that would represent their interest. Even some in Louisiana backed the alternative. Most of the sugar-planting Whigs in that state were also Catholic, but they were willing to ignore the anti-Catholicism if the new party would adopt a platform of popular sovereignty in all the territories and back the Fugitive Slave Act. These are the issues that wracked the national conventions of 1855 and 1856. In 1855, it looked like the Southerners would get their way, but in 1856, the Northerners won out. This caused the failure of the Know-Nothings in the South and eventually the complete failure of the party.

The Republican Party

Northern Whigs and some Northern Democrats became the foundation for a new party, which would not only survive but also find success while making no effort to appeal to the Southern voter. The prophecies of Calhoun had come to pass. In the 1860 census, the Northern population was more than twice that of the South, including the slave population. Initially, it required the split of the Democratic Party to win the White House for the Republicans, but as we will see, by the end of Reconstruction, the new party had become solid without any Southern support and eventually would even be able to abandon the black Southerners.

The mere existence of the Republican Party affirms the Librev interpretation of antebellum politics and the role that slavery played. The Whig party did divide and die as the Southern Whigs deserted them since they could not adopt a pro-slavery platform. The Democratic Party would split since the Northern choice of Stephen Douglas refused to support the pro-slavery Lecompton Constitution. The Know-Nothings would not conform to the slavery platform. In the election of 1860, the South would succeed from the Union as it became clear to them that they could not retain any power and influence in the national government. Not only did the black Republicans have no concern for the Southern voter, but they also became more and more aggressive in their criticism of Southerners. Led by the abolitionists, they used strong language in their condemnation of slavery in which they clearly expressed feelings of moral superiority, the same attitude many Northerners continue to embrace in their attacks on our Southern heritage today.

Some Other Slavery Issues

Some other national issues helped to fuel the political divided between North and South. The Dred Scott case drew national attention, but when the Supreme Court backed the Southern slave view, it further agitated Northern hatred and prejudice. More and more writers expressed their contempt for Southerners, the most famous being Harriet Beecher Stowe and her book *Uncle Tom's Cabin*. The Lincoln Douglas Debates of 1858 helped to bring national attention to the future president and the man who would lead the way in the destruction of the South. Perhaps the most devastating was the raid on Harper's Ferry.

John Brown had demonstrated his hatred for Southern slave owners in Kansas, but in the fall of 1858, he attempted to lead a slave rebellion.

Though the terrorist was tried, convicted, and hung for treason, many in the North looked at him as a martyr. It was bad enough that Northerners would politic to limit the spread of slavery into the territories. It could even be understandable that some would campaign to end slavery in America; even many of the slave owners had learned to regret the system they had inherited from their ancestors. But with the venom put out by some writers and the determination of John Brown to not only kill but also to mutilate Southerners, it was becoming clear that there was no future for the South in the United States of America.

Northern Hatred of Southerners

Many, if not most, Northerners would protest my accusations that they hate Southerners today almost as much as their ancestors did more than a century and a half ago. The more liberal-sounding would simply call it disagreement, or better yet, they would say that we Southerners are still fighting the Civil War. The fact is that, like our ancestors in the 1860s, we are simply defending ourselves. The battles that we fight today are a defense against Northern aggression. The verbiage of the South haters who attack our heritage is very similar to the language used by the Northern abolitionists and the radical wings of the Republican Party. Northern identity was founded on hatred of Southerners, and it is alive today.

I find that the following words from Major General Isaac Ridgeway Trimble best sums up the Northern attitude. Keep in mind that Trimble was born a Quaker; raised in the border South; and that neither he nor his family owned slaves. He graduated from West Point but spent the thirty years before the war working for the railroads, the vanguard of modernization in America.

> Our Connection with you never had, from the early settlement of the colonies till now, any bond but that of political interest. Your bigatry [sic] & hatred of every thing Southern drove us from you-the Union was at variance with our feelings, tastes, pursuits, honorable aims & religion and time instead of removing these, has strengthened them, untill [sic] on the great principles of

self preservation and self respect, the Union has been sundered forever. Let the calm verdict of a future age, be awarded on the merits of this contest. The South has no fears for her reputation either on account of the wisdom of her statesmen or the valour [sic] of her soldiers-If she perish, she can go down to the grave of nations, with the proud boast that she has abundantly nourished with her blood the seeds of Liberty, which will spring up & bear fruit to bless mankind in comeing [sic] time.[9]

I feel confident that the majority of Librevs would disagree with what I am saying on this subject, but there are those who have covered this topic. Eric Foner claimed "Northerners came to view slavery as the very antithesis of the good society, as well as a threat and an affront to their own fundamental values and interest."[10] Howard Floan studied Northern literature in *The South in Northern Eyes* and concluded that the Northern view of the South was basically a view of slavery. A more interesting account can be found in *North over South* by British historian Susan-Mary Grant. She saw the Republican Party as the origin of a national identity which, because of their success, became a Northern identity. This is what Lincoln was doing when he created the national holiday we now celebrate as Thanksgiving. The first declaration of such a day for thanks did not occur in Massachusetts. However, the creation of this national holiday has altered reality by generating the myth that the United States begin in Massachusetts and New England. Thus, many think that the founding fathers of the United States were Puritans, even though Jamestown predates it. This holiday became more powerful since it combined the patriotic founding of America with the religious sanctification of the Puritans. This was what Lincoln and the Yankee Army fought for. To recap in the words of the most famous Southern historian C. Vann Woodward, "the South has long served the nation in ways still in great demand. It has been a moral lightning rod, a deflector

---

9   Isaac Ridgeway Trimble, "The Civil War Diary of General Isaac Ridgeway Trimble," *Maryland Historical Magazine*, March 1922, 15.

10   Eric Foner, *Free Soil, Free Labor, Free Men: The Ideology of the Republican Party before the Civil War* (New York: Oxford University Press, 1970), 9.

of national guilt . . . a floor under self-esteem."[11] He went on later to say, "the legend that the Mason and Dixon Line not only divided slavery from freedom in antebellum America, but that it also set apart racial inhumanity in the South from benevolence, liberality and tolerance in the North." He continued "Looking back through the haze of passing years that obscured historical realities the myth-makers credited the North with the realization in its own society of all the war aims for which it fought."[12] If you doubt my word, a humble California Okie, perhaps you will believe Woodward, generally acknowledged as one of the greatest historians on the American South. This is pretty much the same concept that I am trying to express with the scapegoat theory. There are those who want to put the sin of American racism on the symbols of Southern culture and then sacrifice the goat to the god of history.

The Fire-eaters

As hatred of all things Southern grew, so did those in the South who preached secession; we call them fire-eaters. They were still a small band, but they were the seed from which the creation of the Confederacy sprouted. They had the most influence in the states, which had the most slaves, which again lends some credibility to the Librev point of view. To reiterate, I do not dispute that the war was caused by slavery, but I do not agree with the idea that it was fought to free the slaves. The fire-eaters did come from those areas which had the most slaves. The three states in which they had most influence included South Carolina with 57 percent slave population, Mississippi with 55 percent, and Alabama with 45 percent. They also had some influence in Florida, Georgia, Texas, and Virginia. The more famous included Barnwell Rhett of South Carolina, William Lowndes Yancy of Alabama, and Edmund Ruffin, who was born in Virginia. They called to reopen the slave trade and promoted filibustering, the term used to describe Southern territorial ambitions. With their leadership, South Carolina began the secession parade following the election of Lincoln in 1860.

---

11   C. Vann Woodward, "From the First Reconstruction to the Second," *Harper's Magazine*, April 1965, 133.
12   C. Vann Woodward, "The Antislavery Myth," *American Scholar* 31 (spring 1962): 316.

The Election of 1860

The secession of the Southern states and the subsequent war was caused by slavery. However, the war was not fought to free the slaves. The fact is that in the month after the election of Abraham Lincoln in November of 1860, South Carolina seceded. Lincoln and the Republican Party, who came about as neither the Democratic Party, the Whig Party, nor any new party, met the demands of a majority of Northern voters. They never adopted a platform to abolish slavery, they merely wanted to limit its spread into the new territories. Most of the abolitionists joined the new Republican Party, but the majority of Republicans were not abolitionists, and there is little doubt that the party would not have succeeded with an abolitionist platform. The conclusion is that the Librevs are right in claiming that the war was caused by slavery.

The Librevs are right too with their claim that many in the South, especially the lower or middle classes, did not support the notions of secession from the Union; however, the actions of Mr. Lincoln led to the Southern abandonment of the nation created by their grandfathers. By February of 1861, six more lower-South states joined the Confederacy: Georgia, Alabama, Florida, Mississippi, Louisiana, and Texas. They founded the Confederate States of America after the successful election of a candidate, who ignored or even vilified Southerners. They saw no political future for themselves. However, Texas is the only state that made the decision by popular vote. For the others, it was the state legislatures that voted, and of course, they were dominated by the planter class. It is quite reasonable to accept the Librev view that the process was started by the planter class. This is very similar to the thinking of Northerners at the time who blamed the whole thing on a planter conspiracy.

When we look at the election results in the case of Texas, it is quite likely that the majority of Southerners did not want to give up being Americans. Only 14 percent voted against secession, however, 43 percent did not vote. If we combined the two groups, we find a minority of those living in Texas actually voted to succeed. Most of those in favor of secession were white protestant and many of them slave holders. It has also been shown that a correlation existed between the counties that voted for secession and those who voted for Breckinridge. If we look at the 1860 election results, this means we need to score another one for the Librevs who claim that the planter class were the ones who pushed for secession, especially when we take into account the fact that the upper South states remained loyal at first.

This does not mean that they caused the war. Even if we accept the possibility that the planters lead the way for secession, the fact is that it is the North who decided to kill Southerners, thus, it was a "war of Northern aggression." I have seen books which have claimed that after the firing on Fort Sumter, the upper tier states, or border South, joined the new country. Those who claim this forget an important step—the demand Lincoln made for 75,000 troops with each state meeting a quota. Many of those in the upper South even objected to the firing on Fort Sumter. However, when told that they must go and fight their fellow Southerners, in many cases relatives, then they chose secession.

Lincoln wanted the South to fire the first shot. However, evidence suggests that the whole thing was a setup. First of all, Fort Sumter was in Charleston Harbor. This would be similar to the Soviet Union building a fort in Manhattan during the cold war and then claiming the United States started a war by firing on it. The United States withdrew its forces from all other forts in the South except Forts Pickens and Sumter. It has been claimed, and it seems reasonable that they held on to these simply as an attempt to draw first fire out of the South. Nonetheless, most people at the time did not accept the notion that it was the South who was the aggressor since their only objective was to end occupation of a fort in their then sovereign nation by a hostile army.

The reasons for Southerners to fight the war changed dramatically since the first votes for secession with not only the demand for 75,000 troops but also the subsequent invasion of the Southern states. Not only did four more states join the Confederacy, but I think it is also safe to assume that many of those in the Deep South who originally opposed secession now supported their new nation. By the time of the first real battle in July 1861, many if not most Southerners saw the issue as one of defense against a foreign army invading their land; and thus, they needed to defend their homes and families—a situation in which war is undeniably justified. I am quite ready to concede to the Librevs that secession was led by the planter class; I will never accept the claims that the majority of the Southern people did not believe in their cause. What may have began as a heated debate over the spread of slavery into the territories was now a war of defense for the Confederate soldier. It is the North who turned a declaration of independence into a war.

Black Southerners

There is not a whole lot to add to the situation for black Southerners during the antebellum period other than what I have already discussed in previous chapters. The most significant event was the Dred Scott Supreme Court decision. Not only did the court reject Scott's attempt to gain his freedom, but in the process, they also stated that all of those of African ancestry, free or slave, were not citizens of the United States. This would have as much impact in the Reconstruction years as it did in the antebellum years.

Conclusions

The period that we now call antebellum is crucial in the defense of our Southern heritage since it is the time that we look to in searching for the causes of the Civil War. The main reason that so many hate Southern icons, especially the Confederate battle flag, is that they see them as symbols of slavery. The liberal-revisionist historians know that Abraham Lincoln and the Republican Party never promoted abolition. They also claim that they are merely objective historians searching for the truth in history. I do not believe them. The vast majority support the attempts to exterminate our culture, and many of the studies focused on the antebellum and Reconstruction periods in American history seem to be attempts to discredit the Southern perspective. They have labeled the traditional Southern historical interpretations as the "lost cause myth." If we can accept their view that the Confederate cause was simply something created by the slave-owning planters for the purpose of protecting their slaves, then we must accept that the North was fighting a noble fight. On this, they base their admiration of President Lincoln. Polls among American historians have consistently shown Abraham Lincoln as their choice for the best president in American history. I do not agree with them. When I hear that Saddam Hussein was an evil dictator who killed 300,000 of his own people, I think to myself that is what Lincoln did. Lincoln created the War of Northern Aggression. This 300,000 figure is based strictly on those Confederate soldiers killed and does not include the 300,000-plus Yankees who died in the process. It also does not include the thousands of civilians, black and white, who were killed or starved to death as a result of Lincoln's war.

CHAPTER FIVE
The War (1860—1865)

Introduction

This chapter is about the War for Southern Independence. However, it is strictly from the point of view of the relationship between the war and the attacks on our Southern heritage. There are thousands of books out there that go into the details on the military and political aspects of the war, so I see no reason to go into detail. I will offer a brief account of the highlights of the war for the sake of those not familiar with it. It is such a large part of Southern history that I do not want to make the assumption that all readers are well-versed on the war.

One of the most fascinating aspects of the Librev view on the war is that this seems to be one of the few cases in which the liberals, who dominate the intelligentsia of America, support the idea of war. Though generally pacifists, most of them look at what they call the Civil War as a just war because it liberated the slaves. They are well aware but seldom mention the fact that the United States is the only nation on earth which found it necessary to kill hundreds of thousands of their own people to end slavery. The Librevs consistently vote Abraham Lincoln as the greatest American president, even though he created the most devastating war in the history of North America. In fact, more Americans were killed in the War for Southern Independence than all other wars combined up until Vietnam. This is to say more than in the war for American independence, plus the Indian Wars, plus the War of 1812, plus the Mexican War, plus the Spanish–American War, plus the First World War, plus the Second World War, plus The Korean War, and finally with the Vietnam War, the total American death toll exceeded that caused by the Librev's favorite president, Abraham Lincoln. In addition, many more were left crippled and maimed. The countryside was in near total desolation as the friends of Lincoln destroyed towns, houses, farms, and even fences. I cannot cite reliable statistics. However, I have little doubt that if we included the civilian loss of life, the American death toll would be considerably greater for this war than all others combined. It has always amazed me that the pacifist liberal American historians most admire the man who generated such death and destruction.

Some Clarification

As I composed my opening comments for this chapter, I realized that there are three main issues I need to discus before continuing. First, the liberals have convinced much of the American public that liberalism is synonymous with intelligence or education. Second, the significance of the name "Civil War" and why Southerners continue to object to that moniker. Third is a reminder of the basic assumption that Adam Smith made in his book *Wealth of Nations*—that people are motivated by the principle of self-interest.

Liberalism is Genius

The majority of liberals in America seem to make the invalid assumption that those who are liberal are more intelligent and more educated than conservatives. I recall a survey of Mensa members done in the 1990s in which the split between those who labeled themselves liberal or conservative was very similar to the same division among the general population. Since Mensa members are chosen for their above average IQs (the top 2 percent), then it seems logical to assume that intelligence is not a significant variable in determining why people lean one way or the other in the political spectrum. In others words, it would seem that liberals are no more intelligent than conservatives, nor for that matter, the other way around.

I can see why so many liberals have this belief; the leftist view does dominate in American academia. I can offer a suggestion on why this is true, but I cannot prove this to be anything more than my opinion.

It has become a self-perpetuating system. A good example of this came with the passing of Grady McWhiney. *The Journal of Southern History* wrote about the death of "an influential if controversial historian of the American South. . ." They mentioned his "provocative work" *Cracker Culture* and later described the historian as "an interesting mix of devotion, gentility, *controversy*, and dedication to his craft and to his students."[13] (I emphasized the word controversy) However, when the communist Southern historian (that is a historian of the South, not a Southerner) Elizabeth Fox-Genovese died, they described her as being of "fiercely independent mind."[14] Perhaps it is just me, but "fiercely independent" sounds more respectful or at the least less euphemistic than "controversial." I remind the reader that Grady McWhiney is the historian who wrote *Cracker Culture*. He obviously did not accept the Librev conclusion that Southern identity was created during and after the war. This is why he was "controversial." He dared to disagree with the liberal academic elite. Again, it may be just me, but I felt that they were saying that not only was he controversial but that he was also wrong. The communist historian, on the other hand, was just "fiercely independent."

Anyway, since the liberals have seized control of the top jobs in the great Northern universities, such as Yale and Harvard, they influence the hiring process so that it is difficult for a conservative historian to find a job at such a school. Perhaps some of the less prestigious Southern or western schools would hire the more conservative, but how could they compare to a Harvard or Yale professor? As these professors seek publication of their findings, they cannot expect to be received in the same way as those who work at Harvard or Yale.

This attitude spread southward shortly after the end of the war. Some of the first "reconstructed" Southern universities were the University of North Carolina at Chapel Hill and Louisiana State University. These schools have become liberal anchors in the conquest of Southern history. They are respected even in the North, though they could never compare to the holy shrines of Harvard or Yale. Southerners have sought recognition by landing a position at these Yankeefied schools. They generally fall into line with the Northern interpretations and make

---

13   "Obituaries," *Journal of Southern History* (August 2006): 738–9.
14   "Obituaries," *Journal of Southern History* (May 2007): 516–7.

sure that they are liberal enough to merit the respect given them by the intellectual elite.

Meanwhile, when someone like Grady McWhiney comes along, they may be able to earn recognition by selling a lot of books, but all the liberal historians know that he cannot be correct. He ended up working in Kansas. He was not in agreement with the dominant historian culture of the Ivy League. This Librev thinking has spread throughout the South like a cancer. Those Librev historians who could not get a job in the North, or at least the prestigious Yankeefied schools of the South, are forced to settle for positions in the less-prestigious Southern universities. They accept jobs with the University of Oklahoma, or Arkansas, or Tennessee with the hope of escaping north some day. When they move down, they carry their Librev culture with them in their carpetbags.

I do not believe that the liberal Northern intellectual elite are any more intelligent or educated than the more conservative historians, who have achieved the same educational level. Merely being on the faculty at Harvard or Yale does not mean that their interpretations are more correct than a conservative-thinking historian. I do feel comfortable in claiming that the Yankee intellectual elite look at Southern history with a Northern slant, not necessarily a better slant.

What's in a Name?

The reason for the controversy over the name given to the war is simply that the term "civil war" is defined as a conflict between factions within a nation. Historians refer to the events of 1776 as the "War for American Independence" or "Revolutionary War," even though when it started there was no declaration of independence. However, even though the Southern states stated their intent from the beginning; wrote a constitution; elected a president; printed their own money and stamps; and built an army, their actions are simply called a "civil war." Since they lost, they are reduced to treasonous rebels. In 1861 and today, the loyal Confederate Southerner views the conflict as one between two independent and sovereign nations and not as a civil war. Therefore they prefer the name War of Southern Independence over Civil War. They sometimes call it the War of Northern Aggression since it is the North which invaded the South.

War of Economic Opportunity

Most Americans, liberal or conservative, have a difficult time accepting the economic motives for the war. The liberal prefers to think of it as a war to free the slaves. Most conservatives, on the other hand, think of themselves as patriotic Americans. They prefer to believe that their nation's soldiers fought and died for freedom and democracy, not imperialism. This creates a dilemma when they try to evaluate the War of Southern Independence. The fact is that the war was one in which the business-driven Republican Party of the North conquered the South. Their main reason was to protect Northern business interest. It is true that it was a rich man's war and a poor man's fight. The war was a battle of the business interest of the Southern planters versus the Northern merchants.

Today our own people are a burden in preserving our Southern heritage. The conservatives have swallowed the glorious principles of Manifest Destiny and firmly believe that America fights war for the principles of freedom and democracy. These same people firmly believe in the principles of capitalism, and I assume that most would equate capitalism with freedom and democracy. The cold war, for example, was democracy versus communism. So what if democracy is a political system and communism an economic system? The reality is that the systems are not mutually exclusive. The odd thing is that even though the basic assumption of Adam Smith, father of capitalism, is that people operate on the principle of self-interest, the conservative will deny that American wars have been fought for self-interest rather than the more noble principles of defending freedom and democracy. As we discuss the war and Reconstruction, we must realize that our Southern ancestors were victims of United States imperialism.

In most other cases, the liberal will not only admit to the notion that American wars have been fought for selfish gain but will even promote the idea. Librevs talk about how the United States military stole land from Indians; unjustifiably invaded Mexico; fought the Spanish because of the capitalist newspapers; and even entered World War I for the sake of the bankers and munition manufacturers. A fewer number will blame World War II on United States imperialism. However, in their mind there is no doubt that Vietnam was an imperialistic war. The Librev historians will use the expression "a rich man's war but a poor man's fight." However, they will generally refer only to the planter conspiracy and gloss over the fact that wealthy Northerners sent immigrants to do their fighting for them. They mention the draft riots of New York City but ignore the implications of this when they vote for Lincoln as the best American president. They instead focus on the evils of the slaveocracy and seem to be in general agreement that the war of Mr. Lincoln was a rare example of a "good war" to end slavery. In their logic, it is only later that Republicans represent business and United States imperialism. I believe that the Republican Party has always represented the interest of businessmen, Northern businessmen.

The Librev Principles

There are a number of issues relating to the War of Southern Independence which have become part of the Librev historiography. These are the liberal assumptions used to justify the extermination of our Southern heritage. First, the war was caused by the planter conspiracy. Second, the war was fought to free the slaves. Third, the poor Southerners, who they have labeled the "pine-barrens folk," did not support the Confederacy or the war. Fourth, they like to emphasize the role that blacks played in winning the war for the North while generally rejecting that notion that blacks played any significant role in defending the Confederacy. Fifth, they have even begun to peck away at the near-deity status of Robert E. Lee. Sixth, and most important for us today, is that they clearly support the idea that Confederate symbols, especially the battle flag, should be thrown on the same historical rubbish pile as Hitler's *Mein Kempf.*

Planter Conspiracy

I personally cannot deny the idea that the planter class of the South are the ones who initiated the momentum which led to the declaration of Southern independence. I believe the idea that all American wars, including this one, were fought to protect the interest of American businessmen. What the Librevs overlook is that the planters led the conflict in the South because they were the leading businessmen in the region, just as the businessmen in the North led their faction. The conflict did not arise over slavery but rather economic competition.

The North and the South were both capitalistic societies. Generally speaking, Southerners have been as guilty as Northerners in looking at the South as a region which resisted modernization. It is true that the South was still predominantly agricultural but not in the same way as a feudalistic society but rather as an agribusiness, a part of a capitalist economy. As N. S. B. Gras, the founding father of business history at Harvard, said in his book *Business and Capitalism*, "A study of the history of capitalism shows that major struggles do not occur between capitalism and some other order of society but between two rival forms of capitalism." Gras's view would indicate that tariffs and other economic issues may have been as important as slavery. And even the issue of slavery was more likely an economic issue rather than due to moral superiority. The South had dominated the federal government and was losing out to the North. They finally became convinced that they would be better off on their own, better off economically. The Northern businessmen could not lose the supply lines for their textile industry. They were determined to retain them even with force. "One group of capitalists may win over another and the victory may be progressive or retrogressive, but some form of capitalism will remain triumphant." Gras did not specifically refer to the War of Southern Independence, but apparently, if he was correct, would agree that the South was not a premodern society. "To be sure, force could be attempted, but a seizure of a capitalistic society without a preparation in the use of investment of capital is like an invasion of an orderly state by Huns and Vandals."[15] From his theories, it would seem logical to view the war between the states as one between two differing capitalist factions.

The War to Free the Slaves

The Librevs still argue that the war was fought over slavery. They know the numerous quotes from Northern leaders including Abraham Lincoln and Ulysses S. Grant in which they said they did not fight to

15   N. S. B. Gras, *Business and Capitalism: An Introduction to Business History* (New York: Augustus M. Kelley Publishers, 1971), vii-viii.

free the slaves. However, the Librevs still see it as the war that freed the slaves and therefore was a "good war." They know that the Emancipation Proclamation did not free a single slave at the time that Lincoln signed it. However, they argue that it is still a great document because as the North conquered the South, the slaves became freed. They ignore the fact that the masters in the North held on to their slaves. The fact is it was the Thirteenth Amendment that freed the slaves and that was not ratified until after the war was over. The war resulted in the end of slavery, but that was not the reason that the North started it.

The Pine Barren (Poor) Folks Did Not Support the Confederacy

Librevs, like other liberals, like to think of themselves as caring people who are the defenders of the poor, and thus, they do not like to think of the poor as being capable of doing wrong. It takes a rich man to be a sinner; this is why I believe they have created a historiography which attempts to show that the poor of the South did not support the Confederacy. This of course is tied to the planter conspiracy theory. I will not deny the leadership role of the planters. However, the Librevs overlook the leadership role of the businessmen who decided to attack Southerners for wanting to be independent. North or South, the average man is not the one who leads a nation into war. The leaders are usually rich, and the rich are motivated by self-interest, at least according to Adam Smith. Hence, the poor too are motivated by self-interest. In their case, self-interest came about when the blue hordes moved south. I will never believe that the poor will not and did not fight to protect their homes from invaders.

The Librevs like to look at the election of 1860 in determining the Confederate supporters. They assume that the Breckinridge supporters were those who led the way to independence and thus the war. The election results do indicate that the average middle-class Southern farmer and even many of the wealthy feared a movement toward a declaration of independence. The Constitutional Union Party was formed by those who could not support the black Republicans but feared a split in the Union. The supporters of Breckinridge did come from those areas with the most planters. I can see no reason to disagree with this Librev assumption; that is up until April of 1861.

The fact is that after the firing on Fort Sumter and the subsequent demand for seventy-five thousand troops and the invasion of the South by the Northern army, it became a different question. It is true that many deserted as they did in the North. It is true that many resented the draft as they did in the North. It is true that the common farmer was worried about the welfare of his family and the protection of his property as they were in the North. The bottom line is the most men in the South did fight in the war. They fought long and they fought hard, and it took the North four years to defeat them, even though they outnumbered them two to one and possessed more weapons and supplies. I cannot accept the idea that this would have been true without the support of the common man. They were the ones who made up the vast majority of the population. Seventy-five percent of the Southerners did not own a single slave. If they did not fight, it would not have taken years to conquer the Confederacy.

The Role of Black Southerners in the War

One of the main objectives of the liberal revisionist since the 1960s has been to include the stories of all Americans, not just the middle-class Anglo-Saxon population. This is a noble objective. All people are part of history, not just the wealthy and powerful and not just the whites. I finished my undergraduate studies in history in 1970 and never heard of the role that black soldiers played in the War of Southern Independence. Even though Elkin's book about the black soldiers, *The Sable Arm*, had been published in 1957, it was not required reading in the university I graduated from. It is a good thing to realize that the blacks were part of American history too.

In more recent times, there are those who have studied the black support for the Confederacy. The Librevs generally dismiss this as a statistically insignificant anecdotal collection of accounts of blacks who fought because they were forced to. I do not understand how they can be enthusiastic in recalling the black role in the war for American independence. These stories involve the grandfathers of the 1860s' slaves helping the grandfathers of the 1860s' planters, even though the British crown promised them freedom if they supported the king. The bottom line is that they want to emphasize the role of blacks in helping the North win while rejecting their contributions to the South. I will discuss the black efforts for the Confederacy later; what I wish to point out now is that these views are part of the Librev effort to provide evidence that the North fought the war to free the slaves and that the Southern side was merely an attempt by the planter class to hold onto their slaves. Therefore, according to their thinking, it is right to look at Confederate symbols as icons of evil.

The Sainted Mars Robert

Lately the Librevs have begun attacking the name and image of Robert E. Lee. General Lee is the only man in the history of the world to be offered command of opposing armies. He has been one of the most respected historical figures not only in the South but also around the world. He has been a symbol of integrity as well as a military genius. He has been such a powerful image that his existence alone justifies respect for the Confederacy. I have no doubt that this is the main motivation for attacking his good name. The only thing I have to say is that General Lee did not suspend the constitution; order an invasion; encourage state-sponsored terrorism; nor oversee the destruction of millions of acres of private property including cities, farms, homes, and businesses. The man who appears on the five dollar bill and the one-cent coin, whose monument looms over the city of Washington, and the continued favorite Librev president did.

Bury Confederate Symbols

In the end, the Librevs have endorsed the attack of our Confederate symbols, especially the battle flag. Most of the previously mentioned objectives of the Librevs seem to be aimed at the principal target of Confederate symbols. The Librevs look at organizations such as the Sons of Confederate Veterans or the United Daughters of the Confederacy as defenders of the "lost cause" who are "still fighting the Civil War." Some seem to accept our pleas that to us the flag is a symbol of "heritage not hate" and that it does not represent racism. Nonetheless, they say that "at issue is not just history but whose history." So while they endorse ideas such as Black History Month, they urge the sacrifice of our heritage. As one college history book explained, "In the interests of reconciliation, it's surely time for Southerners to follow Robert E. Lee's final order to his men and 'Furl the flag, boys.'"[16] What more do I need to say. I, for one, do not believe that I should be expected to sacrifice the memory and honor of my ancestors to the gods of political correctness and diversity. No one should be made to feel ashamed of their heritage, black or white.

The South Lost the War

We may not like to admit it, but we lost the war. People like to look for simple one-line answers to questions, including the answer as to why the South lost. We all know that the North outnumbered them two to one and that they had more factories, railroads, and munitions from the start. They also had a navy, which allowed them to build a blockade and thus limit the ability to acquire the needed weapons and other supplies. These all fit into the category of military causes for defeat.

Less frequently discussed are the political problems. The South had to create a new government along with all of its infrastructure, whereas the North already had a government. It dramatically changed with the parting of the Southern states, but nonetheless, it had been operating for many decades.

Some like to say that the South just copied the government of the Union, but do not forget that government was partially constructed by Southerners. The few changes made highlight what the Southerners saw as problems with the old government, which needed to be fixed. These included a nonrepetitive presidential term of six years, line-item veto, limits on federal taxation, and limits on the central government interference with slavery in the states or territories. Clearly we cannot deny that slavery played a role in the issues that led to disunion.

The Southerners' reasons for fighting were a big part of their problem. They claimed that they stood for states' rights, which means that they stood for a weaker central government. Like most controversial issues, there is some good and some bad to be said for each point of view. A weaker central government affords more individual freedom, but it can

---

16   David Goldfield et al., *The American Journey: A History of the United States* (New Jersey: Prentice Hall,), 560.

be a problem in times of crises, such as a war. There were times when the states resisted the control that Jefferson Davis tried to exercise in order to present a more unified defense of the new nation. Thus, while we love to talk about the tyrant Abraham Lincoln, we want to overlook the cries by some Southerners that Davis was a tyrant. Lincoln had the advantage of defending a strong central government while Davis supposedly fought for states' rights, so we must admit that we cannot call Lincoln a hypocrite as it relates to this subject.

Underlying the military weaknesses as well as some of the internal issues was the Southern economy. They had to pay for a war when they had no money. The states' rights advocates of course wanted to limit the taxation powers of the new federal government. It was difficult to find foreign financiers for a country which had not been recognized by the greatest financial powers of the world such as England and France. Stocks and bonds of a new company will always be more risky than stocks and bonds issued by an existing company that has a good debt history.

The Border States

Some claim that the term "border states" is a Northern invention. These are the states which had slavery but according to Mr. Lincoln did not join the Confederacy: Delaware, Maryland, Missouri, Kentucky, and an illegally formed state called West Virginia. The most obvious contradiction about these states is that Lincoln claimed them all as loyal to the Union. However, they all had slavery (though West Virginia did agree to end the institution). How could this have been a war to end slavery if states that were still part of the United States had slavery? Slavery was not abolished in some of these states until the ratification of the thirteenth amendment, which happened after the war. Basically, the term border state meant those slaves states which did not join the Confederacy.

In the case of Missouri and Kentucky, the state governments split into factions in which one claimed to be loyal to the Union while the other sought and received admission as a Confederate State. Delaware had very few slaves, but they voted for Breckinridge in 1860 and failed to come up with their quota for the seventy-five troops, which Lincoln had ordered. In their case, they claimed a loophole in which their state had no militia system and therefore did not have the mechanism to come up with their quota. The most controversial of the so-called border states is Maryland.

I have no doubt that Maryland would have voted to follow the lead of Virginia if Lincoln had not taken such giant steps to squash democracy in that state. Again, there are numerous books which get into the details, but suffice it to say that the Union arrested many Marylanders after Lincoln suspended habeas corpus. Some spent only a few days behind bars while others served until they submitted to the might of the Union. Meanwhile, General Butler occupied one strategic point after another before finally entering the city of Baltimore and establishing a rule that would have left Hitler envious. By the time that the state legislature voted on the issue of secession, the Union army had been established and the legal system dismantled to the point that it was clear that a vote for secession would lead to immediate arrest. I am sure many feared the consequences of such arrest, and this is why they voted down secession. The vote did not come until after Union military might had been well-established.

The Librevs often take the position that Maryland would not have seceded since Lee and the Confederate army twice marched into the state in an attempt to liberate them but failed to find the anticipated support. This could be a valid point, but I firmly believe that by the time Lee arrived, the opportunity had passed. Many of the pro-Confederates had either left; joined the Confederate army elsewhere; or feared the consequences of their actions if they failed in an attempt to overthrow a well-established Union military. A relative stability had been achieved by the time Lee arrived in the state, and to upset the cart at that point would have been at great risk to property and family.

The War

As stated earlier, I will offer here a mere outline of the military aspects of the war. I do this for those who have little or no knowledge of the subject. For those already familiar with the generals and the battles, do not expect to find new material. In fact, because there are so many books on the war is another reason why I feel it is wise to make sure we are all on the same page.

Overall Strategy

Both sides believed it would be a short war when it started. The original Union enlistments were for ninety days. For the South, victory could be achieved when the North recognized Southern independence. Many in the South believed that the average Northerner would never support Lincoln in his attack on fellow Americans. For the North to win, they had to get the South to abandon their claims of independence. As it turned out, this meant that they had to totally conquer the new nation.

After the loss at the Battle of First Manassas, Winfield Scott convinced Lincoln that it would be a long and difficult path to victory. They would continue to travel that long road to Richmond, but in the meanwhile, they would follow Scott's Anaconda Plan. With this, they would strangle the life out of the Confederacy. First, they would form a blockade to limit Southern trade, and second, the Army would follow a plan of divide and conquer with a march down the Mississippi River.

The Trans-Mississippi

The struggle west of the Mississippi began with the attempt to subdue the Confederate government of Missouri. Governor Jackson had led the pro-South faction of the state to the Southwest corner. The Union army tried to defeat them, which led to the battles in that part of Missouri and overflowed into Northwest Arkansas. The climax came with the battle of Elk Horn Tavern and then later at Prairie Grove, both in Arkansas. The Confederates lost and never did get reorganized west of the Mississippi.

The Five Civilized Tribes signed a treaty with the Confederacy, and they became a buffer zone for Texas. They held off the first invasion, but with the second, the Union captured Fort Gibson and the Cherokee capital of Tahlequah. The Yankees took the principal chief, John Ross, to Philadelphia where they operated a puppet government. General Stand Waite led the Confederate faction. By the summer of 1863, the

Union had gained control of much of the Cherokee nation, Fort Smith in Arkansas, and by September, Little Rock fell. After that, the war in the West degenerated into guerilla warfare, which resulted in terrible destruction and numerous cases of torture and murder on both sides. At times, it spilled over into Kansas. Some major campaigns occurred in 1864. The Confederate General Price led a raid into Missouri, and the Union attempted an invasion of Texas going up the Red River.

The Trans-Mississippi is one area where the desertion rate did get very high. The contemporary Librev historiography likes to use this information to paint a picture of the common farmer and soldier as lacking dedication to the Confederate cause. I have done a lot of research on Arkansas since most of my ancestors in the war were from that state. I have not collected statistical data, but I have noticed that the desertion rate of Arkansas soldiers serving on the other side of the Mississippi did not seem any higher than from other states. I believe the desertion rate was higher on the west side of the river because they were being invaded and conquered. I have seen a few Librev accounts in which they admitted that the high desertion was probably due to the fact that the invading army occupied the home and farms of many of the soldiers. It seems like a natural response to feel that your place is with your family at such a time rather than to remain with the army.

The West

When we talk about the western front, we are referring to the war involving the Army of Tennessee rather than the far west. This is where we saw the most direct impact of Scott's Anaconda Plan. U. S. Grant made a name for himself by leading the attacks on forts Henry and Donelson, which defended the Tennessee and Cumberland rivers. Shortly after that, he led his army down the Tennessee River and met the enemy at the Battle of Shiloh in April of 1862. From there, the Union army went into Northern Mississippi, over to Chattanooga, and then into North Georgia where they finally took Atlanta in the summer of 1864. After Atlanta, the Union army went on its rampage through Georgia and up to the Carolinas while the remains of the Confederate army of Tennessee headed back toward Franklin and Nashville where they faced total annihilation.

The East

Robert E. Lee and his Army of Northern Virginia basically defended Richmond for most of the war. Lee did not assume command until 1862. He defended the capital, though he did invade Maryland twice with the assumption that the people of that state were awaiting liberation. I discussed this earlier. This is what some Librevs use to support their belief that Maryland would not have joined the Confederacy even if Lincoln had not disposed of the Constitution and denied the people any voice in their future. Lee reversed his defensive strategy in the summer of 1863 when he led his army into Pennsylvania. He failed to accomplish what he hoped to but did make it back to Virginia, where he continued the struggle for another year and a half. Following the siege of Petersburg, the Army of Northern Virginia fought its last battle at Appomattox where Lee surrendered on April 9, 1865.

Major General Philip Sheridan and his accomplices in front of his tent in 1864. Sheridan bragged about his destruction of civilian food in the Shenandoah Valley of Virginia, though such behavior was condemned by the Geneva Conventions later in the same decade. He followed Sherman in similar destruction of civilian property after the fall of Atlanta. Left to right: Wesley Merritt, David McGregg, Sheridan, Henry E. Davies (standing), James H. Wilson, and Alfred Torbert. (Courtesy National Archives)

Final Days

It is often assumed that the war ended at Appomattox. It did not. After the fall of Richmond, Jefferson Davis attempted to take his government across the Mississippi to Texas where they would continue the struggle for freedom. He did not make it. As stated earlier, the Army of Tennessee was decimated after Franklin and Nashville. The Army of the Trans-Mississippi under Kirby-Smith did not surrender until May of 1865. It was the following month when the conquering Union army occupied Texas and informed the slaves that they were free. This is why we still have the holiday celebrated by black Southerners called Juneteenth.

The Cherokee general Stand Waite was the last Confederate general to surrender in Doaksville, Indian Territory, on June 23, 1865. Some former Confederates could not live in the United Yankee States and so they fled the country. Some eventually came back while others were buried in foreign lands. Edmund Ruffin, for one, preferred death over living in an occupied nation. As we will see in the next chapter, the military aspects of the invasion and defeat of a proud people was over. However, the conquest was not complete. Some have described Reconstruction as being worse than the war.

Ethnic Diversity

The earlier quote about furling the flag came from the Southern but Librev historian David Goldfield; it is a prime example of the main rationalization for the extermination of our Southern heritage. He called for the furling of the flag "in the interest of reconciliation." Those of us who are old enough to remember America before 1965 realize that it is much different today. We called the nation a "melting pot," but it, in no way, resembled the amount of diversity that is the United States of today. Whereas we grew up in a country that had some Africans, a few surviving Indians, and in some areas a number of those with Mexican background, for the most part, diversity meant being Italian, Jewish, Polish, or some other non-Germanic Europeans. With the increased diversity that we have since 1965, some, especially educators, have promoted the concept of diversity. This is a value talked about much today but which I never heard of before 1965, not in the way it is used now. The America I grew up in told ethnic jokes, stereotyped nonwhites in television and movies, and treated them as second-class citizens.

I am not complaining about this change in America; I am simply setting the stage for discussion of the role that diversity plays in the annihilation of our Southern heritage. With the promotion of "diversity" some like to promote the notion that this country has always been about diversity. The new America represents democracy, freedom, opportunity, and "diversity." Even though the Librevs have never been shy about pointing out the faults of the United States, they have gone off in the direction of blaming past racist attitudes on Southerners. I have covered this topic in previous chapters, but it is the most crucial in understanding why the scapegoating with Confederate icons is not only unjust but based on misconceptions. The fact is that the Confederate army was diverse. I cannot support my claim with exacting statistical data; however, it is clear from some recent books that the Confederate army was in all probability more diverse than the Union army was. The Confederate symbols that Dr. Goldfield and his friends wish to sacrifice for the sake of "reconciliation" in fact generated patriotic pride from people of many backgrounds other than the white Anglo-Saxon protestant background that most of those from New England came from. I am not attempting to compete with books which have been written on this topic; I present here only a brief recap of what the ignored scholarship says.

Let me also remind the reader that I am not attempting to paint Southerners as lovers of all mankind. They were racist as most Americans were until well after World War II. I attempt here to point out that they were no more racist than those in the North. The minorities who supported the Confederacy or the Union did so because they saw their choice as the one that would most benefit their people. Some of different racial and ethnic backgrounds turned to the Union, but others turned to the Confederacy. In many cases, it seems that these ethnic minorities saw greater advantage for them to side with the Confederacy.

Indian Confederates

As mentioned previously, the Cherokee general Stand Waite was the last Confederate general to surrender. In the early days of the conflict, the

United States Army evacuated the forts in Indian Territory and made no attempt at catering to the Indians. I believe that it was Northern racism that led them to ignore any interest in an alliance with the red man. Albert Pike of the CSA went into the present state of Oklahoma and negotiated an alliance with all five of the Civilized Tribes and also signed treaties with some of the western Indians. Those from the Five Tribes (the forces of political correctness does not like to use the term "civilized tribes" these days, the implication being that the other Indians were not civilized) had reasons to support the North. It is the people of the South who drove the Indians from the lands of their ancestors. Perhaps the most compelling reason to support the Union is that the government of the United States still owed them annuities payable to them from when they agreed to vacate their ancestral homes. Opposition to the Union would probably mean that they would sacrifice these future receipts.

The fact is that the Five Civilized Tribes were Southerners. They had assimilated into white culture but mainly Southern white culture. They had economic bonds to the region; grew cotton; and owned slaves as many white Southerners did. By 1860, there was a large population of mixed bloods which had established familial bonds with Southern whites. Not all agreed with the Confederate alliance. Opothleyahola led a faction of Creeks and assorted others, including runaway slaves who fled to Kansas in November of 1861 and became involved in the first Civil War battle in Indian Territory known as Round Mountain.

Annie Heloise Abel, one of the first to study the war in Indian Territory, gave us a good explanation for the reasons why the Indians chose the Confederate States over the United States. The Indians promised alliance and, in return, were given political recognition they never received from the old country. The Confederates allowed them representation in the Confederate Congress and promised them the status of statehood. "The Southern white man, embarrassed, conceded much more than he really believed in, more than he ever could or would have conceded, had he not himself been so fearfully hard-pressed." She went on to say that "it was quite otherwise with the Northern white man . . . he, self-confident and self-reliant, negotiated with the Indian in the traditional way, took base advantage of the straits in which he found him." The Northerners asked the Indians "to help him fight his battles, and, in the selfsame moment, plotted to dispossess him of his lands." She went on, "the very lands that had, less than five and twenty years before, been pledged as an Indian possession 'as long as the grass should grow and the waters run.'"[17]

I persist in claiming that the North was as racist, if not more so, than the South, and this is reflected in their attitude toward the Indians. At first, they did not consider them worth catering to. Then they treated them with the same attitude of racial superiority that they had always used when dealing with nonwhites. After the battles at Elk Horn Tavern and Prairie Grove in Arkansas, the Northern press complained of the savages employed by the Confederate army who had removed scalps from the poor Yankee soldiers they defeated in battle. The Indians were more concerned with their own welfare more than either Northern or Southern whites. In the end, the majority of the Indians believed they would be better off supporting the Confederate States of America. The Confederate symbols represent Southern Indians as well as Southern whites.

Jewish Confederates

About one-third of the Jews living in America in 1860 lived in the South, where recent research claims they were more widely accepted than in the North. Historians are usually handicapped by restricting their comments to what they consider proven facts. As a Southerner, I have an advantage over all of those Yankee Librevs who are writing the "true history" of our people. I was raised by Southerners and know them. Many, and probably most, have their prejudices. They also have the ability to overlook their prejudices for the sake of kindness to someone they see as a good person despite his defect of being black, or Indian, or Jewish. In other words, if "he's still a good ol' boy." When you realize this aspect of the Southern nature then historical facts make more sense. Most of those of the North think of the typical Southerner as a racist bigot who can only express hatred and contempt for those they see as their inferior. This is definitely not the case for the majority of Southerners.

Most of the Southern Jews immigrated in the 1840s and 1850s from what is today Germany although back then there was no Germany, so they came from places such as Bavaria, Prussia, Alsace, Hesse, Baden,

---

17   Annie Heloise Abel, *The American Indian as Slaveholder and Secessionist* (Lincoln: University of Nebraska Press, 1992), 18–9.

Swabia, or Westphalia. Some came from other areas such as Poland or Russia. "American Jewish experience reached a consensus long ago that the Jews were more accepted in the antebellum South than in the North." Their "loyalty to the Confederacy often was a matter of intense personal gratitude. Nowhere else in America had they experienced such fullness of opportunity or achieved comparable political and social acceptance."[18] It should not be surprising that three of the six Jewish congressmen came from the South, even though the North had twice the Jewish population.

As I have repeatedly stated, I do not deny Southern racism; I'm only pointing out that the North was as bad or worse. The first known Jew in Boston was "warned out" in the 1640s. They flourished in Charleston but were not allowed to live in liberal Boston. "John Quincy Adams referred to David Yulee as the 'squeaking Jew delegate from Florida' and Rep. Albert G. Marchand of Pennsylvania as 'a squat little Jew-faced rotundity.'" As the war approached, the *Boston Evening Transcript* "blamed secession on the Southern Jews." *The New York Times* referred to Senators Benjamin and Yulee as "president and vice president of a Southern Jerusalem," and in 1864, "castigated the Democratic Party because its chairman, August Belmont, was 'the agent of foreign jew bankers.'"[19]

"Jewish soldiers . . . fought for the South for many reasons, but the chief reason was to do their duty as they saw it."[20] The Librevs and the haters of our Southern heritage would like us to believe that our part of America bares the sin of American racism. Robert N. Rosen, author of *The Jewish Confederates*, clearly does not buy that thinking. The Jews of the South fought so hard in Tennessee that Grant expelled them. They remained loyal to the cause to the end. According to Rosen, "They had grown accustomed to breathing the free air of Dixie and were determined, like the Jews of Shreveport, to stand by, protect, and honor the flag of the Confederacy." Rabi Korn said, "The Jews of the Confederacy had good reason to be loyal to their section. . . Nowhere else in America - certainly not in the ante-bellum North - had Jews been accorded such an

---

18   Robert N. Rosen, *The Jewish Confederates* (Columbia: University of South Carolina Press, Inc., 2000), 31.
19   Ibid., 35.
20   Ibid., xiii.

opportunity to be complete equals as in the old South."²¹ The Confederate symbols represent Southern Jews as well as Southern whites.

Hispanic Confederates

Thousands of Hispanics fought for the Confederacy, many of them documented in books written by John O'Donnell-Rosales, originally of Cuba but now a resident of Alabama. Entire companies were raised of Spanish or Hispanic men. Rosales said, "I must honestly admit that although I love the United States, I have never felt American, but instead I feel Southern." He went on to add "This land is our sacred birthright, each group having earned it by their blood and toil." He spoke of his Confederate ancestor, Pvt. Kelvin (Carlin) Rosales of Louisiana and said, "he was wounded many times and surrendered with the last Confederate units still active in June of 1865."²² Between 1762 through 1813, Hispanics settled in two pockets. The coastal settlements included New Orleans, St. Bernard Parish, St. Louis, Biloxi, and Ascension, Assumption, and Iberville Parishes of Louisiana. Some other settlements include those in Arizona and New Mexico, St. Augustine, Florida, Saint Elena, South Carolina, and of course, many in Texas. There were also Spanish Jews in New Orleans, Savannah, Charleston, and parts of Virginia. The fact is that Confederate symbols belong to Hispanic Southerners as well as white Southerners.

21   Ibid., 54.
22   John O'Donnell-Rosales, *Hispanic Confederates* (Baltimore: Clearfield Company, Inc., 1998), v.

Black laborers on a wharf, James River, Virginia. Both Union and Confederate armies used slave labor during the war. There is no doubt that the slaves just did as they always did, what they were told. However, if they had turned more toward resistance, the war would not have lasted as long as it did. When the Union army destroyed food, they were also starving the slaves. (Courtesy National Archives)

Black Confederates

There have been numerous recent publications about black participation in the Confederate cause. I will make no attempt here to compete with them but instead will point out that it is a fact regardless of how many Librevs wish to deny it. The undeniable reality exist that if the slaves were prime for a rebellion such as that imagined by John Brown, then the time would have never been better. It is true that tens of thousands of slaves followed the Union army as it invaded the South. However, hundreds of thousands remained on their plantations. Their labor in the fields allowed many more whites to serve in the army. If they had broken out in rebellion, those same white soldiers would have been needed to quiet said rebellion instead of fighting Yankees. The

Confederacy would have fallen in a matter of months, maybe even weeks, if this had been the case.

We may never know the exact numbers of blacks who fought for the South; they did not serve in segregated regiments as in the North. The Confederate army utilized thousands of slaves in the construction of defenses. The first black regiments formed were Confederate regiments, not Northern ones. Some Librevs and South haters will say that many of those who served the Confederacy did so as laborers. They overlook the fact that the same could be said about many of those in the Union army—a policy which continued through World War II. Some blacks had not only gone to the front as servants for the Confederate masters but also participated when the time to fight came. I have seen numerous cases of those who had served as substitutes for their white master. Anyway, the anecdotal evidence is overwhelming supporting the notion that numerous blacks fought for the cause of Southern independence.

The main reason for resistance to this fact is that many cannot believe that a slave would fight for the nation that enslaved them. I cannot blame anyone for questioning this. First of all, I would suggest that maybe they did not see this as a war to free the slaves. Lincoln and most of his general officers denied that on numerous occasions. The second thing I don't understand is how these same liberals can talk about the blacks who fought for American independence. Did they not fight for the country that was enslaving them? In most cases, those in 1861 would have been the grandsons of the slaves who served in 1776, and their masters would have been the grandsons of the masters of the Revolutionary-era slaves.

In 1776 and in 1861, the blacks thought of themselves as Virginians, Carolinians, and Louisianans, not Americans. The free blacks who first joined up would have done so out of a "sense of community responsibility which impelled them to throw their lot with their neighbors." I could give many, many examples, but one of my favorite is the black servant who had been captured along with his master. When questioned by a white Northern officer of why he was fighting he answered, "I had as much right to fight for my native state as you had to fight for your'n, and a blame sight more right than your furriners, what's got no homes."[23]

---

23   Richard Rollins, *Black Southerners in Gray: Essays on Afro-Americans in Confederate Armies* (Murfreesboro, TN: Southern Heritage Press, 1994), 6.

Many Southerners resisted the arming of black troops; no doubt because they realized that to do so would greatly reduce the possibility of returning to slavery. In March of 1865, the Confederate Congress finally passed legislation which called for the conscription of black soldiers. Not long after, Davis sent his secretary of State to Europe with the message that the Confederacy would abolish slavery in exchange for recognition of the new country by France and England. It was too late at that point.

The bottom line is that not all but many blacks fought for the Confederate army. Like the white Southerners, I am sure there were many different reasons for why they did. Regardless, Confederate symbols stand for black Confederates as well as white ones.

The Loss of Civilian Life

The Librevs underplay or completely ignore the atrocities committed against Southern civilians by their President Lincoln's invading hordes. They do admit to Sherman's march to the sea and render a little more than a footnote account of the destruction in the Shenandoah Valley, but they seem to accept the idea of collateral damage justified by the fact that they resulted in a greater good of freeing the slaves. The liberals of America love to complain about atrocities committed by the United States Army in other wars but seem to be quite accepting with this one. I have seen estimates as high as 2 million total deaths, which would mean well over a million civilians. Most sources I have seen put the number at about fifty thousand. In either case, they almost completely ignore the fact that many of these were the blacks that they were supposedly there to rescue. The Librevs speak of the thousands of blacks who tagged along after the liberating Yankee Army but assume that the millions who remained on the plantation did so out of fear. I think it is quite possible that many of them feared the Yankees more that the white Southerners. A great many of the civilian deaths were due to starvation; the invading army was starving the slaves too. The sad thing is that much of the food was destroyed and not simply consumed by the invaders. There are a number of books that list some of the destruction, none that I am aware of, written by the academic historians. I suspect that they would say that it is because such stories are part of the "lost cause myth." I tend to think it is because such stories contradict their preconceived ideas about what makes Lincoln so great.

A refugee family leaving a war area with belongings loaded on a cart. The Yankee textbooks rarely mention the civilian cost of the war. Some have estimated more the fifty thousand civilian deaths. In addition, many lost their homes; families were separated; and no one talked of post-traumatic stress in those days. (Courtesy National Archives)

Conclusions

The Confederate cause probably had a greater racial diversity than the Union cause. The North did have more immigrants—mainly Irish, German, and other Northern Europeans. The South had Indians, Jews, Hispanics, as well as blacks. They too had a number of immigrants. Those who wish to eradicate Confederate symbols claim that they are divisive symbols that should be sacrificed to the gods of diversity for the sake of peace and harmony in the modern United States, the nation they forced upon us. They encourage respect for different cultures; they believe that to be the glory and beauty of diversity. One exception is those of Southern Confederate background. They believe that our ancestors do not deserve to be remembered, much less honored. The absurdity of their whole attitude is that Confederate symbols were important to many of diverse backgrounds. It is only the attitude of the political correctness supported by the Librev historians that prevents many of those from diverse backgrounds in recognizing their Confederate ancestors. So many Americans have been brainwashed into equating racism with the South. This has led most non-Anglo-Americans to identify with the North. They do not even consider the possibility that their people may have been supporters of the Confederacy since they come from a minority so persecuted by our people. Fortunately the Sons of Confederate Veterans have some of the descendants of diversity among their membership today. I have seen the white members of the SCV repeatedly demonstrate respect and appreciation to those who are willing to step forward and be recognized. The Confederate symbols are meant to honor the Confederate soldiers who sacrificed for the cause of our independence, regardless of racial or ethnic background.

CHAPTER SIX

Reconstructing Reconstruction, 1865–1877

Introduction

Reconstruction is the pivotal point in understanding the Librev interpretation of Southern history. The consensus among Librev historians is that we unreconstructed Southerners believe in what is called the Dunning School interpretation, which has been relabeled "the lost cause myth." Dunning School is the interpretation applied in the movies *Gone with the Wind* and *The Birth of A Nation*. Professor Dunning was from Columbia University of New York, and so the Librevs do not deny that this view was widely accepted by Americans from the North as well as the South. As stated in the introduction of one college-level history textbook, Southerners viewed the war not "as a lesson in humility, but as an episode in the South's journey to salvation." Some have been kind and try to sound understanding as to why Southerners are so wrong; "The Southern white view of the Civil War [and of Reconstruction - LT] was not a deliberate attempt to falsify history, but rather a need to justify and rationalize the devastation and loss of life that accompanied the Confederate defeat." I cannot be so kind in understanding the Librev motivation for their point of view. They would like to believe that their motivation is purely academic. To me it seems that their view is just as distorted, if not more so, than what they call the Southern "lost cause myth."

My thesis is an expansion of what most recognize immediately, that history is written by the winners. For generations, the Northern historians have let the South write their own history as they focused on the New England village and other such topics. With the civil rights movement and growing revisionism, they developed more of an interest in black history. This combined with the fact that they have done more histories of New England than there were puritans, they turned their attention to the South. They were motivated to revise the view of Civil War and Reconstruction history. With the increased popularity of Confederate bashing, they acquired a new motivation. At first, the "lost cause myth" manifested itself in the erection of Confederate memorials "erected typically on the most important site in a town, the courthouse square." It also included "commemorations of Confederate Memorial Day, the birthdays of prominent Confederate leaders, and the reunions of veterans." It was created and fostered by organizations, such as the United Daughters of the Confederacy and Sons of Confederate Veterans, who saw to it that "the white history of the South was implanted into young minds and the legacy carried down through the generations." This "insured that the Lost Cause would not only be an interpretation of the past, but also the basic reality of the present and the foundation for the future."[24] Therefore they can accept our claims that the "neo-Confederate" is not motivated by racism but that we are simply victims to the brainwashing of our ancestors.

The Yankee arrogance that led to the war in the first place continues to guide the Yankee Librev historian of today. They have recruited an army of scalawag historians who know they better accept the Harvard and Yale interpretations or abandon all hope of being an academic historian. They can see so clearly our self-interest in history, but they are completely blind to their own. The basic assumption that guides them is that the war was not only justified but also necessary for the elimination of the evil institution of slavery. One Yankee Librev historian who is at the vanguard of this thinking is Eric Foner. He has defined Reconstruction as being the story of the new South in which the black is a freedman rather than a slave. For him, Reconstruction included the so-called border states, even the ones who made no attempt at becoming part of the Confederacy. According to him, if they had slavery, they had Reconstruction. He sees the freeing of the slaves as beginning with the Emancipation Proclamation, completely ignoring the fact that every historian is aware of—that that document never freed a single slave at

---

24   Goldfield et al., *The American Journey: A History of the United States.* (New Jersey: Pearson Printice Hall, 2004), 499–500.

the time it was issued. In addition, some of the border states, especially West Virginia, began emancipating or attempting to emancipate the slaves. Therefore the Fonerites see Reconstruction as beginning in 1863. This serves to heighten the nobility of the war and Reconstruction in that the North is simply trying to create a better world for black Americans while the South resisted this.

Foner thoroughly combed the historical records, and I would not criticize his abilities as a researcher; I do take exception to his conclusion that the history of Reconstruction has now been corrected. In the preface of his book *Reconstruction: America's Unfinished Revolution, 1863–1877,* he claims "no part of the American experience has, in the last twenty-five years [the book is copyrighted in 1988 - LT] seen a broadly accepted point of view so completely overturned Reconstruction." He sees his book as a need to fill the void left by scrapping the Dunning interpretation. As he said, "yet despite this change in consciousness, so to speak, historians have yet to produce a coherent new portrait of the era." I am impressed with his history of the ending of slavery, but I am not convinced that the War of Southern Independence and the oppression of the Southern people that lasted until 1877 and even beyond was justified.

It may be that some of the Yankees had noble intentions, but not all of them did. It may be that some simply wanted to help the black people, but this does not negate the fact that the Republicans used them as the foundation on which they tried to build their party in the South. It is true that during this period, Southerners cultivated the image of their efforts as the "lost cause," but that does not mean that it was a "myth." The fact is that the people of the South, like their grandparents did in the late eighteenth century, declared independence. Like then, they were invaded as the forces of centralism attempted to deny them the right to self-government. The difference between the two occasions is that in the latter they were defeated. This does not mean that they were wrong. In the end, the slaves were freed, but this does not mean that the atrocities committed against the South by Yankee imperialism were justified. It may be that after the South took control of their reconstruction that the blacks were reduced to second-class citizenship, but it does not mean that Northerners were any less racist nor does it prove that America would have produced a much better society for all if they had not abandoned their noble crusade. It may even be that race relations were worsened by the fact that they used the blacks as pawns in their attempts to control and dominate the hearts and minds of the Southern people.

Dunning School (Lost Cause Myth)

In the early twentieth century, North and South had somewhat of a consensus regarding Reconstruction regardless of any disagreements over the war. William Dunning and John W. Burgess saw Lincoln as trying to achieve sectional reconciliation, which Andrew Johnson tried to follow after he came to the White House. They blamed the radicals of the Republican Party as being responsible for turning Reconstruction into the debacle that failed with the Compromise of 1877. Librev historians of today see this as the dominant interpretation in both the South and the North from the late nineteenth century through World War II. They see this as the simplistic views expressed and solidified in the American conscience with films, such as *Gone with the Wind* and *The Birth of a Nation*.

I for one see *Gone with the Wind* as a soap opera, both the book and the movie. This movie is still loved by many today thanks to Scarlet's beautiful dresses, the romantic balls and the colorful backdrop. There are others who despise the film today; they see it as portraying the blacks as simple-minded buffoons who speak and behave in the stereotypical ways with which many whites viewed their fellow Americans. I have shown the Reconstruction scenes from the movie to some of the history classes because they were classic Dunning School. Nonetheless, I have the opinion that the movie is better than most Hollywood productions as far as historical accuracy. They may have shown Mammy as being loyal to her white mistress, but the fact is that this was quite often the case with house servants, such as the one she portrayed. The field slaves were gone; that is why Scarlet had blisters on her hands. They showed the Ku Klux Klan as simply trying to restore law and order where the carpetbaggers had failed. It is obvious that this organization served other purposes, but this was one of them. Scarlet, as a symbol of the New South, surrendered her morality to modernization as she greedily pursued wealth at any price; however, Karl Marx would have agreed with this as an example of one of the weaknesses in the capitalist system. My greatest objection to the movie is the general portrayal of the South as resisting modernization and the Confederate soldiers as defenders of a feudal society, which was "gone with the wind" after the war.

It is a movie and like most movies not a reliable source for history. It is classic Dunning School, but I am not convinced that this alone is the cause for its deficiencies. Margaret Mitchell knew many who had lived through the war and Reconstruction. I have no doubt that she used stories which she had picked up from her family and acquaintances. There were Confederate veterans who attended the premiere of the movie in Atlanta in 1939. The Librevs believe that their memories were distorted by the "lost cause myth." This is so typical of Yankees', especially Yankee intellectuals, arrogance. They are the only ones wise enough to see the true history of the events which tore apart the United States. They know more with their research than those who were there. I realize that an eye witness may have a more distorted view of reality than someone who has studied several sides of a story, but we cannot simply ignore the eyewitness account when it is contrary to the conclusions of researchers. It may be that one or two eyewitnesses believe they saw something that did not happen the way it appeared. When we are looking at the accounts of the Southern experience during the war, we are talking about thousands of eyewitnesses. It seems unlikely that they are all wrong or deluded.

The racism in *The Birth of a Nation* should be a source of embarrassment for all Americans, Northerners as well as Southerners. The movie is of historical significance. When it came out in 1915, it was the first epic film. The silent movie was the story of two families who lived through the war and Reconstruction. We think of Adolph Hitler and his Nazi Reich as an evil empire that had delusions of Aryan superiority. What we try to forget is that the United States as well as most other European powers held similar beliefs. In our country, we called it Social Darwinism. In the United States, North as well as South, we assumed that the natives, meaning those of colonial stock, were superior to either the immigrants from Southern and Eastern Europe or those with African ancestors. Those of American Indian, Asian, or Mexican were also inferior, but in most parts of America, they were not numerous enough to be as much of a threat. In the final scenes of *The*

Birth of a Nation, a line of Klansmen prevents blacks from casting their votes on election day. This reflects an obvious pride in reestablishing Aryan superiority. In 1915, most Americans clearly saw these clansmen as heroes who were helping to keep our country pure. Such racism may embarrass us today, but it was the way that not only Americans but also most of those of Western European culture saw the world.

Through the 1920s, this thinking was prevalent as can be seen by the revival of the Ku Klux Klan, increased activity of nativist organizations, and an increase in violence against the non-Aryan intruders of the United States. This new Klan was as popular in the North as in the South. The largest single chapter was in Chicago. They took over the state legislatures in Oklahoma and Texas, but they did the same in the non-Southern states of Oregon and Indiana and came close in California. In the North, they were more opposed to the immigrants who were Catholic or Jewish or Communist. In 1924, they passed the first of the quota acts, which seriously limited further entrance of non-Aryans into this country, a law which was refined further and lasted until 1965. Remember, the United States Army which invaded and conquered the Third Reich was segregated.

The Birth of a Nation was clearly a Dunning School interpretation of the war and Reconstruction. It was also clearly a racist point of view. I do not agree with the racist philosophy of our ancestors during the period nor during the days of slavery, but that is the way people thought back then. I do not wish to disown them because things have changed. That is what history is all about. I repeat once more, my Southern ancestors were no more racist than most in the North nor in other parts of Northern Europe. Racism is how the Aryan nations rationalized their conquest of other peoples. The racism evident in this movie is not relevant to the Yankee conquest of the South. It does not mean that they were justified in what they did to the Southern people. It does not mean that Confederates were wrong to declare independence from the North. It does not mean that they went through some sort of mass self-hypnosis where they created a "lost cause myth" to rationalize their position. Colonel John Washington Inzer wrote in a letter to his grandson, "Glad that you were pleased with *The Birth of a Nation*. That part of the of the show that attempted, or sought, to illustrate the conditions of the South during Reconstruction Days—to your mind—was most horrible, but I am sure that it did not begin to illustrate things as they really occurred in those days." He went on to say "I passed through that period, and I could give you only a faint idea of the occurrences of that time."[25] Am I to believe that this man who served in his country's army was under some kind of mass-induced delusion when he wrote this? The Librevs want me to believe that thousands of his contemporaries who recorded similar descriptions were likewise misled.

The Specific Myths

I see seven specific areas in which the Librevs believe they have successfully corrected American history. There are some aspects of the traditional interpretations of our history that should be revised, but I disagree with what they now call the "lost cause myth" and with their assumption that the "broadly accepted point of view" has been "so completely overturned."[26] First, the Librevs are convinced that they have proven that the carpetbaggers and scallywags were not as corrupt as Southerners have claimed all these years. Second, they have shown that they did not leave the Southern people saddled with intolerable debts and taxes. Third, they have shown that the blacks did not run rampant through Southern cities as they seized control of the Reconstruction governments. Fourth, they claim that they have proven that Reconstruction was not merely an attempt by the Republicans to establish control. Fifth, they also say that the South was not occupied by the United States military. Sixth, they think they have shown that not only did the Yankees not commit horrible atrocities against Southerners but also that they even accomplished a number of beneficial reforms. Seventh, some have even begun to attack the near deification of Robert E. Lee as they attempt to show that he is not the man Southerners have painted him to be in their "lost cause mythology." I will now go into more detail on these myths, but they will also be themes in the remainder of the chapter.

Perhaps the greatest criticism which Southerners have levied on Reconstruction has traditionally been the charges of corruption. The

25 Mattie Lou Teague Crow, ed., *The Diary of A Confederate Soldier: John Washington Inzer, 1834–1928* (Mattie Lou Teague Crow, 1977), 159.
26 Foner, xix.

Librevs do not try to deny that there are proven examples of this corruption. There are many stories of the Northmen who came and got themselves appointed or elected to public office from which they resigned and took the treasury back North with them. I believe there are some who had noble intentions, but many more came South seeking profits and in some cases what could even be described as plunder. Even the famed carpetbagger Albion Tourgee admitted that he did not head South on any kind of crusade but rather because "the South seemed to offer economic opportunities to the man with initiative."[27] He was not about the devil's work, however, he did posses Yankee arrogance, which was demonstrated by the fact that "he shared the hope of other Yankee settlers that the South would be quickly transformed into a duplicate of the North 'by the power of commerce, manufactures, and the incursion of Northern life, thought, capital, industry, enterprise.'"[28] There have been a number of the revisionist histories that have demonstrated that some of these men had good intentions, but like European and American imperialists around the globe, they end up forcing their improved lifestyle on people who do not necessarily want it. As to those who clearly were corrupt, the Librev response is that the Grant administration was noted for corruption, not just in the South. And they accuse us of rationalizing? It amazes me that these liberal types who have consistently been critical of American imperialism as simply spreading truth, justice, and the American way have been wrong. Yet in the case of the conquest of the South, they seem to have swallowed that type of thinking hook, line, and sinker.

One of the myths that the Librevs are satisfied that they have disproven is that of the big debts and high taxes which the Republicans saddled Southerners with. Like the corruption charges, they confess that in some cases the large debts accumulated by the Republican Reconstructed governments were due to the corruption, especially in North and South Carolina and Georgia. Nonetheless they feel that they have still destroyed the Dunning interpretation. In some cases, they have demonstrated that the debts were simply the result of poor decision making. Others came about following Johnson's plan for

27   Albion W. Tourgee, *A Fool's Errand: A Novel of the South during Reconstruction* (New York: Harper Torchbooks, 1961), x.
28   Ibid, x.

Reconstruction, which ended up being spent to develop railroads. These and other needed postwar rebuilding expenditures led to more debts than those caused by corruption. The debts led to increased taxation. Somehow they have concluded that by showing that some but not all the increased debt and taxation was the result of things other than corrupt carpetbaggers that they have thus disproven the traditional view of Reconstruction. To me it seems that they have shown that not all the debts and high taxes were due to Republican Reconstruction governments, but some were. They may have shown that this aspect of Reconstruction may not be as simplistic as some have considered it, but they certainly have not demonstrated any "lost cause myth."

Another "disproven myth," at least according to the Librevs, is the Southern complaints that the Reconstruction South was dominated by black Republicans. I have no doubt that this has been exaggerated, but it does have a foundation of truth. Before the war, there were some free blacks, a significant population in some areas such as Virginia, Maryland, and Louisiana. There were even some who were well-off financially, including some who owned plantations or business worked by slaves. However, compared to the way things were after the war, it must have seemed to the white Southerners that the tables had been turned. It is a fact that there were 735,000 black registered voters in the South compared to 635,000 whites in 1867 in the ten unreconstructed states. The Librevs are self-satisfied at disproving a Dunning myth, pointing out that only sixteen blacks served in Congress. They held other high offices throughout the region, but the only state legislature that they dominated was South Carolina. This may not have been as dominating as some have implied over the years, but it is still a radical change compared to the prewar South. I find it completely understandable that some Southerners felt that the blacks had taken control. Other Librev studies have a valid point in that they showed that the black politicians were more competent that has been claimed. This is an improvement in our history, and I see no error in their conclusions, but it does not destroy the overall Southern interpretation of our history and certainly does not justify what the Yankees did to our people.

The most ridiculous claim of Librev victory is in disputing that a primary objective of the Republican Party during Reconstruction was to build and maintain a strong presence in the South. As far as I am concerned, that was their purpose. I will discuss this in greater detail later.

Related to this is the "myth" of occupation by the United States military. Like the Southern view of black domination, I have little doubt that this was exaggerated in the minds of Southerners. They had lived all of their lives in a nation which was not patrolled by soldiers. Law enforcement was left to civilian authorities. On this particular charge, we have the statistics. Only 18.000 troops remained in the South in 1866 and by 1876 the number dropped to 6,000. These troops were rarely used against the whites. The Librevs do point out that those occasions generally involved incidents in which the Southern whites were trying to impose their will on Southern blacks; the implication being that this was a good thing. The fact is that the United States military occupied the land in which such things had been previously unheard of. It may not have been as big a deal as implied by some, but it did happen. There is little else to say about this issue; ten states fell under martial law during Reconstruction. I am sure that if any states today were placed under martial law enforced by a military presence, the liberals would be leading the protest, yet in this case, they do not seem to think it a big deal.

The Librevs feel that they have shattered the Dunning myth of Reconstruction by focusing on some of the accomplishments of the Republican occupation of the South. This is an approach still used by United States occupying forces as did the Romans before them. They may conquer a land and impose their will, but they do offer rewards and eventually will even turn over political control to natives as long as they are friendly to the conquerors. The Freedmen's Bureau spent $1 million on relief for Southern blacks and whites and $5 million on education. Literacy rose impressively among blacks who were enrolled in schools for the first time. Rail systems were restored and expanded by nearly 7,300 miles. There were some improvements made by the conquering United States government. Surely this justifies killing hundreds of thousands of people; burning their homes and towns; killing their live stock; and forcing Yankee morality and lifestyle on them? Again, I must point out that liberals have traditionally not accepted these rationalizations in other examples of American imperialism, yet they believe it was a great good when the North conquered the South.

The Librevs have pointed out that even though some bad things did happen, they were not as bad as they could have been. Some wanted to charge Davis with crimes, but they didn't. The military occupation and plunder of what treasures were left could have been even more widespread. I suppose that there is no denying that it could have been worse. Hitler could have gassed two or three million more people than he did. He too could have been worse than he was. Is that a logical justification for the evil he did commit?

Of late, there are some Librevs that have attacked the image of Robert E. Lee. Not only has he been the father figure of the South, displacing George Washington in the minds of many Southerners, but he has also been the object of respect for many others around the world. He is the only man in history to be offered command of opposing armies. He is the only man to have changed the course of the Mississippi River. He began his career by graduating West Point without a single demerit and tried to live his life with the same kind of discipline and integrity. It is no wonder that they feel compelled to cut the man down; he was indeed a giant. He was a man and no doubt was not as perfect as some imagine him to have been, but people need to have someone to look up to and admire. Someone who can at least approach perfect. I cannot think of anyone who has come any closer, and it seems to me that those who attack him have only demonstrated how mean-spirited they are. The deeds of heroes are often exaggerated in the minds of admirers, but there are usually reasons that they have been given so much respect.

Chattanooga, Tennessee, in time of war. Soldiers, tents, and supply wagons beside the city building, 1864. (Courtesy National Archives)

Shells of the buildings of Richmond, Virginia, silhouetted against a dark sky after the destruction by Confederates, at least according to what we are always told. It may be that the Confederate government did not want some things to fall into Union hands, but the destruction of civilian property across the South was massive. (Courtesy National Archives)

Ruins seen from the capitol, Columbia, South Carolina, 1865. The capitol of the first state to secede was a primary target for revenge destruction by the Union army. (Courtesy National Archives)

Ruins of the navy yard at Norfolk, Virginia, December 1864. (Courtesy National Archives)

The ruins of Mills House and nearby buildings, Charleston,
South Carolina, 1865. (Courtesy National Archives)

Ruins seen from the Circular Church, Charleston, South
Carolina, 1865. (Courtesy National Archives)

Anecdotal History

The ideal in trying to say we can prove some historical issue is to have some statistical data to support our conclusions. The reality is that this can rarely be done to the degree that we can consider it proven, and that is the reason why history is so often open to reinterpretation. Much of the history of slavery, the War for Southern Independence, and Reconstruction are based on anecdotal evidence. Because of the high literacy rate, we have a treasure trove of letters, diaries, and other documents written by eyewitnesses. As a result, we have a near infinite number of interpretations of the events. This is the main reason why those researching these topics can find evidence to support almost any thesis. The Librevs also use this type of evidence, but they seem to want to dismiss those to the contrary. The main reason is that the ones they don't like were written by Southerners and therefore are biased.

There are some statistics that can lend credibility to one interpretation or the other. One good example that the Librevs have used in recent years is the election results of 1860. Texas is the only one of the states that held a popular vote on the question of secession, and so that is the only one in which we have a good picture of how the various parts of the state divided over the question. For most of the states, they have looked at those counties that voted for Breckinridge as the most likely to have favored secession. This, of course, cannot be considered to be a 100 percent correlation, but it does seem to be a reasonable assumption. I do find it interesting that they ignore the fact that Maryland and Delaware voted for Breckinridge. This may be a valid assumption in 1860, but all changed after the firing on Fort Sumpter and Lincoln's demand for 75,000 troops and the subsequent invasion of the South by the Yankees. It is logical to assume that many who may have initially opposed secession now saw it as a war to protect home and family. This is a concept ignored by the Librevs.

I believe that many of the basic accounts written by the Southern people during the war years and the so-called Reconstruction that followed were basically accurate. I am confident in stating that they believed in the cause that they fought and sacrificed for. I do not believe that they were so stupid that they created a "lost cause myth" to cope with the fact that they had been conquered. I do believe that they may have exaggerated some aspects of their occupation. I also believe that some of the Yankees believed in the cause that they fought for. In both cases, I believe that most of the anecdotal evidence was real and not based on delusions, lies, or myths. I also accept that politicians are among the most heavily motivated to lie, deceive, and distort the truth for the mere sake of their political ambitions. If my assumption is correct then the Republicans would have been the most motivated to lie about the years after the war.

Republican Domination of the South

My thesis about the Northern motivations behind Reconstruction rests on the same basic assumption that Adam Smith made in his *Wealth of Nations*; people operate out of self-interest. Despite the Librev claims that they have disproven the importance of Republican ambition, common sense seems to dictate to the contrary. There are a two other assumptions that I make. First, political parties are organized to accomplish what the members feel is in their best interest. Second, I also believe that the members of political parties become so obsessed with their objectives that at times they function to the detriment of those not in their party. If these assumptions are accepted then it is easy to see what concerned Republicans. They were a minority party that got elected because of a split in the majority Democratic Party. If the Union was reconstructed without slavery then the differences that divided the majority Democratic Party would be gone; therefore the Republicans would have to do something to survive. In other words, the basic objective of the United States government during Reconstruction reflected the self-interest of the dominant Republican Party. They worked out a plan where they could try to build Republican support and cut Democrat voters.

The South had become Democratic by 1860 and after their military defeat by a Republican president could not be expected to change their party loyalties. The fact is that for a century after the war, the South was solid Democrat, which should be no surprise. There were numerous measures taken by the Republican Reconstruction establishment to limit the return of Southern Democrats to positions of power and to even limit their voting abilities.

The source for new Republicans was obvious—the newly freed slaves who made up about 40 percent of the Southern population. I think it is safe to assume that the majority of slaves were ecstatic to be free. It would be an easy sale for the Republican conquerors to point out to the freedmen that Abraham Lincoln and his Republican Party are the ones that freed them. If the Republicans could make certain that the freedmen could vote then their numbers combined with the white Unionist would at least come close to a majority vote. It could still be close in some areas, so it could be necessary to limit the voting of Confederate Democrats. My thesis is supported by the fact that they did go to great lengths to limit the white voting and to assure black voting.

My thesis explains and is supported by many of the events that unfolded during the period. They did pass laws, including the fourteenth amendment, designed to weaken the Southern Democrat ruling class. They passed laws to insure the voting rights of freedmen. Southern whites countered this strategy by trying to limit the voting of blacks. They even turned to terrorism with groups such as the Ku Klux Klan which not only attacked blacks but also carpetbaggers and scallywags. It even explains the Republican desertion of blacks after 1877. By that time, they had built their party and found a constituency based on the businessmen of the Industrial Revolution. At the same time, they were losing votes as the Northern racist found appeal in Democratic politicians who preached against racial equality. I see no problem in understanding why the Republicans abandoned the blacks after 1877. They found Republican support elsewhere and saw that continued preoccupation with the blacks could lose them votes among the majority of the American population who were racist. This includes the more numerous Northern voters.

I will concede that some of the Librev criticisms of traditional Dunning interpretation are valid. I am sure that there were many who went South with the desire to give help to the freedmen. There were people who firmly objected to slavery on moral grounds. I have no doubt that some of them were prepared to practice what they preached and sacrifice their time to help the people they felt empathy for. Likewise,

I am equally confident that there were many who simply saw an opportunity to make money. This is a characteristic of capitalism which many have criticized. I also believe there are those who supported the Republican Party and its legislation with the conviction that they were doing the right thing. Nonetheless, I believe the greatest force behind events that transpired was Republican self-interest.

No One Likes Someone Else Telling Them What to Do

When looking at Southerners, the Librevs seem to be overlooking a common human feeling—no one likes someone else telling them what to do. It is no wonder that Librevs ignore this since they have the delusion that Southern identity is a myth that did not come about until shortly before the war or even after. Because of my own personal experiences, I cannot accept their nonsense. No arrogant intellectual Yankee is going to make me believe that my Southern identity is a myth and not real.

When the Librevs talk about the "lost cause myth," they should understand that national identity is an emotional thing and not intellectual; that is why I will now submit to an emotional outburst. That is also why I know that their thesis is nonsense. It is common that those of us who spent a significant part of our lives outside of the South are quite often the most patriotic. I am a California Okie. I was raised by parents that never spoke of evil Yankees. I graduated high school and even college with an identity of being a Californian. I knew of my Confederate ancestors, but I had to learn to hate Yankees by myself. I was aware that we ate different food than most of my friends (beans and corn bread) and that we went to a different church (Southern Christian) and that my parents listened to different music (country and gospel). My parents even spoke a different language, but since I was a child, I learned to talk like my friends. I should say that I was ridiculed into talking like my friends and classmates; hillbilly was my native language. In time, I learned that the people I disliked the most because they were arrogant, self-righteous, pretentious, and at times downright mean had something in common; they or their families came from the North. I started doing genealogy at an early age, and I eventually realized that I was Southern. It all came together for me—the food, the music, the religion, the Confederate ancestors; I am Southern. I may have been raised in California, but that is not my ethnic background. I also began to realize that I had lost much of my culture and began to embrace what I had left. I now value that culture as part of my identity. I guess at times my native language comes back because one night, a salesman got mad at me because I did not want to listen to his pitch. He attempted to insult me by accusing me of being from Kentucky. I began to realize how much some people hated us and did not think it an insult to be accused of coming from Kentucky. They call us bigots, but many of these people hate Southerners. They hate our music, the way we talk, our fundamentalist religion, our fried food, and just about anything else. They do like our sunshine, but they retire to the Sunbelt, not the South. We are a different people, ask them. They know that Southerners, black and white, walk slow, talk slow, and are slow-witted. Our Southern identity is not a delusion that our people developed to rationalize the war that we lost. Our Southern identity is what we are, and I, for one, will not allow arrogant Yankees to take it from me, no matter what uppity school they got their PhD from.

The Yankees conquered us, but this does not mean that we liked it. The story of Reconstruction from the Southern perspective is that our people did all that they could do to preserve what self-respect they had after accepting the reality of military defeat. They were told by the lying, thieving Yankees that they would be accepted back into the Union with forgiving arms, but when they tried to rebuild their lives, they found that there were many more restrictions than they anticipated. We could not fight anymore, but that did not mean that we believed that we had been wrong. You cannot beat your beliefs into someone. Even the famous carpetbagger Albion W. Tourgee understood; thus, he emphasized the fact that in the years immediately following the Civil War, the former Confederates had control of their own state and governments. It was during this period "that they clearly demonstrated their unwillingness or inability to face up to the implications of surrender at Appomattox."

The South had put down their guns but did not comprehend what this meant. Some fled the country rather than to live under Yankee rule. Some, such as Edmond Ruffin, chose death. The others faced the humiliation and focused on what was left of their homes and families. They had all lost loved ones and many lost limbs. No doubt their self-esteem suffered considerably. They made these sacrifices for a cause they believed in, but they did not suddenly experience a change of mind or belief. Like Governor Stockdale of Texas said, "but they have none of the spaniel in their composition. No, sir, they are not in the least like the dog that seeks to lick the hand of the man that kicked him." They did what they had to do. "They know that they resisted the federal government as long as any means of resistance was left, and that any attempt at resistance now must be in vain, and they have no means, and would only make bad worse."[29]

The charges that Northern cruelties were nothing but the delusions of Southerners who wanted to rationalize their unjust war is arrogant and absurd. The Librevs love to quote Lee about furling the Confederate flag, but they ignore what he told Governor Stockdale: "if I had foreseen the use those people designed to make of their victory, there would have been no surrender at Appomattox Courthouse; no, sir, not by me." He went on to add, "Had I foreseen these results of subjugation, I would have preferred to die at Appomattox with my brave men, my sword in this right hand."[30]

The following words of "I'm a Good Old Rebel" were not delusions: (said to have been written by Major James Randolph, a Virginian and member of General J.E.B. Stuart's staff)

Oh, I'm a good old Rebel,
Now that's just what I am;
For this 'fair land of Freedom:
I do not give a damn.
I'm glad I fit against it'
I only wish we'd won.
And I don't want no pardon
for anything I've done.

29   James R. Kennedy and Walter D Kennedy, *The South Was Right* (Baton Rouge, LA: Land and Land, 1991), 23.
30   Ibid., 24.

I hates the constitution,
This great Republic too;
I hates the Freedmen's Buro,
In uniforms of blue.
I hates the nasty eagle,
Will all his brag and fuss;
but the lyin' thievin' Yankees
I hates'em wuss and wuss

I hates the Yankee nation
And everything they do,
I hates the Declaration
of Independence, too;
I hates the glorious Union
Tis drippin' with our blood
I hates their striped banner,
I fit it all I could.

I followed Ol' Marsh Roberts
for four years, nearabout,
got wounded in three places
and starved at Pint Lookout:
I cotched the rheumatism
a' campin: in the snow;
but I killed a chance o'Yankees,
I'd like to kill some mo'.

Three hundred thousand Yankees
Is still in Southern dust;
We killed three hundred thousand
befo' they conquered us.
They died of Southern fever
And Southern steel and shot;
And I wish it was three million
Instead of what we got.

I can't take up my musket
And fight' em now no mo',
But I ain't a-goin' to love 'em,
Now that is sartin show';
And I don't want no pardon
For what I was and am;
And I won't be reconstructed,
And I do not give a damn.

Freeing the Slaves (Beginning Reconstruction)

The latest thinking by the wise and all-knowing Librev historians is that Reconstruction began with the freeing of the slaves. It seems to me that their whole illogical interpretation unravels at this point. They know the numerous quotes from Lincoln and his friends that they were not fighting to free the slaves, yet the Librevs keep insisting that the war was a war to free the slaves. Since they accept Foner's thesis that Reconstruction was really the abolition of slavery then they must insist on the concept of "border state" to describe those parts of the South which for one reason or another are not accepted by them as "the South." As far as I am concerned, these "border states" are part of the South. If the term is used simply to distinguish them from the "Deep South," I would much prefer the term "upper South." Good or bad, as far as I am concerned, the definition of the South are those states that still had slavery as of 1860. I will first talk about those who were definitely not part of the Confederacy: Maryland and Delaware. I will then cover the two states that had Union and Confederate governments: Kentucky and Missouri. The Librevs generally refer to the latter two as remaining with the Union and completely ignore Confederate claims and the two extra stars on the battle flag represent the Confederate states of Missouri and Kentucky. I will conclude with West Virginia.

Maryland and Delaware

Maryland continued to have a divided population even after Yankee occupation. I have already discussed the question of Maryland secession and how I believe that they would have been Confederate if allowed the right to democratic process, but now I will look at abolition of slavery since that is what Foner and the Librevs say we must do. They had about 87,000 slaves, mostly in the Southern part of the state. They had a long tradition of antislavery sentiment and, as a result, had the largest free black population. Naturally they added to the abolitionist fire. The slave owners accepted the inevitability of abolition but attempted to gain compensation. The 1863 elections called for a constitutional convention to reconstruct a state that supposedly remained part of the Union. Foner did offer a quote from one Maryland Unionist after the constitution passed:

> [It] must be a source of mortification that emancipation has . . . not been from high principle, . . . but party spirit, vengeful feeling against disloyal slave holders, and regard for material interest. There has been no expression, at least in this community, of regard for the negro - for human rights, but . . . many expressive of the great prosperity to result to the state by a change of the system of labor.[31]

Lincoln did carry the state in 1864, but the whole thing has the same stink about it that it did in April of 1861. They clearly tried to exclude those who had not only served the Confederate cause but were also known to have expressed any sympathies for the Confederacy. This, of course, is in addition to those who had fled Maryland after Yankee occupation. I do see evidence for my oft repeated claim that Southerners were no more racist than Northerners. The Yankeefied Marylanders did not give the blacks the vote.

Delaware was a collection of inconsistencies, which may explain why Foner did not delve into that state. Most people do not think of Delaware as the South, and I must confess I have a hard time accepting it as such despite the fact that it meets my simple definition of the region—those states which had slavery in 1860. The fact is that the history of the state was different from the others. It was closely connected to Pennsylvania and its Quakers, and so that suggests an antislavery outlook. Though introduced earlier, the institution did not take serious root until Dutch

31   Foner, 41.

involvement as in New York. (Remember, the first slave ship in Virginia was a Dutch ship.) With the Enlightenment and Quaker influences, Delaware discussed the end of slavery during the early days of the United States and the Constitutional Convention. This was common in other states too, including Virginia. One of the biggest barriers in Delaware, as in the country as a whole, was American racism. Even many who did not approve of slavery did not want a lot of freed blacks living among them.

Nonetheless, the freeing of slaves continued so that by 1810, 78 percent of the blacks in that state were free. After Nat Turner's Rebellion in 1831, they began to pass "black codes" to control the inferior population. Soon Delaware was "the least hospitable place in the Union for freedmen prior to the Civil War."[32] This unique background accounts for the inconsistency of the states voting on slavery issues. They opposed the extension of slavery during the days of the Missouri Compromise and passed resolutions against the annexation of Texas and the spread of slavery into the territories after the Mexican War. In 1860, they voted for Breckinridge thus fitting the Librev definition of those places that would have supported Southern secession. Despite attempts by Lincoln to talk them into abolishing the institution during the war, not only did they fail to do so, but they also did not ratify the Thirteenth Amendment until 1901. It is interesting that Lincoln offered the state compensation at the average rate of about $500 per slave if they voted in abolition. No doubt the confusion in trying to explain Delaware is due to its diversity. Some talked of states' rights, some may simply have reacted to Lincoln and his telling people how to live their lives, and some, if not most, had the racist fears of an uncontrollable freed black population that dominated in America, North and South.

Missouri and Kentucky

These two states share the fact that not only did they have factions that supported the Union and the Confederacy, but each also had men who claimed to be the real government of these states. Most Librev historians seem to ignore the Confederate states of Kentucky

---

32   William H. Williams, *Slavery and Freedom in Delaware, 1639–1865* (Wilmington, DE: Scholarly Resources, 1996), 171.

and Missouri. Not only did both states have factions that claimed they were Confederate, but they also both provided armed regiments to each side. The inconsistency of the Yankee and Librev perspective is evident when looking at Kentucky and Missouri. How can states need reconstructing if they never left the Union? The Librevs need Foner's thesis to explain Reconstruction of states, which they say never left the Union in the first place.

Kentucky had the largest number of slave-owning families among the "border states," and at the end of the war still had 65,000 slaves. They denounced the Emancipation Proclamation as unconstitutional, but of course, it did not apply to them anyway. The slaves in that state were freed by the Thirteenth Amendment.

The pro-Confederate faction of Missouri fled to the Southwest corner, and the Union's attempts to bring them under their control led to the first major battles in the far west. The region near the borders of Missouri, Kansas, Indian Territory, and Arkansas experienced long and painful years of guerilla war and bushwhacking. Both sides committed great atrocities against the other, each claiming revenge. Foner used the term "internal reconstruction" to describe those states like Missouri, which were not reconstructed because of conquest but rather to free the slaves. In 1864, Union Missouri required loyalty oaths for voters which helped to get Radical Thomas C. Fletcher elected governor and to call a convention to devise a plan of emancipation. They gathered in January 1865. They passed the new constitution utilizing the Republican strategy of recruiting black voters and barring "rebels" from voting and holding office. They also barred the "disloyal" from acting as teachers, lawyers, and ministers. They failed to pass proposals to confiscate the lands of the planters to compensate loyalist for their wartime losses.

West Virginia

The best example of Yankee logic is the creation of the state of West Virginia. The Unionist usually claimed that secession was unconstitutional, yet they accepted the secession of numerous counties from Virginia. Neither the Yankees of yore nor the Librevs of today seem worried about Section 3 of Article IV of the constitution: "nor any state formed by the Junction of two or more States, or parts of States, without the Consent of the Legislatures of the States concerned as well as the Congress." No doubt those men who gathered in Wheeling would have been able to get approval from the remaining congressmen, but I am sure the subject was never even submitted to the Virginia Legislature. If the Union is denying the right of states to succeed then there should only be one state legislature. I see no provision in the constitution for any state whose legislature claimed to have seceded while the federal government says that such claims are not legal. West Virginia was accepted into the Union in 1863 with the proviso that they abolish slavery.

There is a social/economic division in the South as in the rest of the United States; that is why I titled this manuscript Corn bread and Magnolias. From the very earliest days of the colonies, there has been a division between the wealthy merchants and planters who grabbed the primo land on the coast and the poor or lower middle classes who usually lived in the west on the frontiers. This is the bases for those persons living in the western Mountain counties of West Virginia. They had only a 5 percent slave population and had a history of dispute with the planter class of the Tidewater. The situation was similar to that which brought about the class conflict of the Regulator movements of North and South Carolina. This is why it has been called a rich man's war. As a historian, I am well aware of the fact that most wars are created by and for the rich. What the Librevs seem to forget is that Union troops invaded the South thus changing the nature of the war. Many of the lower classes now saw the war as the defense of their homes from foreign invaders. There were, however, many in the South who continued to favor the Union. Southern Unionist did tend to be in the most rural and often mountainous regions of the South, such as Northwest Arkansas, East Tennessee and the upper counties of Alabama and Mississippi as well as those in western Virginia.

I do not deny these accounts which are often pointed out by the Librevs. What I fail to see is how this is relevant. They seem to conclude that this somehow distracts from the rights of the Southern people to self-government. I suspect that their attitude is more a reflection of their general liberal philosophy that most of the world's problems are caused by rich white guys. I do believe that the planters led the South down the road to secession. However, I also believe that the rich merchants of the North turned secession into war and destruction. This is the part that the Librevs tend to ignore. If they didn't, they would lose much of their current anti-Confederate rhetoric in assuming that the war was a noble cause.

Louisiana

The situation in Louisiana is the best example of how the Librevs stretch their imaginations so that they can defend their view of Lincoln as a noble man who defended the poor slaves rather than as a typical sly politician who would do almost anything to accomplish his objectives. Louisiana was a Confederate state in which he attempted pre-Appomattox reconstruction. New Orleans especially was unique, but I do not see this had as much to do with the situation as the political motivation.

Foner pointed out that the city of New Orleans had strong business connections with the North and Europe. However, so did the other economic centers of the South. I will discuss this under a separate topic in the next chapter. Foner mentioned the large free black population of the crescent city but ignored the fact that they formed the first black regiment which was committed to the Confederacy. Lincoln endorsed a program for the Free State Association and urged General Nathaniel P. Banks to organize a constitutional convention that would abolish slavery in Louisiana. However, he excluded these parishes under Union control in his Emancipation Proclamation. By January of 1864, Lincoln endorsed the enrollment of freeborn blacks as voters in Louisiana. However, Banks was concerned about how such a policy would jeopardize his attempts to reconstruct.

The Librev Lincolnist embrace the notion that the 10 percent reconstruction plan of Lincoln's is an example of what a caring empathetic man he was, who just wanted to make it easier for the Southerners to rejoin the Union. Occam's Razor and the nature of politicians support my interpretation of the situation in Louisiana. As November 1864 approached, Lincoln became more and more convinced that he could lose the election in November. The fact is that 45 percent of the Northern population voted against him. I think most of the Librevs would agree that if Atlanta had not fallen in the summer of 1864, the 5 percent swing needed to put McClellan in the White House would most likely have been the case. Lincoln needed to get electoral votes. The Republicans in Congress would have interest in seeing their party retain power, but they did not have to worry about electoral votes. Lincoln did. I believe this is why he got Nevada admitted to the Union in 1864, and I think this is why he pushed to get Louisiana readmitted. I understand that I cannot prove that this is the case, but it does seem to make more sense. They claim that Lincoln was simply kind-hearted. Ninety percent of the people in Louisiana could be wearing grey uniforms and shooting at Union soldiers, but he wanted to readmit the state? That sounds more like the desperate act of a politician.

Lincoln's Reconstruction

So the Librev Lincoln worshipers see the former president as a kind and gentle man who simply wanted to make it easy for Southerners to rejoin the Union; I see him as a typical politician who had plans on how to win the election of 1864. He did seem to have some concern about the slaves. However, he was a believer in the colonization effort. He was a disciplinarian at times, but at other times, he was merciful. Motivation is a hard thing to prove, but the fact remains that by the time of the Lincoln presidency, democracy had become prevalent enough that the greatest skill that a politician needed to be successful was the ability to get elected.

Congress did not agree with the presidential Reconstruction. The Republican congressmen did not have the same interest. The survival and future of their party was of equal importance. However, during his years in the White House, Lincoln had usurped many of the powers that belonged to the legislative branch of government. No doubt some allowed this as long as the outcome of the war was unclear. As it drew to a close and victory became certain, Republican congressmen were in a better position to defend their self-interest. Lincoln never got a chance to implement his plan at war's end since he died shortly after Appomattox.

In July of 1864, Congress challenged the president with the Wade–Davis Bill. They were more interested in creating Union state governments. They required that at least half of the voters take a loyalty oath. This does seem much more logical than Lincoln's plan. How could anyone consider a former "rebel" state as reconstructed if up to 90 percent of the men are still shooting at Union soldiers? They provided for some protection of black Southerners, but they did not give them the vote. They needed the blacks to build their Party. At first, they were only interested in the Southern black voters, but they recognized the inconsistency of not allowing Northern blacks to vote too. They would make this sacrifice. By 1877, they realized that they did not need this strategy for the postwar Republican Party to thrive. This is why they "abandoned" the black Republicans of the South.

Johnson's Reconstruction

Andrew Johnson had interests different from either Lincoln or the Republican Congress. He came from the corn bread part of the South, but he was still a Southerner. I do agree with the Librev claim that the movement toward secession was spearheaded by the planter class. However, once the invasion began, the average yeoman and poor Southerner divided into two main groups—those who would fight for the cause because they felt a need to defend their homes and families and those who would still remain loyal to the Union. Johnson obviously fell in the latter category. He was still a Southerner, and as such, he did not hate Southerners. Like many of the corn-bread South, he did not have much use for the rich guys. The Librevs see Johnson as one who remained loyal to Lincoln. This may have been part of the logic in his actions. Nonetheless, he was Southern and did not hate the people of the South. He felt empathy for the majority of the Southern population, but he did want to restrict the planter class from regaining control. He was still a racist as most Americans were and did not favor the plans that involved giving the freedmen the vote. His policies and actions pleased the defeated Southerners as much as possible under the circumstances. He proved to be contrary to the ambitions of the Republican Congress, especially the radical portions.

The Uppity South

In the spirit of Johnson's plans, Southerners began to feel that they could come back into the United States and carry on business as usual. Their lives had been shattered by the tragedy of war—homes burned; livestock gone; many of the men dead or crippled; destroyed railroads;

and heavily disrupted market economy. They suffered the humiliation of defeat at the hands of the girlish Union army, but their sense of self-esteem had not been totally sucked out of them. They may have lost, but they did not think they had been wrong. As they rebuilt their land, they would not have slavery, which for many was just as well. Most of them never owned a slave before the war, and many of those who did regretted the system they had inherited from their ancestors.

The majority of the South had fought for the Confederate cause, regardless of whether or not they quit fighting before Robert E. Lee did. The Librevs love to point to the high desertion rate as proof that most did not really support the new nation in the first place. I think this is utter nonsense. The degree of loyalty to the Southern cause varied considerably. However, I see the main reason for the desertion to be the results of giving priority to family. As their land was invaded and occupied by foreigners, more and more men felt a need to be home rather than in the army. I could produce numerous letters to support this interpretation as others could produce their anecdotal evidence to support the contrary. The fact is that the Confederate army fought long and hard and did not do bad for a people who were outnumbered two to one. They did not act like a people who did not really believe in what they were fighting for. Why would the North have so much problem with uppity Southerners if they did not really believe in their cause in the first place? The Librev response would be that this is why they created the "lost cause myth." Bull!

I cannot tell if they believe the lower- and middle-class Southerners to be smart or dumb. On one hand, they want us to believe that they never fell under the spell of the planters and thus did not really support the Confederacy. On the other hand, they paint these people as mindless dupes who are manipulated into believing the "lost cause myth." Which is it?

The first reports by Union officers who occupied the South indicate that the people did not act like a people who had done wrong, and most did not seem all that eager to embrace the Union flag nor Reconstruction laws. Mississippi and Texas refused to ratify the Thirteenth Amendment. Mississippi and South Carolina would not repudiate state debts. Several of the state constitutional conventions would not fly the Union flag. The newly elected Southern congressmen included seven Confederate cabinet officers, nine ex-Confederate congressmen, four generals, four colonels, and from Georgia, the former vice president Alexander Stephens.

Overall, they had met Johnson's demands for reconstruction. Most accepted emancipation; granted some civil rights to the freedmen; swore allegiance to the Union; and formed new state governments. The Radical Republicans led the crusade that would attempt to remove Johnson from office with the first impeachment of a president. They proceeded to subjugate the South to their rule. The Librevs believe that they have disproven the Dunning view of Reconstruction by writing about the New England schoolmarms who worked in the freedmen schools and the nobility of such Radical Republican leaders as Thaddeus Stevens. This is what Stevens had to say about Reconstruction: "Hang the leaders—crush the South—arm the Negroes—confiscate the land . . . Our generals have a sword in one hand and shackles in the other . . . The South must be punished under the rules of war, its land confiscated . . . These offending States were out of the Union and in the role of belligerent nation to be dealt with by the laws of war and conquest."[33] This attitude would explain the previous quote from Lee in which he said he would have preferred to die at Appomattox. I am not a smart Harvard graduate, but it seems to me that the Reconstruction Yankee government was not so noble.

Congressional Reconstruction

How could we possibly prove the motivations behind Congressional Reconstruction? On one hand, the Librevs are right about some of the issues. There were carpetbaggers who honestly wanted to help the freedmen. White Southerners did much to restrict the social equality of black Southerners. Not all the corruption and economic problems of the postwar South was due to carpetbaggers. On the other hand, the Dunning-type interpretations are partially true. Many men did move into the region from the North like the barbarians into Rome. They were conquerors who saw the opportunity to loot and pillage. Some did want revenge and foamed with a genuine hatred of not only slavery but also the Southern people and just about every aspect of their culture.

---

33   Kennedy, 105.

Congress had a need to not only establish domination over the South but also to recoup some of the power they had lost to the executive branch of the government. In December of 1865, when Congress reconvened, they refused to seat the newly elected Southerners in the House or the Senate. In the election of 1866, the Republicans gained a three to one majority in Congress. With Johnson subdued by impeachment, Congress had no trouble gaining control. In 1868, they got Grant elected to the presidency, and under him, things pretty much proceeded as Congress wanted.

They began to pass legislation intended to restrict the Southern ruling class and to empower the freedmen. The Thirteenth Amendment satisfied the slavery question once and for all. They continued the Freedman's Bureau, which was established to aid the former slaves. After the impeachment of Johnson, they were able to pass their laws restricting the black codes. Nonetheless, many of the Republicans and most of the Northern Democrats did not endorse a philosophy of racial equality. If they believed such things, we would have never had a need for a revolutionary civil rights movement in the 1950s and 1960s, which involved the North as well as the South. The reality is that Americans were racist up to the end of World War II and even beyond.

The Librevs like to think that they have disproven the Dunning view of military occupation, but the Republican Congress did pass the Fourteenth Amendment. The Librevs like to praise this amendment as the grounds for civil rights cases in this country until the civil rights movement. It does offer some rights for the black people. However, I have no doubt that the intent was to protect Republicans more than blacks. Clearly it enforced the voting rights of the freedmen. I cannot prove that this was not altruistically motivated, but if one accepts my interpretation of being politically motivated, it would be more consistent with Section 3 of the Amendment, which forbid those from taking office who had "engaged in insurrection or rebellion" against the United States government. It would also be consistent with Section 4, which repudiated Confederate debt. Section 5 guaranteed that "Congress shall have the power to enforce, by appropriate legislation, the provisions of this article." I won't even go into the legalities of the passage and ratification of this amendment. The New Jersey legislature said, "the origin and objects of said proposed amendments were unseemly and unjust . . . "[34]

New Orleans, Memphis, and the Question of Race

The riots in Memphis are examples of how white Southerners were not about to recognize the equality of black Southerners. Slavery may be dead, but the new black citizens would not be equal to the founding white citizens. This would be true in the North as well as the South, but the South had many more blacks and thus more reason to be aggressive in maintaining the traditional racial domination. The situation in Memphis was more the product of the frustration which accompanied the surrender, whereas the New Orleans case was more political.

The riots in Memphis began in the spring of 1866 and appear to have been aimed at the Unionist as well as the freedmen. Following the collision of two carriages, one driven by a white man and the other by a black man, rioting broke out involving blacks, former Confederates, and Irish immigrants. Such violence only fueled Northern Republican anger and not only their desires for revenge but also fears that the Democrats would regain control in the South. If reunited, the Democratic Party would dominate in the United States government as it would have in 1860 if it had not divided into Northern and Southern factions.

The New Orleans situation made it clear that the Democrats intended to control the South and that the political struggle would center on the prospect of the new black voters. The resulting violence produced thirty-eight fatalities which included thirty-four blacks, three white Republicans, and one white Democrat. The Louisiana Democratic Party had declared the government as one of white people, "made and to be perpetuated for the exclusive benefit of the white race. . . ," and that there would not be "any equality between the white and other races." Similar situations occurred in Chattanooga, Louisville, and Vicksburg. This is the kind of fuel the liberals love to use to prove the offensive nature of Confederate symbols. The North responded with the passage of the Fourteenth Amendment and subsequent legislation to protect black voters. However, I do not see that they did so out of

---

34   Kennedy, 192.

any sense of racial justice rather than the utilization of the freedmen as political pawns.

The Librevs struggle with weak explanations for why the noble Republicans deserted the cause of racial equality in 1877, but I do not have the same problem with my interpretation of the events. The way I see it is that by 1877, the Republicans concluded that they did not need to depend on black Republicans for survival. They could surrender the South to the Democrats. They began to realize that with the enlistment of blacks in their party, they not only gave fuel for the racist Northern Democrats, who frequently campaigned against what many considered a repulsive platform of racial equality. The Republicans alienated some of their Northern Republicans who were also racist. The Radical Republican Senator Charles Sumner proposed legislation to prohibit racial segregation in public schools, in selection of juries, on all forms of public transportation, and in public accommodations. The Southern Republicans endorsed it, but Congress had reservations as to the constitutionality of it and feared the reaction of their voters. After Sumner's death in 1874, they did push through a memorial Civil Rights Act in 1875, but the Supreme Court threw it out in 1883. I repeat once more, it was not just Southerners who were racist but the majority of Americans. The way I see it, the Republicans gave up on the Southern blacks because they no longer needed them and were losing support among the white Northern voters.

Reconstruction in Indian Territory

Having roots in Indian Territory, I have always resented the way historians have ignored their sufferings during Reconstruction, but I also see it as a good example of how the Republican policies were designed to serve their dual purposes of revenge and the promotion of their political agenda. In September of 1865, Washington officials summoned the tribes to a conference in Fort Smith. They were told that they had made unprovoked war on the United States and that they had forfeited all of their annuities and lands. But then they were informed that the president would forgive them "of their great crime." The Indians did point out that some of their people supported the Union and that the United States had abandoned the nations to the Confederacy.

The final treaty had some points which support the noble purposes claimed by the Librevs. The Indians agreed to abolish slavery and give their freed slaves citizenship and property rights. However, other changes indicate that the government was not so altruistic. They had to accept one north–south and one east–west railroad through their lands. They did not have to submit to a territorial government but did consent to an intertribal council. One reason I resent the ignoring of Indian Territory in Reconstruction is that they, in fact, were the only Southern state or territory which lost land because of the war; that is unless one wants to consider the creation of a new state out of Virginia. It is clear that the reason for taking away the western lands was to provide a place to which they could remove the plains' Indians as the United States government opened the western lands for white settlement. The great liberating United States apparently had no problem with forcing the Indians into submission to the white men. The poor Seminoles had to sell their old lands to the U.S. government for fifteen cents an acre and then pay that same government fifty cents an acre for land which they had purchased from the Creeks for thirty cents an acre. The facts seem to indicate that the main purpose of the new treaties was to allow for the advancement of the white Americans, more specifically the Northern white Republicans.

Ku Klux Klan

The existence of the Klan is probably the greatest source for the liberal revulsion of all things Confederate, if not Southern, and one of the first images they conjure related to the Confederate battle flag. I certainly make no attempt to justify the freaks who call themselves the Klan today, and for that matter, I do not take any pride in the racist attitude which was part of what they stood for in the beginning. The main thing that we need to understand about the original Klan is that the racism was only part of what they did. They were more comparable to terrorist groups we see in Iraq today rather than the odd balls in sheets that appear on the Jerry Springer show. Their primary objective was to resist occupation of the South by United States military. Books have been written about the Klan, so I will make no attempt at an in-depth analysis, but according to Albion Tourgee, the Invisible

Empire was "fundamentally a political organization aimed at frustrating the Negro voter and blocking the federal government in its efforts to transform the South."[35] These are the words of one of the most famous Reconstruction Republicans.

The Southerners were racist; many of the activities that involved the Klan or similar groups involved attempts to force the blacks into a subservient role as well as the political motives, but even some of those in the North understood why this happened and the role that the conqueror played:

> After having forced a proud people to yield what they had for more than two centuries considered a right, - the right to hold the African race in bondage, - they proceeded to outrage a feeling as deep and fervent as the zeal of Islam or the exclusiveness of the Hindoo caste, by giving the ignorant, the unskilled, and dependent race - a race which could not have lived a week without the support or charity of the dominant one - equality of political right! Not content with this, they went farther, and by erecting the rebellious territory into self-regulating and sovereign States, they abandoned these parties like cocks in a pit to fight out the question of predominance without the possibility of national interference. They said to the colored man . . . "Root, hog, or die!"[36]

The resulting violence against black Southerners was partially due to the whites' desire to maintain dominance over them but was primarily a political conflict because of the Republican use of the blacks as pawns. I am not trying to justify what the whites did to the blacks, but rather point out why it happened. Violent change, by definition, produces violence. Perhaps if the change had not came so rapidly or been forced on them by outsiders, maybe the results would have been better for the blacks too. It is one of those things we will never know for sure.

---

35   Tourgee, xiii.
36   *National Anti-Slavery Standard*, October 19, 1867.

The Redeemers

"Redeemers" is the name given to those who regained control of the South for Southerners. They are considered to have accomplished this with the Compromise of 1877. Although I attempt to include Southern blacks in my study of the South, in this particular statement, I am talking about white Southerners only. Redeemers were white Southerners who gained control of their respective states for white Southerners. In doing so, they established the South as a solid Democratic region which would remain as such until late in the twentieth century. Those black Southerners who could still vote remained predominantly Republican.

Even the Librevs have difficulty defining the Redeemers. Most of them were former planters. Some were supporters of the New South, others were not. There are those who have tried to define them as defenders of the feudal South and thus those who rejected modernization, but this is not true. They did hope to preserve as much of the Old South as possible, but they accepted the reality of military defeat and knew that talk of secession was dead and so was slavery. They were the perpetrators of the Lost Cause, though I firmly disagree with the Librev's declaration that this was a myth.

Though I reject the notion that Southern identity evolved with the "lost cause myth," I do realize that Reconstruction Southerners begin to refer to the war as "the lost cause." Whereas Librevs insist on calling it a myth, I see it as refusal to admit that our people did anything wrong. This is the same reason I call myself "unreconstructed." First, the Confederacy was founded on a correct constitutional principle. Second, the South lost because they were outnumbered. It was not due to lackluster support of the poor, but rather they were overwhelmed by superior strength with men and materials. Third, though I do not see the hand of God in the outcome, I do believe that the Southern people were and still are religious. The South is more of a Christian society. I am not saying that there are not religious people in the North. The North, on the other hand, is more into moneymaking. This is not to say there are not those in the South who seek the rewards of capitalism. I do believe that more Southerners are fundamentalist Christians and that they are the same ones who went political by supporting the Republicans in

2000 and 2004. I also believe the stereotype that Northerners are more moneygrubbing.

The unique situation in Virginia offers a glimpse into the less-talked-about South, the division between corn bread and magnolias. I am referring again to the application of self-interest across class lines. Virginia did have some unity, which, combined with the fact that they had a smaller black population than many of the conquered states, enabled them to resist occupation by Radical Republicans. Thus, they did not have the same need for Redemption and thus no need for Redeemers. After gaining enough solidarity to block Radical takeover, they ended up splitting over the issue of state debt. The more conservative wanted to pay all debt despite the extreme burden on the state treasury. It has not been proven, but it seems that self-interest may have been as much a part of their desire to pay the bonds rather than simply the matter of doing the most honorable thing. The Readjusters, under the leadership of William Mahone, wanted to reduce the interest and the payment. Mahone did win a lot of support from the working people. When the dust settled, Virginia came out looking similar to the other Southern states, even though they did not have the same need to oust Republicans. Virginia too was a state where the whites were Democrats and dominated over the blacks who had little political power.

The Compromise of 1877

With the Compromise of 1877, the official occupation of the South was ended. Southerners surrendered control of the federal government to the Yankees, but under the leadership of the Redeemers, they regained control of the local communities and states. The abbreviated story is that following the election of 1876, the Republicans rejected the Democratic victory of Samuel Tilden. Though Tilden clearly defeated Rutherford B. Hayes, they insisted that the elections in Louisiana, South Carolina, and Florida were not fair because of terrorist-type actions that kept black Republicans from the polls. After a long drawn-out contest, Hayes's representatives engaged in negotiations with the Southern Democrats and struck a bargain in which the Yankees got their president, and the South got what they wanted. First, federal troops would be removed from the South. Second, the Republicans would no longer prop up their governments in South Carolina and Louisiana. Third, Hayes agreed to appoint a Southerner to the cabinet and give some patronage to moderate Southern Democrats. Fourth, Hayes claimed to support the idea of federal funds for more internal improvements in the South, mainly railroads.

The Librevs have proclaimed that the North won the war, but the South won Reconstruction. I really have no problem with this claim. The basic idea is that before the war, the Southern economy and politics were controlled by the planters. They returned to power after Reconstruction despite being briefly deposed by the Fourteenth Amendment and other such Republican legislation. Slavery was dead, but the planters still owned their plantations, and by 1877, most of the blacks were back in the fields picking cotton. In a way, the planters profited from the change to sharecropping; they now had poor whites as a source for cheap labor. They may have taken a hit on the balance sheet with the loss of "personal property," the category in which the slaves fell in on the census records, but soon after the violence of Reconstruction had settled, the income statements looked the same or, for some, even better.

Socially, the foundations for American society and the Dunning School had been laid with the Compromise of 1877. The Librevs like to focus on black subservience in the South and their so-called "lost cause myth," but the reality is that it established apartheid America, which included the North and the South. I have a belief that one of the main reasons that the Northern population found the terms of the Compromise acceptable is that the majority of them disapproved of the notion of racial equality. I can accept that many of the carpetbaggers believed in the racial equality which they tried to establish in the South, but I also believe that many simply saw it as a strategy to increase the strength of their party. The fact is that the North failed to achieve racial equality too. The Librevs boast of the achievements of Massachusetts; however, I see that as due to the fact that very few blacks lived in that state. My assumption is that the main reason for race hatred is fear. Whether it be economic competition or feelings that the presence of foreign elements will weaken the social fabric. Many people fear the presence of strangers, especially when they appear in large numbers. Blacks were rare in Massachusetts, whereas they were a majority in many parts of the South. Therefore Southerners viewed blacks as more of a threat than the people of Massachusetts did.

The Compromise of 1877 did bring about a social and economic system that would leave black Southerners as well as all black Americans as second-class citizens. Most Americans believed in the intellectual and moral superiority of white people and, in fact, of the Aryan race. The American belief system was not a whole lot different from Germany where the Nazis rose to power with their theories of Aryan superiority. There is nothing Southern or American about this belief; it seems to have been the dominant philosophy among most people of Northern European background. French and British history is full of examples of this philosophy. I can see no reason why Confederate or Southern symbols should be singled out as emblems of racism.

Black Southerners

We need to be careful in defending our Southern heritage by not falling back on the defense that our ancestor used. When the Librevs complain about the Dunning School, they are thinking in terms of the old belief that the "darkies" were happy with the way things were. Some do not see slavery as whips and chains but rather as a time when the happy-go-lucky darkies would gather and sing songs and dance when not busy in the cotton fields. This thinking was probably a carryover of the old belief system that Africans needed to go through slavery to achieve the intellectual growth that would allow them to adapt to the superior European civilization. No one in the old days thought in terms of civilizations as simply being different. The Europeans were the ones conquering the world; it is natural that most of them felt that they were superior over those they dominated. Again this was nothing uniquely Southern. The fact is, as stated above, black Southerners would be second-class citizens. However, they did make some gains which have been acknowledged by the Librevs.

The negatives were plenty and obvious. The majority of black Southerners did not have jobs as good as whites, and even if they did the same work, they rarely received equivalent pay. As a result, they did not have as much money and all that money buys in a capitalist society: food, housing, clothes, entertainment, and political clout. After the

Compromise of 1877, their political power began to diminish so that by the next century most would not even be able to vote, much less hold public office. More blacks would be lynched by vigilantes; imprisoned for longer terms; and less likely to receive justice in the courts. Black women would be less safe from sexual harassment, and black men would be more likely to face complications while simply trying to defend themselves against aggressive white citizens. Life for black Southerners was not as good as it was for those with white skin. It would be nonsense to dispute that.

Nonetheless, there were some improvements for black people that even the Librevs recognize. They were not slaves. This meant that they no longer feared the unexpected breakup of family units that came with the selling of slaves. Violence, rape, and other such aggressive behavior would be less likely to happen since the perpetrators would face the possibility of being arrested, even though they would probably not receive the same kind of protection that whites would. They did have the sense of working for themselves, even if someone else actually owned the land. They would have more freedom to live and socialize in black communities and worship in their own black churches.

> Though we should be careful about describing the life of black Southerners as contented, either under slavery or shortly after, I do think that there existed a relationship between black and white Southerners. Black Southerners are different in many ways, but there are many characteristics which black and white Southerners share. As stated earlier, most blacks still identify with being Southerners. I repeat the words of Ann Moody, "I got a feeling that there existed some kind of sympathetic relationship between the older Negroes and whites that the younger people didn't quite get or understand."[37]

Conclusions

At this point, I think the situation of Reconstruction can best be summed up by one of those who took part in the attempt to capture

---

37   Anne Moody, *Coming of Age in Mississippi* (New York: Dell, 1968), 109.

Southern hearts and minds as well as their country and homes. The following was stated by Tourgee, one of the most famous carpetbaggers. He is one who was there, and one who admitted going South with an attitude of superiority. It sounds to me like he might agree with my interpretation of Southern identity and disagree with the Librev notion that it came about as some sort of "lost cause myth."

Undoubtedly. The North and the South are simply convenient names for two distinct, hostile, and irreconcilable ideas, - two civilizations they are sometimes called, especially at the South. At the North there is somewhat more of intellectual arrogance; and we are apt to speak of the one as civilization, and of the other as species of barbarism. These two must always be in conflict until the one prevails, and the other falls. To uproot the one, and plant the other in its stead, is not the work of a moment or a day. That was our mistake. We tried to superimpose the civilization, the idea of the North, upon the South at a moment's warning. We presumed, that, by the suppression of rebellion, the Southern white man had become identical with the Caucasian of the North in thought and sentiment; and that the slave, by emancipation, had become a saint and a Solomon at once. So we tried to build up communities there which should be identical in thought, sentiment, growth, and development, with those of the North. It was A Fool's Errand.[38]

---

38   Tourgee, 381.

CHAPTER SEVEN

The New South, Rednecks, and Jim Crow (1877–1920)

Introduction

After winning Reconstruction, Southern patriotism began a period of decline. The Librevs like to talk about the "lost cause myth," but after the Compromise of 1877, I see a decreasing interest in the issues relating to the war. There are a number of reasons for this. As each year passed, the number of veterans of the Yankee invasion, both military and civilian, declined while the population of those born after the war increased. The children and then grandchildren grew up hearing the tales of great battles and Yankee atrocities, but with each passing year, such tales slid into the realm of legends and history. During Reconstruction, the concerns of the Southern people were part of the political system and, in effect, was the ironing out of the final details of surrender. After the compromise, the people did not change in their thinking about who was right and who was wrong, but new issues gained priority. They started down the path to becoming Americans again, and by the late twentieth century, not only were they once again American, but they also became the most patriotic region in the United States.

There were three main changes that diverted the attention of our people during the period between 1877 and 1920. First, the middle classes and wealthy became absorbed with the notion of the "new South." The Librevs will be the first to point out the new mantra. The South lost the war because the North was more industrialized and had a more diverse economy. The South must follow in their footsteps. Second, the American dream of the family farm progressed down the same road to extinction that the Confederacy had gone down. We all know about the Industrial Revolution and the growth of big business in America, but we don't usually think of what this means to the small businessman. In addition, we rarely think about the small farmer as being one of these small businessmen. After the war, they had to compete with the freedmen and the planters. The economies of scale that gave the manufacture an advantage would also give agribusiness an advantage. Third, the rise of the new kind of imperialism which would send the United States Army across the seas would end up increasing American patriotism. At first, the average Southerner would display little interest in such things, but as time passed and the United States became involved in one war after another, the Southerners would end up fighting the wars and as a result coming home more American.

Two other negative developments came along during the period this chapter covers which would contribute to the decline of Southern patriotism. Here I make a distinction between Southern patriotism and American patriotism; it is difficult to serve two masters. As Southerners became more American, they became less Southern. The first problem, and the one most relevant for those of us who take pride in the display of our Confederate heritage, is the rise of the Jim Crow South. Black Southerners may have been slaves before the war, but they were not segregated. How could they be? Black and white Southerners lived together and worked together. One was master and the other slave—an established order which the whites worked hard at maintaining. What most Americans do not realize is that the Jim Crow system which Martin Luther King fought against did not come into being until the late nineteenth century. This of course is what many claim to be the main reason to ban the Confederate flag. They say it represents the system of segregation and racism.

The second negative thing to occur by the end of the nineteenth century is a decay in the Southern economy, which led the Southern Diaspora. Southern industry grew in both quantity and diversity, but apparently, the prosperity remained in the hands of the few while the working class and poor, both black and white, became more and more entrenched in Southern poverty. The Librevs have focused on the black exodus from the South, and in the true liberal fashion, have explained it as the product of black resistance to Jim Crow. I see it as primarily an economic problem which affected all the lower classes regardless of color. I mention this now but will not go into detail until the next chapter. It began at the turn of the century, but most of those who left did so later, and so I will cover this issue in greater detail later.

The Economy after the War

When the war ended, the Southern land lay in ruin. Many of the men in their prime were dead or wounded. Even more lost their homes, farms, plantations, businesses, and had to face the humiliation of defeat. I certainly don't mean to defend the institution of slavery. However, it represented the end of an economic system and thus required major adjustments. The freedmen faced their own economic and legal hardships. Most felt giddy with freedom but sobered up to the reality that they now had to support themselves. They no longer feared being separated from their families but had the new worry of providing for them. The white Southerners were determined to keep them in the cotton fields and to keep them in a subservient social status. From chaos, all Southerners, black and white as well as a mixture of Hispanic and Indian, needed to restore order. They all served a new master—the Union.

I have already pointed out the error of looking at the South as resisters to modernity. The business and economic leaders understood that they trailed the North in most respects, but they were on the road to modernization. They remained entrenched in agriculture, but the production of cotton and other cash crops was their way of participating in the world-market economy. Their greatest sin had been the lack of diversity. The former Southern Whigs would lead the way in correcting that error with the battle cry of "the new South."

Southern Poverty

The South had lagged behind the nation as a whole since 1840. After the war, they dropped to their lowest point with the average per capita income of only 51 percent of the national average. It would be the 1950s before the region as a whole would approach the level it had been before the war, but that would still be three quarters of the national level.

The western part of the South actually exceeded the national average before the war. They paid for the sin of joining the Confederacy though they still did better than the region as a whole. The fact is that poverty became part of being Southern and would lead to one of the greatest mass exoduses in world history where almost twenty-nine million would leave the South in search of more economic opportunity.[39]

The division between magnolias and corn bread had been there since the early days of the South, and they would only get worse during the century that followed the war. Before the unpleasantness, there were the planters who fancied themselves as American aristocracy. They had slaves to work their manors while they raced their horses, hunted, and danced the night away at their balls. However, before the war they did recognize the peerage of white men. After the war, the poorest of the whites would be reduced to the new social class of redneck. There were wealthy people who prospered while the majority went shoeless and lived on beans and corn bread. The planters not only had the blacks picking their cotton but now also had white sharecroppers. They could play the poor blacks and whites against each other while they achieved the economic diversity they sought for the new South.

The New South

The merchants joined the planters in becoming the leaders of the New South. Both were what I call the magnolias. Planter or merchant, they were probably Whigs before the political polarization of the 1850s, which left the Republican Party and the divided Democratic Party. Many of the Librevs see this period as one where the merchants seized control of Southern communities. I am not convinced that this is the case. Before the war, the merchants and larger agribusiness planters helped each other in the popular American pastime of accumulating wealth. This is what I have been saying all along; the South did not resist modernization. They did not advance as rapidly as those in the North, and that is one of their big disadvantages when the war came, but they were still building railroads and had some big cities, such as New Orleans, Memphis, and Charleston. I believe that the most important

---

39   Richard A. Easterlin, "The Regional Income Trends, 1840–1950," in Seymour E. Harris, ed., *American Economic History* (New York" McGraw-Hill, 1961), 28.

aspect of the concept of the New South is the push for economic diversity. A number of new industries blossomed in the late nineteenth and early twentieth century.

Sharecropping

A few brief words are needed about sharecropping. The Librevs rightfully see one of the main reasons for the black codes which followed the war as a way to put the freedmen back in the cotton fields. It is important for us to understand the basic idea if we are going to understand the turn of the century South and an important reason for that mass exodus from the South through much of the twentieth century. Quite simply put, the small farmer worked the planters land for a portion of the crop. On the surface, it seemed like a reasonable capitalistic business arrangement. Unlike forced servitude, the worker benefitted from increased efficiency and hard work. Apparently the system had some appeal to working people as many whites also became involved with the tenant system. The Librevs accuse them of recreating the slavery system as the tenant became chained to the land by debt. The debt was usually to the local merchants where they purchased seed, tools, work boots, and other supplies on credit. Much of their share of the crops went to pay their tab to the local merchant. Many times the planters had connections to the merchants or may have even owned the mercantile themselves. The Librevs often look at the high-interest rates charged for the credit as an additional link in the chain of bondage. First of all, interest rates do traditionally represent the risk for the lender. Generally speaking, a tenant farmer will be a greater risk than a property owner. Second, the national financial policies dictated by the Yankees produced high-interest rates which the Southern merchant or planter had no control over.

Banking and Finance

There are a number of financial reasons that the South struggled for the next century after the war. First of all, many of the wealthy lost capital. The main loss would be their slaves, a major asset on the balance sheet. Much of their cash had been invested in Confederate notes and bonds, both of which were worthless. They suffered major damage to buildings and equipment as a result of war damage; any cash they did have access to would be used for needed repairs. In addition, there were few banks in the South. Another this is that the North won in the struggle for a tight monetary policy which worked to their advantage but not for Southerners.

The South trailed in banking prior to the national conflict, and it got worse after. In 1863, Congress passed a Banking Act that increased the reserves required to charter a bank. This made it more difficult for the new South to open new banks. By 1900, the former eleven Confederate states had only 252 of the 1,737 banks in the United States, with only $26 million of the $417.6 million. New York alone had 252 banks with $75.9 million. The banking regulations of the time did not allow for the easy transfer of funds from one region to another so that little could be done to meet the increased demand for capital. The increase demand with low supply resulted in high-interest rates.

In addition, the United States had policies which created deflation. The Resumption Act of 1875 halted the green backers and silverites who wanted to increase the money supply. The deflation cut the cost of cotton but Republican protectionism increased the cost of manufactured goods. The Gold Standard Act of 1898 and low federal spending further aggravated the situation. By the 1890s, the leading demand for the Populist Party would be the increased demand for the minting of silver, which would increase the money supply and thus stimulate inflation. The small farmers of America, mostly in the West and the South, hoped to pay back their mortgages with cheaper inflated dollars.

Return to Cotton on a Confederate Grave

As soon as the veterans returned from the war, they planted cotton. In 1850, the South produced 2,469 bales of cotton which increased to 5,385 by 1860. Production dropped in 1870, but at 3,011 bales, it still exceeded the 1850 levels. By 1880, they topped the 1860 production with 5,709 bales. Likewise they returned to other favorite crops in other parts of the South, such as tobacco in Kentucky and sugar in Louisiana. Nonetheless, the business leaders of the region developed other industries. Among the numerous journalists singing the praises of the New South, none had greater influence than Henry Grady, editor of the *Atlanta Constitution*. With the rise of the new South, they began to cut away at Southern patriotism. He said, "There was a South of slavery and secession—that South, thank God, is dead. There is a South of union and freedom—that South, thank God, is living, breathing, growing, every hour." Grady praised Abraham Lincoln whom he called "the first typical American" who had "within himself the strength and gentleness of this republic . . . the sum of Puritan and Cavalier." This attitude conflicted with the redeemers as far as generating Southern patriotism.

"Guthrie Cotton Market," 1893. Not only shows the return of King Cotton but how the Southerners took their industry into Oklahoma Territory and points west. (Courtesy National Archives)

Railroads & Other Industries

The existence of railroads in the South alone challenges the notion of resistance to modernization. The 9,000 miles of track which the region had in 1860 was not that deficient compared to 11,000 in the Northeast and 11,000 in the Middle West. Of course, Sherman and his friends greatly reduced the mileage in the1860s. By 1880, the region had more than doubled the prewar mileage with 19,430. They saw railroads a key to the New South. Every Southern state created their own railroad commission, and Southerners played a key role in the passage of the Interstate Commerce Act of 1887.

By 1900, lumbering was the largest industry in the region. Congress opened federally owned lands in the South without restriction, which gave an already growing industry a boost. Much of the land originally intended for former slaves was sold, almost 5.7 million acres by 1888. Northerners as well as English investors profited with help from the railroads, which built lines to haul the Southern pine. Poor whites and blacks found an alternative to working a tenant's share of cotton. Hardwoods also came in demand for furniture making. It is hard to determine the importance of the availability of cheap labor. Rich men of all backgrounds got richer on the sweat of those who lived on beans and corn bread. The supply of cheap labor is what made the South attractive to some industrialists.

The South had no shortage of minerals. The proximity of coal and iron gave boost to an Alabama city which would carry the same moniker as a steel-making center in England— Birmingham. Yankees and rich Southerners reaped the profits while the poor, black and white, risked their lives in the mines. The western regions of the South benefitted from oil discoveries in Oklahoma, Texas, and Louisiana. The ranks of the wealthy picked up some new recruits from the lucky wildcatters who struck it rich. This even included a few of the Indians from eastern Oklahoma. Today some of the wealthiest families in the western part of the South made their fortunes in oil. They rarely came from aristocratic tidewater families but rather from those who happened to have been lucky enough to own a farm with oil in the fields.

Medicines and elixirs became popular, and to this day, fortunes ride on those remedies that became soft drinks. The most famous was the product of Asa Candler. The man purchased the rights to a headache remedy in Atlanta and turned it into Coca-Cola. By 1892, he sold 35,000 gallons of the carbonated drink compared to only 25 gallons in 1886. Coca-Cola utilized the power of advertising and this became the key to success.

In addition to the growing of tobacco, which has been in the South since the first colonies, there were the developments in the manufacturing of cigarettes. By 1880, tobacco production approximated the 1860 level, nearly doubled it by 1900 and doubled it again by 1920 and continued to grow until 1980. During the war, soldiers were introduced to the tobacco grown in the Durham, North Carolina area. The former Union and Confederate troops loved it. Bull Durham led the way in production. To challenge the highly successful company, Washington Duke and his sons became the first company to use the Bonsack cigarette machine in 1881. Within two years, Duke cigarette production increased by 600 percent. In the later part of the decade, they boosted sales further with the use of advertising and gimmicks. In 1890, Duke and four other competitors formed the American Tobacco Company. They created another industry that made the capitalist wealthy and provided work for those less fortunate.

Before the war, most of the cotton went to mills in the North or in Europe. Between 1880 and 1905, the South increased the number of mills turning the Southern staple into cloth. There are an assortment of statistics which show the increased production. Spindles increased from 11,898 to 110,000 which helped to increase the production of raw cotton seven times between 1880 and 1900. The value of Southern cotton mills increased from $11.1 million to $124.6 million, and the number of workers went from 16,714 to 97,494. Compared to 22,423 workers in the steel industry, we can see the advantage textiles had was due to the much lower requirement for start-up capital. Like the other industries in the South, the wealthy benefitted from the lower cost of labor, both black and white and thus widening the gap between corn bread and magnolias.

Urbanization, Working Class & Such

The increase in Southern manufacturing, whether it be in minerals, steel, tobacco, or textiles, had an effect on the region by increasing the number of working class and the growth of cities. Railroads probably did the most to increase the number of cities from 119 in 1880 to 320 in 1900. Steel helped Birmingham, oil helped Dallas and Tulsa, but even though many of the textiles mills had their own "mill towns," the increase agricultural production contributed to the development of urban centers. We are not talking about large cities, 80 percent of these towns had populations of less than 10,000. Nonetheless, this still means that more people in the South had moved off the land and into working-class jobs.

Librevs and the unreconstructed alike have a tendency to look at the South as being a land of planters, poor blacks, and farm families. Most of it was before the war and continued to be until the last half of the twentieth century. Some of the needed cash for development came from Northern businessmen, but the majority of the new manufactures were Southerners. They profited most from the low cost of labor. Southern attitudes helped to limit the popularity of labor unions though there were some exceptions. Men like Huey Long in Louisiana preached "sharing the wealth," and in Oklahoma, the Socialist Party had more success than any other state in the Union. This is why Woody Guthrie and some of his fellow Okies were feared when they went to California during the days of growing anticommunism.

Through the years, there have been those who have proposed the notion that the wealthy encouraged racism as a way to keep the working class from uniting. Such theories have been used to explain the lack of appeal that socialism and communism had throughout the United States and not just the South. I can see why some have been drawn to this thesis. However, I am skeptical of the conspiratorial nature of the charges. I do believe that the ethnic and racial diversity of the laborers made it more difficult for the workers of the United States to unite. Whether it be the Italian immigrants in New York or the blacks in Alabama, the numerous ethnic communities would naturally look after their own interest and thus look at the others as competition. I am sure that there were times when management took advantage of these divisions. However, Americans of the North or the South were racist, just like the Aryans of Germany, France, and England; and thus, racial and ethnic disunion should be the expected.

This is what I have been saying all along and will continue to say throughout this essay; racism is not a Southern thing. The white workers may have realized that the blacks were working people like themselves and that their sweat was helping to make the capitalist wealthy, but they still believed that white people were superior. Likewise, the white owners and management may have realized the advantage they had in keeping the working people divided. However, they too believed in racial superiority. Those in the North had an even more complicated situation because of the larger and more diverse immigrant population. Those of white Aryan background also believe themselves to be superior to some other whites. They did not look at some of the other Europeans as white. The Italians, Greeks, and others from eastern and Southern Europe tended to be darker in complexion, and so the native white American population of Germanic extraction considered the darker-complexioned Europeans to be inferior. This is why Italians were called Guineas, a name that is derived from an African nation. To the Anglo-Americans, the Italians were no better than blacks.

From Yeoman to Populist

I cannot prove it, but I firmly believe the main explanation for the delayed economic development of the South during the century following the war had nothing to do with either the Southern resistance to modernization or the evil carpetbaggers. The Librevs like to blame racism, the Southern lack of respect for education, the twisted code of honor, disease, the long hot summers, and overall Southern backwardness for the extreme poverty which plagued the region. Many Southerners, especially the unreconstructed, like to blame Yankee imperialism. To them, it is the greed and corruption of Reconstruction which laid the foundation and the powerful Northern Republican businessmen who profited from the continued oppression. Perhaps all of these variables contributed. However, I believe that the key is the fact that not only did the region continue to be predominantly agricultural, but they also depended on the traditional American mechanism of agriculture, the family farm. Though many, if not most, of the crops grown were commodities, such as cotton, much of it was still produced on the small family farm. Agriculture was becoming agribusiness. However, the South retained the impression of being a land of small farmers since so many were sharecroppers.

The main reason for the success of the sharecropping system is that it allowed for more of the poor farmers, especially the freedmen, to assume the role of the traditional American farmer who continued to be the majority of the population until the 1920s. They may not have owned the land, but like the majority of white men, they worked the land and reaped the profits of their labor. This may have been more theory than reality according to the Librevs. I do not consider these charges to be as important as the fact that it left agricultural production to families, and thus, the agricultural industry could not benefit from the lower cost associated with the returns to scale found in manufacturing during the Industrial Revolution. Today the vast majority of agricultural production in America is agribusiness. Between 1865 and the late twentieth century, the small family farm advanced down the road toward extinction because it could not compete with agribusiness. Between 1865 and 1900, the pain of the small farmer was expressed with the development of the Populist movement. This happened in the West too but dominated in the South.

My intent is not to give a detailed analysis of Populism but rather simply an outline. The small farmers of America blamed their problems on the railroads for their high rates, the bankers for their high interest, and the Republican capitalist for their adherence to the gold standard, which produced deflation. There is no doubt that these are the more direct causes for the decline of the family farm. However, the more inclusive problem is modernization. Economic survival under industrialization depended on cutting cost. This would allow the successful to bury the competitors who could not control cost. This included agricultural goods too. The cost of goods produced on the family farms were higher than those produced on the larger tracts of land owned by the agribusiness. This was just as true for those who operated as sharecroppers as those who owned the land they worked.

The first attempt by the farmers to attack what they saw as the enemy was the Grange. This was more a social club than a political movement. The Grange became replaced by the Alliance movement. When Kansas and both of the Dakotas joined the Southern Farmers Alliance, they formed the National Farmers Alliance. In 1890, they met in Ocala, Florida, and drafted the demands that identify for us what their main concerns were. Top of the list was the free minting of silver. This they hoped would increase the money supply, which would create inflation, which would benefit the small farmer who could get a rise in prices and allow them to pay mortgage debt with cheaper dollars. They also wanted to abolish national banks; surrender railroad lands not actually needed for the operation of their business; lower tariffs; and implement a subtreasurey plan. Some of their goals were downright socialistic, such as graduated income tax and government control or even ownership of the public means of communication and transportation.

In the 1890s, they formed the Populist Party. The depression of 1893 no doubt contributed greatly to the demise of the political party which experienced rapid growth and some success before its equally rapid decline. Historians point out how many of the demands became implemented under the Progressives, which they usually dismiss to the lack of political sophistication of the Populists. I believe that the real significance of the failure of the Populist movement is that it could not do anything about the main reason for the problems in the first place; the family farm could not compete with agribusiness and the sharecropper who had maintained a delusion of independence became replaced by machines.

From Populist to Redneck

With the changes that came after the War of Southern Independence, the most significant has been the decline of the small Southern farmer. Before 1860, they were not only the majority of the Southern population, but they were also still the majority of the American population. The American dream since the founding of the first colonies was to own their own land. This is why most crossed the ocean; killed the Indians; and fought nature and any other perceived enemy. The Librevs love the book by Edmond S. Morgan, *American Slavery, American Freedom*, in which he put forth the notion that democracy grew in the South because of slavery. The black slaves occupied the lower rungs of the social ladder, which lifted even the poor whites to a level of equality that fostered the spirit of democracy, at least among whites. In other words, the white population who owned their own farm, no matter how modest, had feelings of equality to even the wealthy planters. The end of slavery, the decline of the family farm, and the industrialization that did occur in the South left a new Southern elite who began to look at the poor whites as "rednecks." The magic of being white in the South began to disappear, which may at least partly account for the rise of Jim Crow.

The Biggest Enemy of Our Confederate Heritage

Though actually symbols of the Confederacy and what the Librevs consider the slaveocracy, the greatest problem we have defending our Southern heritage are due to the use of these symbols, mainly the Confederate battle flag, in later years. Images of Jim Crow and our Southern kin who waved the Southern banner in defense of segregation and the destruction of American apartheid are what gave us the most grief. Most of America was segregated prior to World War II. However, in the South legislation made it official. In the case of Oklahoma, it was even part of the state constitution. Most who want to extinguish the symbols of the Old South see them as representing "white only" signs, lynchings, and voting restrictions, etc. Blacks in the North suffered the same kind of discrimination, but it is easier to put the burden of American racism on the shoulders of the South. Since more blacks lived in the South, there were more laws limiting black freedom. It was the federal courts, however, which opened the door for the Jim Crow laws in the first place.

In 1883, shortly after the Compromise of 1877, the Supreme Court ruled the Civil Rights Act of 1875 unconstitutional. All the indications are that it was more than an abandonment of the freedmen when the North allowed the white Southerners to establish domination over black Southerners. I have no doubt that most of those to the North did not accept the liberal notion that the two races were equal. If the Republicans of Reconstruction succeeded in forcing equality on the people of the South then it would be logical to expect the same in the North. In the nineteenth century, few white people, especially Aryans, doubted the superiority of their race. When the Supreme Court upheld "separate but equal" with the Plessey v. Ferguson decision of 1896, it opened the floodgates of Jim Crow.

More important in politically castrating blacks was the virtual elimination of voting rights. During Reconstruction, not only did blacks vote but many were also elected to public office. There are those who argue that the real attacks came in the 1890s in an attempt to limit the Populist white voters as well. Most of the laws followed the example of the Mississippi Plan of 1890. This legal mechanism circumvented the Fourteenth and Fifteenth amendments. The new state constitution required voters to have resided in the state for at least two years and in their election districts for one, to have paid all their taxes for two years before registering, and to pay their two-dollar poll tax. In addition, they had to prove that they could comprehend any part of the constitution when it was read to them. The traditional accusation is that the examiner could control who passed and who failed. It has been claimed by some that this type of law had also been used to limit the power of the Populists.

It has not been firmly established what the role of lynching has been in the establishment of the Jim Crow South. The liberals of the America have assumed that it served to establish control over the black population. Between 1882 and 1951, 4,900 people were lynched in the United States. More than 80 percent were black, and 80 percent of the cases took place in the South. The most gruesome involved torture or mutilation. Many involved accusations of relations between black men and white women, and a good many do doubt involved making certain that the blacks accepted their status as second-class citizens. Some were no doubt criminals who inspired the ire of the local population to the extent that they could simply not wait for a trial. On one hand, the evidence is that many such group crimes were racially motivated. On the other hand, this is an average of about seventy per year with less than sixty in the South, some of which were not racially motivated. I am not convinced that these numbers prove the importance of lynching in the Jim Crow era. I am sure that it had some impact, but I am not sure it is that much of a deviation from the American tradition of violence. New York City, for example, has at least that many murders in a year. It certainly does not compare to the violence against the Jews in Nazi Germany.

The Atlanta Compromise

The Atlanta Compromise tells us a lot about the attitudes of blacks and whites during the founding of the Jim Crow South. Booker T. Washington made a speech at the Cotton States and International Exposition in Atlanta in which he advised his fellow blacks to work hard, educate themselves, and be patient in advancing in white America. The predominantly white crowd applauded him. Some blacks were glad to have one of their own praised by the whites, but others objected to the comments. W. E. B. DuBois began to challenge Washington for leadership of black rights. DuBois would later be involved in founding of the NAACP. The first black to earn a PhD, he felt that the blacks should not have to wait any longer.

What I see from this incident and the events following is that white people had an attitude of racial superiority, and blacks were still divided on the best way to improve their lives. On one hand, it reflects that most of those whites present did not hate black folks. On the other hand, they clearly did not see them as equals. They reflected the same attitude that had been used to justify slavery for generations; blacks were not equal, but with white guidance and time, they could be. Some blacks were pleased with the advances they had made. In 1895, there were many who remembered slavery. I suspect that many accepted what they had always been told and believed themselves to be inferior to whites. When people are razed from infancy with the idea that they are inferior, I am sure that it is easy to accept that philosophy as fact. Others understood that the education that Washington provided for blacks was the best way to achieve equality with the dominant race. However, the reaction by DuBois tells us that some blacks already believed themselves to be equal. This, after all, was the claim of Thomas Jefferson when he said all men were created equal.

DuBois is admired by the Librevs, and in my opinion, he had a good grasp of the situation during the turn of the century. The following quote is revealing in its description of black/white relations and also distinguishes between the lower and upper classes of Southern white society, or what I have called magnolias and corn bread.

> To-day even the attitude of the Southern whites toward the blacks is not, as so many assume, in all cases the same; the ignorant Southerner hates the Negro, the workingmen fear his competition, the money-makers wish to see him as a laborer, some of the educated see a menace in his upward development, while others - usually the sons of the masters - wish to help him to rise. National opinion has enabled this last class to maintain the Negro common schools, and to protect the Negro partially in property, life, and limb. Through the pressure of the money-makers, the Negro is in danger of being reduced to semi-slavery, especially in the country

districts; the workingmen, and those of the educated who fear the Negro, have united to disfranchise him, and some have urged his deportation; while the passions of the ignorant are easily aroused to lynch and abuse any black man. To praise this intricate whirl of thought and prejudice is nonsense; to inveigh indiscriminately against "the South" is unjust; but to use the same breath in praising Governor Aycock, exposing Senator Morgan, arguing with Mr. Thomas Nelson Page, and denouncing Senator Ben Tillman, is not only sane, but the imperative duty of thinking black men.[40]

Some Gains, Some Losses

During the period between 1877 and the end of World War I, blacks had made some gains and then suffered some losses. Whereas only a small minority had been free in 1860, by 1877, all had gained their freedom. They no longer had to take orders, at least in theory; they no longer had to allow their women to be victims of white passions; they no longer had to see their families split up because the master decided to sell them. With Reconstruction and the Republican Party, they had gained the right to vote, and they listened to promises of land and a mule. By 1920, most had lost their voting rights, most had been reduced to the quasi-servitude status of sharecropper, and they were forced to accept second-class citizenship in the country that they and their ancestors had lived in since 1619. The bottom line is that they were still better off than they were in 1860. They were still free, and they had established their independent community identity. They may have had limited power in the white-dominated world, but they had their own corner of that world with their own leaders.

Imperialism, another Issue in Southern Identity

First of all, let me make sure that everyone realizes that the United States is an imperialist power. This is a repeat of material I have already

---

40 W. E. B. DuBois, *The Souls of Black Folk* (New York: Dover Publications, 1994), 33–34.

covered, but so many Americans deny that we are imperialist, I feel compelled to repeat it. Any nation which started with thirteen states and ended up with fifty states spanning a continent as well as numerous possessions and interest around the globe is imperialist. The techniques utilized by this country are not signs that they are different from European imperialist but rather that they are employing the modern imperialist strategy. The Europeans do not use the old style imperialism as they too have converted to the new.

The new style is what Americans have called Mahanism. Alfred Thayer Mahan is the author of late nineteenth-century American imperialism. His two books on the benefits of a strong navy laid out the plan. First, industrialization leads to surpluses. Second, surpluses lead to the need to enter the world markets. Third, world market competition requires a merchant marine. Fourth, a merchant marine needs a navy to protect it. Fifth, the merchant marine and navy need fueling stations. Sixth, fueling stations mean colonies. The key difference between the old imperialism is that the fueling stations mean only minimal occupation of foreign lands. Remember, the main objective of imperialism, old or new, is to make money. The modern imperialist have realized that the fewer colonial possessions require fewer expenditures to support the empire and therefore produce more profits. They have also realized that global expansion can be for the distribution of goods as well as the acquisition of raw materials.

The new imperialism is for the advantage of the industrialist. In the United States, that means those with money in the Northeast. Some Southern merchants, manufacturers, and other businessmen also benefitted from this new imperialism. However, most people in the South between 1877 and 1920 were farmers, not merchants. They too were part of the world-market economy, but their struggles, which were many at the time, revolved around domestic issues. They had more interest in limiting the power of Northern railroads and bankers rather than in helping them.

During the late nineteenth century and early twentieth century, the South offered little support for the rise of modern American Imperialism. However, in the end it would eat away at the number of unreconstructed Southerners. Politicians with support of Southern Democrats such as Grover Cleveland and Williams Jennings Bryan as well as Southern authors such as Mark Twain were members of the anti-Imperialist League. I would guess that the majority of Southerners were at best indifferent concerning the rise of America in the international imperial competition. Most were Populists or Populist sympathizers who were more concerned about the state of the American farm family than in the quest of Northern businessmen as they competed with the other great powers.

There is one side affect that helped to eat away at Southern patriotism, and that is the growth of American patriotism in the South. Some were glad from the start to be back in the United States, the land of their birth. Others resisted being conquered and occupied by the imperialist American military. This was the struggle of Reconstruction. After the Compromise of 1877, most Southerners were satisfied with the fact that they controlled their local governments; they were back to planting cotton; and that the blacks were back to picking it. Whereas I object to the term "lost cause myth," most Southerners spoke highly of the "lost cause" and the glory and bravery of the Confederate soldier. In 1898, the United States sent troops overseas for the first time. The proportion of Southerners serving in the foreign wars was higher than expected based on the ratio of Southerners to the total population. Many Southerners like to think that this was due to our patriotic enthusiasm. I tend to think it was more due to economic consequences. The poorer classes tend to fill the ranks of enlisted men in wars. This is true for the American military as it has been for others throughout the ages. The South was worse off economically during this period, and I believe that it is the main reason they served at a higher ratio.

Regardless of the reason, the more that Southerners served in the military, the more veterans they produced. The veterans came back and supported their kind. As the numbers of American veterans increased, including those from the South, so has American patriotism. The increase in American patriotism decreases Southern patriotism; as I said earlier, it is hard to serve two masters. There are still many people in the South who continue to speak highly of the Confederate soldier and the Confederate cause of states' rights, but most today place their American patriotism on a higher pedestal. As far as I am concerned, a truly unreconstructed Southerner feels greater pride in being Southern than American; that is our nationalism.

Conclusions

The period 1877 to 1920 has produced a number of variables that has led to a decrease in the number of our people who can be called unreconstructed Southerners. The changes were primarily economic. The wealthy and middle classes profited from being part of the American empire again and what they enthusiastically labeled the "new South." The lower middle-class farmers and white sharecroppers struggled for survival so that their money worries overshadowed any interest in the "lost cause." Black Southerners who may have supported the South during the war years, but were probably indifferent or even pro-Union, became convinced that the conquest of the South and the wonderful deeds of Abraham Lincoln is what set them free. I would say that more than 90 percent of those in the *Slave Narratives* looked at Abraham Lincoln as their liberator. I am sure that this was largely due to Reconstruction propaganda, but nonetheless, that is what they believed, and that is what they taught their children and grandchildren to believe. Meanwhile, more and more Southerners became involved in American empire building by serving in the military. This has produced an ever-increasing number who considered themselves Americans first, Southerners second. During this period, there were many who abandoned their heritage, and their children and grandchildren would find it even easier to do. By the time we get to the late twentieth century, most Southerners seem to be willing to leave their Confederate past in the dust as they cling to their American patriotism. This will be the trend in the next two chapters. By the beginning of the twenty-first century, many more Southerners will adorn their cars and pickups with "United We Stand" bumper stickers, which display the Stars and Stripes while increasingly fewer will brandish the stars and bars.

Chapter Eight

The Fall of the South, 1920–1970

Introduction

I have titled this chapter "The Fall of the South," primarily because of the first part of the period. The time between the two world wars left the region at its lowest point since the fall of the Confederacy and the resulting occupation. After World War II, the South went through a racial crisis and then began to rise. Unfortunately, this new South would be American and those of us who are unreconstructed would become the minority. This intrawar period began a great diaspora that resulted from a defective economy, and this great exodus diminished the self-esteem of Southerners. The intellectual activities of the same era served to lower our self-esteem as well as further tainting the image of our people with Northerners. Many Southerners served in the two world wars, and thus, the survivors were veterans. They were veterans of the United States Army; and thus, they were patriotic Americans and, as a result, became a little less Southern. This period was also a time when the foundation for change would be laid for black Southerners. It began with a change in political affiliation for black Southerners as this is when they shifted their loyalties from the Republican Party to the Democratic Party. I recall one elderly black lady saying that she can explain the change in one word: "Roosevelt." She also pointed out that this happened at a time when the Democrats of the South were the main enemies of black equality.

Remember that one of the main objectives of my analysis in this essay is to explain the decline in the number of unreconstructed Southerners. In many ways, this was a time in which the Old South was demolished to create a vacant lot for the rise of a truly new South. The traditional

New South is the time between 1877 and the turn of the century, but in reality, the New South did not come until after World War II. The traditional New South was more of an adjustment to a new labor system that went from slavery to sharecropping. In the end, they still had a culture where the majority depended on the traditional American family farm. The South has been agricultural since its beginnings. It is different today in that it has a more diverse economy though it is still heavily agricultural. It is not so much that the South is less agricultural as the fact that fewer people depend on that industry for their livelihoods. What is most important to the common people of our land is the demise of the family farm, and this is what made it a true new South.

Since the beginning of the colonies, people came to America for the opportunity to own their own farm and to obtain the status and independence which came with being land owners. At the end of the War of Southern Independence, even most Northerners still dreamed of the family farm. By the end of the Industrial Revolution, most in the North had made the transition to some alternative. It may not have been good, but the majority no longer depended on the land for their living. About1920 was the turning point where the majority of the American population lived in urban areas. This means that the majority did not make their living off of the land. However, let us not forget that this is true for most of the American population in total, but in the North, the change was much greater than in the South. Southerners, black and white, still clung to the dream of the family farm. By 1945, it was clear that the dream was over and only then could the economic diversity dreamed of by Henry Grady be realized.

The transition was brutal for many people. Perhaps it was the conservative nature of the Southern people that made it so that they had to be forced off the land, but then again, it may have been simply due to the fact that Southern participation in the world-market economy included the making of products that came from the land. The South today is still the leader in many agricultural products. The new production method is called agribusiness. There are a few in the South and West who cling to the concept of the family farm, and they are the ones who need Willie Nelson to help them out once in awhile. When we get to the next chapter, we will see a greater diversity in the Southern economy which produced a reversal in the Diaspora. The period between 1920 and 1945 would ultimately separate our people from their dream of a family farm, and because of this, millions would flee from the region altogether. They did so not because they wanted to but because they had to survive. This naturally had a negative impact on Southern identity.

The King is Dead (Cotton)

Cotton did not become king in the South until the early nineteenth century, but it has become a classic symbol of the antebellum South. That South is also known as the "Old South." It is an exaggeration to proclaim the king dead; the reality is that production in terms of bales of cotton was close to 13 percent higher in 1950 than in 1920. What I really mean by this proclamation is that the labor system that produced the cotton has died, and thus, a much smaller part of the population depends on cotton production for their living. In some parts of the region such as Oklahoma, production declined. In 1920, that state produced 11.5 percent of the South's cotton; by 1950 production declined to 1.9 percent. Most think it was the dust bowl that hurt Oklahoma, but it was much more than that. Economic competition led to new methods of production, which included a shift from manpower to machine power. A great number of people living in Oklahoma were Southerners who learned that the way to make a living was to grow cotton; after 1920, they began to look for other ways to make a living.

Cotton production evolved from the small family farm toward the large agribusiness. The large producers changed from using slave labor to sharecroppers to machines. The later meant they no longer needed people. These people were the lower or working classes. The middle-class family farm producer had a harder time competing. For the most part, all but the great planters would be forced off the land. Between 1920 and 1930, the number of farm owners in the South declined by 350,000. Approximately 60 percent of the Southern farm operators worked someone else's land. Other forces helped to rob the Southern families of their land. The boll weevil came up from Mexico. California became more of an economic threat with its agribusiness. Foreign competition took its toll as did the manufacture of synthetics. After so many turned to sharecropping as an alternative to starvation, economic forces began to dismantle the sharecropping system. The

Agricultural Adjustment Act paid farmers not to plant crops; this money did not go to the tenants, and thus, they no longer had a job. During the Second World War, the cotton-picking machine would remove the remaining families from the jobs and their homes.

There were not enough other jobs in the South to provide for those forced off the land. This led to the great exodus to the North. The Librevs like to reinforce the myth that sharecroppers were black and that the Southern exodus, which they call the "great migration," was mostly blacks. The fact is that in the early twentieth century there were 5.5 million white tenants, sharecroppers, and laborers in the United States and only 3 million blacks. Historically, whites made up two-thirds of the farm hands in Tennessee. In Mississippi, 36 percent of whites were not private farmers while 60 percent of the blacks fit in this category. Blacks may have suffered more during this period as was most often the case in American history; however, many whites also paid the price for the transition to machine-powered agribusiness. In the South, the changes in cotton production had the greatest impact, but almost all Southern agriculture went through similar changes.

Rearview of an Okie's car passing through Amarillo, Texas, on its way west in 1941. "Okies" were anyone in California with a Southern accent and no money. Though made famous by John Steinbeck, they were only part of the Southern Diaspora. (Courtesy National Archives)

The Southern Economy in General

Immediately following World War I, there were some good times in the South. At first, the demand for cotton decreased because of the war, but by 1920, the prices had risen from five cents a pound to twenty-seven cents. Even the black tenants were reported to have "come to town with their pockets stuffed with paper money" to pay off their bills. Other Southern industries prospered during the war years, including chemicals, timber, and oil. Cigarette smoking became more acceptable, which helped the South's tobacco farmers.

Cities represent merchant economy; the growth of Southern cities during this time suggest that there was some development in the nonagricultural segments of the economy. New Orleans remained the largest city in the South in 1930, but Houston was closing in and Dallas was not far behind. Urban growth spread across the South and included cities, such as Louisville, Atlanta, Birmingham, Memphis, San Antonio, Richmond, Oklahoma City, Fort Worth, Nashville, Tulsa, Jacksonville, and Norfolk. Cities divided the Southern people between the sophisticated urbanites who had electricity, more store-bought goods, more automobiles, and more education and those who remained in the rural areas and who heated with wood-burning stoves, read by oil lamps, and had less education. The cities became governed by civic elites who cared less and less about the Old South and the lost cause. The division, which I call magnolias and corn bread, took on a new flavor.

The South suffered during the Depression as did the rest of the nation. They had some advantages; since so many more lived on the land, they at least had food that they grew. Of course, this is the time when the sharecroppers were hurled out onto the roads and highways as the government paid the land owners to not grow crops. John Steinbeck burned the image of the dust bowl into the minds and hearts of Americans, but it was the demise of the sharecropping system that pushed most of the Okies off the land. Remember too that the Okies came from Texas, or Arkansas, or even Kansas as well as Oklahoma. Anyone arriving in California in a dilapidated car with only a few dollars in their pocket and spoke with a Southern accent was an "Okie."

The dust bowl itself was centered in the high plains of the panhandles of Texas and Oklahoma. However, severe erosion was a price paid for the generations of land abuse throughout the West and South. The images of the Joads became part of the great Diaspora. People fled the South in the 1930s, but this continued and escalated during the war and shortly after as black and white Southerners searched for jobs in the Northern cities. In the western part of the South, they went to California; in the central parts they went to Chicago, Detroit, or Ohio; and in the east they went to New York, Washington D.C., and Boston.

As part of the New Deal, Roosevelt implemented the Tennessee Valley Authority. This project brought jobs, flood control, but most importantly, rural electrification. With the electricity produced by the TVA and other such projects, the majority of the Southern population who still resided in rural areas had greater access to radio and later, television. This brought the South closer to the rest of the nation and helped considerably in making its people American. Southern identity remained strong during this period, but with the ties to national networks and the president's fireside chats, the spirit of being American grew at the expense of being less Southern.

World War II brought more rapid change to the South than they had experienced since the War of Southern Independence and Reconstruction. The economy of 1945 differed considerably from that of 1940, which in turn sparked considerable social and political change. Cotton, segregation, and one-party politics were weakened so that in the years after the war, these would no longer be characteristics of the region.

The South received a disproportionate share of military bases. The climate played a part in this policy, especially with the increase in air power. Airplanes have a greater dependence on good weather so that their takeoffs and landings are not limited. However, Roosevelt did recognize the South as being the most impoverished region in the nation, and he saw the military installations as one way of helping to resolve that problem. The federal government invested more than $7 billion on the bases and industrial plants. Many of these bases were expanded and made permanent after the war, and even some of the post-1970 population growth came from retired military personnel who remained in the region. Industrial capacity of the region grew 40 percent from 1939 to 1947. The number of production workers increased by almost 50 percent, from 1.3 million to 2 million. Personal income rose from $13.6 billion to $32.1 billion, bringing the South from 59 percent of the national average to 69 percent.

Despite the economic growth, the greatest exodus from the South occurred after 1940. More than 4 million served in the armed forces. However, many more fled to the war-related jobs on the coasts or in Northern cities. The Librevs focus on the blacks who left, and even though they admit that economic factors played a big part, they prefer to emphasize Southern racism as a major reason, if not the major reason, for "the great migration."

The Great Migration Myth

Most of the United States textbooks these days have a topic called "the great migration." This is not to be confused with other such periods in American history, such as the puritans who went to New England in the early seventeenth century. I believe this to be largely due to the error of trying to separate the story of black Southerners from white Southerners. I believe the main implication is that they left because of Southern racism. One textbook I read used the terms "push" and "pull." With "pull" they recognized the economic reasons. However, with the "push," they talk about "the poverty, indebtedness, racism, and violence most blacks experienced in the South."[41] The main reason I believe the push variables to be less significant than do the Librevs is that blacks were never treated as equals.

I call this a myth not because there was no great exodus of blacks from the South, but rather because they talk of the black population only. This is typical of ways in which they focus on and emphasize racism in the South. When they cover this topic, they admit that the blacks moved into a segregated North also and that they did not get as good jobs as the whites and that they lacked in education and so forth, but the Librevs imply that blacks were still much better off than in the South. Later I will give some statistics showing ways in which the North was as bad as the South. It is a fact that some of the blacks

---

41   Alan Brinkley, *A Survey: American History* (New York: McGraw-Hill, 2007), 623.

themselves promoted the North as being a better place. The black-oriented newspaper *Chicago Defender* wrote in the early 1900s: "To die from the bite of frost is far more glorious than at the hands of a mob. I beg you, my brother, to leave the benighted land." However, I can recall a number of songs from that time period, such as the one by Louis Armstrong, in which he longed for the sunny South. The bottom line is that the *Defender* may have influenced some in their decision to move North, but the fact is that it was an exodus of all Southerners, not just blacks, which to me indicates that it was primarily for economic reasons. Of the more than 28 million Southerners who left the region, only 28 percent were black, 68 percent were white, and 4 percent Hispanic.

The Librevs did not create the term "great migration." It is the Northern white media that first begin to write of the increase in the black population among them. I am sure that it was not because they were boasting of the greater opportunities for people of color in the North but more in the same way California press wrote about the Okies in their state in the 1930s. They were writing about a topic of distress, not praise. By the 1940s, they were using the term "great migration." The blacks who went to Chicago before World War I, when the *Defender* started publication, did find jobs. However, they were replaced by white immigrants so that the black weekly journal complained about the fact that they had taken the jobs previously filled by blacks. Even in the 1960s, I can remember when Martin Luther King, Jr. took the civil rights movement North, and after a night of rioting in Chicago, he claimed that he had never seen so much hatred, not even in Selma, Alabama.

As far as I am concerned, this entire subject is a perfect example of why I try to include both black and white Southerners in my study of our history. They may have lived in segregated neighborhoods and communities in the South, and they likewise moved into segregated neighborhoods and communities when they moved north, but they were both part of a greater trend. They were part of a Southern Diaspora. I remember in the 1960s working at Hunts cannery in Hayward, California. I usually ate supper with some of my fellow workers who were black. We were on the graveyard shift, and we all seemed to enjoy conversation as much as food since the facility had such a high noise level that we wore earplugs when we worked. One night, they started talking about "soul food." Before long, I joined in as they discussed the pleasure of eating foods like greens, pinto beans, corn bread, fried chicken, and okra. I began to realize that either I was black or that "soul food" simply meant Southern food. There are some things they seemed to eat more than white Southerners, such as chitlins, but most of it was the same. Likewise with the music; they favored blues and jazz while we whites leaned more toward country; however, we all knew Southern music. The black and white Southerners who moved North during the twentieth century had a major cultural impact on that region. Southern Baptist churches appeared in communities where they had never existed before. They both helped to change the North as Blacks would later be elected in Northern communities for the first time, and Southern whites would help in building the political careers of men like Ronald Reagan. The South suffered a loss of population, but the Southern people influenced the nation as a whole in ways they had never done before.

The sad thing to me is that this Diaspora had a negative influence on our Southern identity. Some would consider this a good thing since it means that we as a people were becoming more American. However, remember that I am writing for those of us who our unreconstructed. There are advantages to assimilation, but I personally regret the loss of our unique cultural identity. As we will see in the next chapter, this became a two-edged sword beginning in the 1970s when the Diaspora reversed itself. During World War II, even though many moved out, there were 6 million outsiders who moved into the South. After 1970, we see a trend where more people are moving into the region than out. Some are returned Southerners such as myself. However, most were not. In recent years, as in the United States in total, many have been foreign born. Since World War II, America has become more Southern because of the Diaspora. However, the South has become more American. The cultural border between North and South is not as well-defined as it was before World War II, and it seems to be getting more and more difficult to recognize the regional differences. There have always been people in the upper parts of the South who did not identify with the region; however, the surveys done by John Shelton Reed and his friends at the University of North Carolina have shown the number in decline.

The Trashing of the South by Southerners

Starting in the 1920s, a number of writers emerged from the South who the Librevs like to describe as being "critical." It seems to be the rule that artists, especially writers, are contrary to the general population whether it is a French artist writing about French culture, English writing about English culture, or Japanese writing about Japanese culture. There are conservative artists and there are conservative writers, but it seems that the most famous are the ones who are critical of their homeland, its people, and its culture. They quite often are critical of the entire human race. I have no problem accepting that many of the Southern writers who came along during the 1920s were critical of our Southern ways. I do not even have any objection to the fact that we have plenty of habits for the writers to be critical of—the treatment of black Southerners is the most obvious example. What I resent is the way this topic is presented in most of the textbooks today. The implication is that the Southern writers were critical of the South in a way that implies we should be following the example set by the great and wise Northerners. Unfortunately, that is what some of them did. I understand this experience since I myself yielded to Northern domination by believing there ways to be superior to ours. Since I was one of those California Okies who was intimidated into adopting their language, I could easily pass for one of them. I have always identified with the lines in the Don Williams song, "I was smarter than most and I could choose, learned to talk like the man on the six o'clock news." I did not think of myself as Southern like I do now. Today I can see that our ways are far from perfect. Every culture has its faults. However, I much prefer the ways of my Southern people over the self-righteous and arrogant ways of Yankeedom.

Perhaps the most famous of these writers was H. L. Mencken, and his most famous attitudinal essay was "The Sahara of the Bozart." Mencken was born in Baltimore in 1880. Some might argue that he was not a real Southerner since he was from Maryland, but I personally have no problem accepting those from that state as fellow Southerners. In his famous essay, he wrote, "Virginia is the best of the South today, and Georgia is perhaps the worst. The one is simply senile; the other is crass, gross, vulgar, and obnoxious. Between lies a vast plain of mediocrity, stupidity, lethargy, almost of dead silence." Mencken was a cranky old man who seemed to hate everything American, but he said, "The North, of course, there is also grossness, crassness, vulgarity. The North, in its way, is also stupid and obnoxious." However, he went on to say that at least in the North they are trying to improve themselves. Where I take exception to his criticism is that he measures these advances by looking at the American imitations of European culture, such as orchestras or little theater. What I love about the South is that the people have culture, and most of it is uniquely American, or more specifically, uniquely Southern. Today, most of the Southern cities do have orchestras who play the classical European music, but we also have Nashville, Memphis, and New Orleans where the music of the South flows from the homes and clubs into the streets. We have created a music that the entire world admires and some imitate. We have some of the best food in America. We do not copy French "haute cuisine" but rather have jambalaya, or catfish and hush puppies, or chicken fried steak and okra, and of course every state in the South claims that they have the best bar-b-que. We have rodeo, we have our own style of clothes, and we have our own literature. Since the days of Mencken, we do more copying of European culture, which is what Yankees think of as culture. What is more important is that we have developed our own culture. It is that culture that I am proud to be part of.

Second to Mencken in importance is Wilbur J. Cash. Coming from South Carolina, twenty years later than Mencken, he was indisputably Southern. He grew up in small towns in North and South Carolina, and in his youth never questioned his culture. He became a journalist and freelance writer when he wrote articles for Mencken's *American Mercury*. One was titled "The Mind of the South," which attracted so much attention from publisher Blanche Knopf that he received a contract to expand the essay into a full book. It took him ten years to accomplish the task. In 1941, the book was published. He criticized the South's bigotry, violence, and anti-intellectualism and influenced historians in that direction since. The scalawag schools like the University of North Carolina or LSU have followed the lead of their Yankee academic heroes and accepted this attitude as the true way to approach Southern history. They see it as the opposite of the "lost cause myth."

I must make it clear that my objective is not to ignore the fact that our Southern culture is not perfect, but I simply resent the implication that we are any less perfect than any other culture. I especially resent the notion that our culture is inferior to that of those Americans to the North. As a historian, I like to study our history as a means to better understand what we are by understanding where we came from. I try to be objective but realize that I cannot be, no more so than the Yankee Librevs. This is the land where I personally come from and where my parents and grandparents before me and so on came from. I resent those who imply that my predecessors are inferior beings, as I am sure that black Southerners have resented being told the same thing about their people for so many years. Some of my ancestors were the ones who told the black people that they were inferior, and some even made slaves out of the blacks. I realize that my ancestors were wrong. Black people are not inferior, but neither were my people. They lived in a different time and place when people lived by different rules than those which we live by today. All of us have ancestors that did things that we consider wrong or even barbaric today. I deny that my Southern ancestors were anymore barbaric than those who came from the North.

The Southern Literary Renaissance

The South had writers in the first half century after the War of Southern independence. However, in the 1920s, they seemed to flower in a way that they received greater respect from those in others places, especially the North. The most important writers of this time were John Crowe Ransom, Allen Tate, Robert Penn Warren, Donald Davidson, Andrew Lytle, Caroline Gordon, Thomas Wolfe, William Faulkner, Cleanth Brooks, Katherine Anne Porter, Carson McCullers, Eudora Welty, Flannery O'Connor, and Tennessee Williams. They did tend to reject the ways of their homeland, which included the New South as well as the Old South. Some leaned in the direction of Mencken and Cash, but others saw a greater curse in the materialism of the New South.

In 1930, Ransom, Tate, Warren, and others wrote *I'll Take My Stand: The South and Agrarian Tradition*. This is known as agrarianism, and the twelve writers involved in the project have become known as the Southern agrarians. These writers actually objected to Mencken and praised traditional Southern values. They did not invent agrarianism;

men like Thomas Jefferson could be put in that category even though they lived generations before the coining of the term. The philosophy sees the good in the cultivation of the soil, which provides direct contact with nature and God. The farmer has a sense of identity and historical and religious tradition as well as a feeling of belonging to a family, place, and region. Farming offers total independence and self-sufficiency. The modern urban life, capitalism, and technology destroy our independence and dignity while fostering vice and weakness. Most of us unreconstructed Southerners are proud of the fact that our ancestors were attached to the land. If you recall, the name of the plantation in *Gone with the Wind* was "Tara," which means land. I confess to leaning in this direction myself and do firmly believe that we pay a price for conveniences that come with modern technology. I do believe we have lost something, and I have little doubt that identity crises is behind much of the drug and alcohol abuse that pervades the land today. Having admitted that, I also realize that this kind of thinking is why many see us as backwards. We may live in big cities like Atlanta and Dallas today, but many of us have an uncontrollable sentiment for the land and the ways of our predecessors who were attached to the land. This does not mean that we are wrong or inferior. There have been plenty of those in the North land who held the same beliefs, from Emerson and Thoreau to the hippies of the 1960s.

Conservatism of the 1920s

We often think of the "roaring" twenties as a time of advances in the modernization process, which included the flappers, booming economy, birth of many technological gadgets and urban fads, but there was also a conservative backlash to the rapidly changing decade. Some of the conservatism took place in the North as well as the South, but more of it has stuck on our people since it fits the negative stereotypes that many prefer to see as Southern backwardness. The revival of the Ku Klux Klan during this period is associated with the South even though the largest single chapter was in Chicago. It makes sense to them that the Klan took over the state governments in Oklahoma and Texas, but they overlook the fact that they did the same in Oregon and Indiana. Tennessee had the famous Scopes Monkey Trial in reaction to the modern teaching of evolution in the schools, but they ignore thriving revivalism that swept the North at the same time, fueled in part by what such people saw as a threat to their religious beliefs.

The KKK of the 1920s was much different than what we think of today when we see the collection of freaks rounded up for the *Jerry Springer Show*; likewise, it was different that the first Klan that came about to resist Yankee occupation during Reconstruction. The birth of the new Klan took place on Stone Mountain in Georgia and was inspired by the popularity of the movie *The Birth of a Nation*. However, it was aimed more at the great influx of foreigners, especially Catholics and Jews, who had infiltrated the country in the late nineteenth and early twentieth century. The Librevs are historians, and they accept the fact that the organization was as successful in the North, but some have tried to claim that it was largely due to the increase in Southerners living in the North because of the Diaspora. To me this is just another example of their determination to pin racism on Southerners. It is the government of the United States which passed the quota laws in 1924 to limit the non-Aryans from coming into the United States, and Southerners were a minority in that legislature.

There is no denying the fact that the majority of the people of the South are religious. However, let us not ignore the fact that there are plenty of those in the North who are also religious. The Scopes Monkey Trial took place in the South, but it could have taken place in the North also. Mencken and the liberal types saw the trial as evidence of the absurdity of the ignorant religious masses, and he even proclaimed fundamentalism dead as a result of the trial. The importance of this segment of the population in recent elections suggests that he may have been wrong.

Fundamentalism 1920–1945

The South is the Bible Belt; some are proud to proclaim this while others see it as an example of why Mencken called the region a cultural Sahara. I firmly believe that the greatest fight we have to preserve our Southern culture is not with the NAACP or such antiflag groups but against our own people, the political fundamentalists that have been created since the 1970s. In the minds of many, they fail to make an important distinction between the religious Southerner who has always been considered to be a big part or our culture and the politically active today that helped to propel George Bush into the White House. Most of the change that I am speaking of came about after World War II, and so I will pursue this topic in much greater detail in the next chapter. However, mainly because of the Scopes Monkey Trial, many associate the South with fundamentalism in the 1920s, so I feel compelled to address the subject to some degree now.

Even the definition of fundamentalism can be controversial. I use it to describe those who believe in a literal interpretation of the Bible. Wikipedia says "The term 'fundamentalism' was originally coined to describe a narrowly defined set of beliefs that developed into a movement within the US Protestant community in the early part of the 20th century. These religious principles stood in opposition to the modernist movement and espoused the strict adherence to and faith in religious 'fundamentals.'" In recent years, with help from the media, the term has been used to describe any group that clings to a set of beliefs whether they be Christian, Muslim, Jewish, or just about any other religion.

The fact is that the historical movement did not begin in the South but began among conservative Presbyterian academics and theologians at Princeton Theological Seminary in the first decade of the twentieth century. After World War I, the movement was more associated with Northern Protestants. However, because of the Monkey Trial in Tennessee and the popular view of the South as being the "Bible Belt," most people think of our region as the center. According to the religious historian Sam Hill, "In the South, Protestant Evangelicalism has long been the largest Christian tradition, its most prominent and dominant religious form." He went on to say "But Fundamentalism was rare before the 1970s."[42] He referred to the Churches of Christ, which have been in the South since the late antebellum period, and he said the Bob Jones element began in the 1920s. In the 1920s and 1930s, they were generally separatist. If they could not remove modernist from the Church, they could remove the Church from the modernist. As one raised in the Church of Christ, I can remember only one time

---

42   Sam Hill, "Fundamentalism in Recent Southern Culture: Has it Done What the Civil Rights Movement Couldn't Do?" *The Journal of Southern Religion*, Vol. 1, No. 1 (1998).

when politics was openly discussed in Church; that was in 1960 when a Catholic ran. The fear and hatred of Catholicism seems to be great among fundamentalists. Generally speaking, they removed themselves from politics and America as well as the South. I will end this discussion for now but will take it up in the next chapter when they began to play a very important role in the termination of our Southern culture.

Patriotism Begins To Take Its Toll

Although I am generally a believer in the Celtic fringe theory, I do take exception to the part of the theory that claims that the Southern people are warriors by birth. I realize that this is the main part of the thesis. What I really like about the Celtic fringe thesis is the part about Southern identity and how the South is predominantly Celtic culture while the North is Anglo-Saxon. In the great nurture versus nature debate, I believe that each plays a role and that there are many aspects of human behavior that are difficult to reach a conclusion on, probably because it is the result of a combination of these forces. I do not believe that one group of humans is more genetically disposed toward warfare than any other. I do believe in Maslow's hierarchy of needs of which the third level says that we all need to have a feeling of belonging to a community. I also believe in his second level, which says that we need to have a sense of safety. Warfare has traditionally been a situation in which a community feels threatened by another. It is true, as stated in the Celtic fringe thesis, that the Scottish people had a tradition of warfare against the English that spanned generations. However, the history of the world has many, many other examples of a tradition of warfare between rival cultures. I do not believe that there is anything unique about the Scottish situation.

The Librevs seem to accept this military tradition of the South because it helps them in looking down on Southerners. Those of the North have a tradition of hatred toward those of the South. They value education, thus, they look at the Southern anti-intellectualism as proof of their ignorance. The tradition of Southern violence is part of the militarism, which has convinced the Northerners that we are savages. Their claims to having liberated the Southern slaves has further demonstrated to them that we are morally inferior.

There has been an increase in American patriotism in the South. Even though there has been a lack of respect from their fellow countrymen to the North, and the Union was forced on our people, in recent generations they have once again embraced their American identity. They have not only become patriotic Americans once again, but most would agree that they have become the most patriotic people in the land. They remember the legacy of the lost cause, whether you want to call it a myth or not, and thus, they still honor their Confederate ancestors. However, with the return of American patriotism, the lost cause has declined in importance.

Many Southerners like to imagine themselves as possessing this martial tradition, and out of self-defense, many Northerners have given them credit for this manly characteristic whether it's true or not. You see, by accepting this as true they have an excuse for why it took them four years to conquer a nation that they outnumbered by two to one. Those in the South and the West have favored a strong army throughout much of American history, but it is more out of self-interest than any military tradition. They have been the ones who kept pushing the frontier westward, and thus, they are the ones who needed an army for protection. For the same reason those in the Northeast have turned their attention to the navy. Their risk for attack by foreign aggressors would be more likely to come from the sea. They had a tradition of fishing and thus sailing while the agricultural Southerners and westerners learned how to ride horses and use their muskets and rifles. This is why one region has been more inclined toward the navy while the other would be better served by a strong army.

There were many in the South who favored a strong army, but in the early to mid-twentieth century there were also many who rejected American militarism and imperialism. Let us not forget the Populists. Most of the aggressive members of the Anti-Imperialist League were from the North. They even rejected the Populist anti-imperialist William Jennings Bryan. This was not because they disagreed with him over U.S. foreign policy but rather because of his favoring the silver standard. Most Populists saw the late-nineteenth- and early-twentieth-century American foreign policy as something for the benefit of the bankers and industrialist of the North and that the governmental funds could be better spent helping the destitute farmers of the South and West.

This no doubt was much of what was behind the American neutrality that delayed the nation's entry into World War I and World War II. The neutrality legislation that came out in the 1930s was the result of the Neigh Committee, which had concluded that the U.S. involvement in World War I was the result of the interest of the bankers and munitions manufactures. They did not emphasize the fact that these were industries of the Northeast, but everyone knew that to be the case.

Many see American patriotism in the South as evidence of a military tradition; I do not see it as being so simply explained. By the time we get to the late twentieth century, about half of the male population of America are veterans. This makes them sympathetic to those who are serving their country at any given time, which in turn makes them sympathetic to the American military. One of the big issues in the Sons of Confederate Veterans these days is the fact that some do not want to include the Pledge of Allegiance to the American flag in their meetings. Since so many of the members are veterans, there have been a great many that resent the lack of respect for the flag they have served under. Even though many of the common people of the South opposed American aggression in the first half of the twentieth century, the fact is that many ended up serving in both world wars. This was not due to patriotism but more because of Southern poverty. The lower classes are less able to resist the draft and the resulting military service. After the world wars, Southerners served in Korea, Vietnam, and ended up stationed in numerous bases during the half-century cold war.

Regardless of whether it was—due to a military tradition or simply Southern poverty or even a combination of the two—the fact is that many in the South have served in the American military and thus are Veterans, and thus, they possess patriotic feelings toward America. They have managed to reconcile this with the pride they still feel for their Confederate ancestors. However, in recent years, such feelings have made it easier for them to abandon their interest in the Confederate flag or other such symbols when they are told that it is in the interest of national unity. They may have some resentment for the sacrifice of their heritage, but the fact is that there are more and more pickup trucks out there with "United We Stand" or "God Bless America" bumper stickers, fewer that have Confederate flags. Even as the military restricts the display of the Confederate battle flag many Southerners accept this as a cost for American Unity. In this way, the growth of American patriotism has contributed to the diminishing of our Southern identity.

Foundations of the Civil Rights Movement

One of the most important things that happened between 1920 and 1945 is that the black people of America began to reject their second-class citizenship in greater numbers. There are numerous reasons for the changes in the early twentieth century that lay the foundation for the greater racial equality that would be achieved in the middle part of the century. Though I have tried to emphasize that, what the Librevs like to describe as the "great migration" was in fact a Southern experience that involved whites as well as blacks; this does not alter the fact that many Southern blacks did move north. Many Southern blacks also served in the American military just like Southern whites. As a result, they began to question more why they should not be treated as full citizens since they were called on to defend the nation. As a result of the migration and military service, more blacks saw more of the world, and this probably contributed to a greater understanding of the status that they had accepted up to that time.

As I have tried to emphasize throughout this essay, I do not reject the fact that white Southerners mistreated black Southerners. I do reject the notion that the discrimination that I am referring to was strictly a Southern thing. For that matter, the belief in Aryan superiority, that such attitude was based on, was not even uniquely an American thing during the early twentieth century. Obviously, that was the basic assumption made by the Germans who followed Hitler. The British may have fought the Nazis in World War II, but it was not because they rejected the belief that white people were superior over those with darker skins. Americans liberated German extermination camps, but the United States displayed numerous examples of their belief in Aryan superiority. The army that invaded Germany was segregated. The Ku Klux Klan of the 1920s were only an example of the groups that pushed into law the legislation that would restrict future immigration by limiting those who did not come from the Germanic Northern European population. The Klan was more of an anti-immigrant thing than an antiblack thing, which explains why the largest chapter was in Chicago.

In June of 1949, George S. Schuyler published an article in *American Mercury* called "'All Over the Country': 1949 Jim Crow in the North." He looked at various aspects of discrimination against blacks and pointed out that conditions were not much better in the Northern states than in the South. He looked at housing, schools, public facilities, and transportation. He found some exceptions but mainly in those parts of the country which had a very small black population. Hatred is most often based on fear; in the case of racial hatred, some perceive one group or another as a threat to their way of life. For example, Schuyler not only pointed out that twenty-nine states (sixteen of them outside the South) had illegalized mixed marriages but that those in the North had the strictest punishment. Georgia had a maximum of one year in jail, and Tennessee and Texas had a limit of five years; but Indiana, North Dakota, and South Dakota put it at ten years. I could go on, but I do not feel it necessary to provide any more evidence that all of America treated blacks as second-class citizens in the early twentieth century.

I see the first stages of change as having come from the decreasing acceptance among the black population, and this is reflected in the growth of the NAACP. Shortly after World War I, the organization grew from twenty chapters (one in the South) to three hundred chapters (more than half in the South). Between 1940 and 1946, they grew from 355 chapters to 1,073 with 450,000 members. This no doubt contributed to the beginnings of change among the white population. It began with the courts. In Oklahoma, for example, they managed to get the grandfather clause declared unconstitutional by the courts. In other ways, the courts showed signs of rejecting an American tradition of segregation that, of course, would lead to even greater change in the 1950s and 1960s. The Roosevelts made their contrition toward a change in attitude. One famous example is when Eleanor gave up her membership in the Daughters of the American Revolution after they cancelled the contract with the black opera singer Marion Anderson. The First Lady also supported the Tuskegee Airmen when she showed her belief that they were smart enough to fly airplanes by allowing one to fly her around.

We can also see this time period as one revealing the defiance that would come from many of the Southern white population. The once-solid Democratic South began to crack as Roosevelt and the Democratic

Party gave support to the birth of the civil rights movement. They had no idea where to turn. They still despised Republicans, not as in the past because it was the party of Reconstruction, but more because it was the party of rich Yankees. The Republicans would not launch their Southern strategy until the 1970s.

The Ku Klux Klan on parade down Pennsylvania Avenue, Washington D.C., 1928. Perhaps we should ban the American flag too since that is the only flag we see in this photo of racist on parade. (Courtesy National Archives)

Conclusions

The period between 1920 and 1945 was an era of great change in the South, and these changes took a great toll on Southern identity. The greatest change was brought about by the continued decline in the economy. Much of that of course was the Great Depression that hit all of America. In some ways, this was easier on those who still lived on the land because they could at least grow food. In the long term, this period in history had a greater effect on the South. There are some

254   Leslie R. Tucker

who like to blame the poverty on Southern conservatism and their stubborn resistance to modernization. Others see it as a continuation of punishment for losing the war against the North, and therefore all of our problems were due to the evil Yankees. As a historian, I see it as part of the trend that has existed since the dawn of the modern age. Modernization has meant that more and more people leave the land because they are forced off by technology. They then turn to the market economy, which later included manufacturing, as a way to make their living. Since the markets are in cities, this means that they move from the country to the city. I believe that the main reason Southerners clung to their agricultural economy is that they found products, such as cotton, tobacco, rice, and sugar for which there existed a great demand in the world-market economy. What changed in the early twentieth century is that new methods of producing these products put a greater dependency on machines and less on people. This made it more costly to compete in the market place, which made it more difficult for the small farmer to compete. To be a successful farmer, one had to be able to invest in expensive equipment. We could blame Roosevelt and his Agricultural Adjustment Act; however, all this did was speed up the process of mechanization. The family-ran farm, whether that be sharecroppers or small land owners, was in decline because they could not compete with agribusiness. The late-nineteenth-century preachers of New South diversity could not lead the people in the direction they wanted to go because the profits in agriculture were still there for those who could compete. They are still there, and these products are still produced in the South. It would not be until the late twentieth century that the South would achieve a more diverse economy. This was not because of better advocates but because technology would force the population off the land and into other endeavors.

The greatest impact of these changes was to send 28 million Southerners fleeing the land of their ancestors; this included black, white, Indian, and Hispanic Southerners. Many of them and their descendants would adopt the identity of their new homeland—the North. This of course would drain much of the Southern pride that our identity lives on. On the positive side, this Northbound and westbound migration made America more Southern. I do not think it a coincidence that much of the music of the 1960s came from the same land that received the greatest influx of Southern migrants. California pop music was greatly influenced by the Southern country and blues sounds of those who went there from Oklahoma, Texas, Arkansas, and Missouri. Likewise, Detroit and New York music was influenced by the Southerners who went to those parts of the country.

More and more Southerners, both those who left and those who stayed, became critical of their heritage. Men like H. L. Mencken and Wilbur Cash not only became critical of our culture, but did so in a way that emphasized the superiority of Northern culture. Meanwhile, the conservative side of Southern society became negative symbols of Southern backwardness to those in the North. Even though the KKK prospered in the North, in the minds of most, they became associated with the South. Even though fundamentalist of the North resisted modern theories such as evolution also, the Scopes Monkey Trial helped to convince the progressive Americans of all regions that religious conservatism was a Southern thing.

At the same time America would move toward greater participation in global competition which brought them into an imperialistic contest. In other words, they had a larger military in which Southerners participated. As a result, more and more Southerners were veterans of the United States Army, the same army they despised during the war and Reconstruction. This had the result of moving more and more of our people toward an American identity. They still came up with clever sayings, such as "American by birth, Southern by the grace of God," but the reality is that dual identity is difficult to maintain. As our people became more American, they became less Southern. They became reconstructed so they were now part of the United States, only this time the nation had been reconstituted in the image of Abraham Lincoln.

This period laid the foundation for change in the relationship between black and white Southerners. The greatest impact would not come until after World War II, but we can see change in the air. The nature of those changes will be covered in greater detail in the next chapter.

All of these together served to diminish our Southern identity and thus the uniqueness of our culture. As of the end of World War II, many, if not most, in our land, the ones still left, would waive the Confederate battle flag with pride. I can remember growing up in California and the Southern Memorial Day and the birthday of Robert E. Lee were still marked on the calendar. These changes were only the beginning. The greatest blows to our culture would come after World War II, and that will be the subject of the next chapter. I would say that in 1945, most in the South at least thought of themselves as unreconstructed; by the year 2000 the majority would be willing to sacrifice our sacred symbols of identity, and those of us who are unreconstructed would become a minority and even a source of embarrassment to many of our fellow Southerners.

CHAPTER NINE

The Real New South, Since 1970

Introduction

In the post–World War II period, the South finally achieved becoming the "New South." Henry Grady and his allies tried to establish a new South in the last part of the nineteenth century, and there are some who still look at this time as the New South, and in fact, I have seen it as a chapter title in textbooks. I disagree with calling the postwar and late nineteenth century the New South for two main reasons. First, the assumption is one in which the South is seen as resisting modernization until after they lose their bid for independence; they then realize that the North was right in wanting to go with progress. In other words, their view of the New South is one in which the South finally accepted modernization. As discussed in earlier chapters, I see the South as having been part of modernization prior to the war; it is just that they did not progress as rapidly as the North. The second reason I do not consider the traditional New South as a real new South is that they resisted being absorbed into the American identity. In other words, many if not most in the South were still unreconstructed. The Librevs call this the "lost cause myth," as I have already discussed. Even though I disagree with them on their basic interpretation that Southern identity was something created by the war, I agree with them that Southerners continued to cling to their uniqueness. After World War II, the South turned into the "Sun Belt" and the North turned into the "Rust Belt," and thus, in many ways, if not most, the South turned into the most prosperous region in the United States by the beginning of the twenty-first century. In the process, and no doubt partly because of this first change, the South became "reconstructed." There are many, and perhaps even most, in the South who are proud of their Confederate past, but the reality is that most of them have stood by while Confederate flags, statues, monuments, and even more subtle symbols of the Old South have been removed. The process was gradual as the South changed from a conquered people who did not celebrate July 4 into that part of the United States which is the most patriotic. One can still be proud of their region, state, or city and be a patriotic American; however, the key to what I am trying to express is that the people in the South changed from being Southern first to being American first. This is the definition of reconstructed; this is why they have allowed the symbols of the Old South to be destroyed. Many became convinced that it was for the good of the United States.

This chapter will be a more detailed description of the three main reasons that this change came about. First is dramatic migration out of and then into the South and the economic forces responsible for that migration. The second is that after the civil rights movement, the South is no longer an apartheid South. Let me make it clear I am not defending segregation but simply speaking of a major change. The third is that by the end of the century, the South is no longer the solid Democrat South. These are the main ways in which the region differed from that which existed before World War II, and that is why I say it became a truly New South. I will discuss these changes primarily as a prelude to discussing how they helped most of the Southern people to become reconstructed.

The influence of massive migration, first out of the South and then into it, is probably the greatest agent of change. It began with the Southern Diaspora, when millions of Southerners left their ancestral homes. This began before World War II. Most are familiar with the Okies going to California and most high school textbooks today talk of the great migration when millions of Southern blacks moved into Northern cities after World War I. These two migrations are just part of the greater movement called the Southern Diaspora. I have already introduced this topic. What most do not realize is that the greatest numbers of Southerners, both black and white, left during World War II and shortly after. After 1970, the trend reversed so that more people entered the South than those who exited. Many of the immigrants were those who left and then returned or the children of those who left and returned to the land of their ancestors. However, it also included millions of people moving into the region who had no past familial ties. Some descended from old Yankee stock; some descended from the new Americans whose ancestors had come from Southern and Eastern Europe; and some are part of the tide of immigrants who have entered the United States since the 1965 reversal of the National Origins Quota Act. The end result of all of this migration and immigration is that America became more Southern and the South became more American.

The South changed dramatically as far as racial relations. Though the whites resisted desegregation, it became a reality. Some have argued that the most important aspect was the Voting Rights Act of 1965, which gave blacks the political clout they needed to end the discrimination which had held them down for so long. I feel that the most important thing is that white Southerners changed socially and accepted the reality of the situation. If this had not come about, the region would still be a political battleground where the two segments of Southern society fight over each inch of ground, the way they did at the beginning of the civil rights movement.

The fact is that white Southerners shifted toward the Republican Party because of the civil rights movement, but there is more to it than that now. The black Southerners had already changed their allegiance from the Republican Party to the Democratic Party during the Roosevelt years, which I discussed in the previous chapter. In this chapter, I will cover the details of change as white Southerners abandon their loyalty to the Democratic Party. During Reconstruction, white Southerners were solid Democrat and black Southerners were Republican. Today a large number, if not most, of white Southerners vote Republican, at least in presidential elections, and the vast majority of black Southerners are Democrats.

The Southern Diaspora Continues

I began discussion of this phenomena in the last chapter and will continue the topic in this chapter. James N. Gregory wrote a book called *The Southern Diaspora*, and I am trying to avoid simply presenting a synopsis of his book. I am more interested in the causes of this change and the social effects upon the South, whereas Gregory was more interested in the ways in which this migration changed the rest of the country or, in other words, ways in which American became more Southern.

As I stated in the last chapter, the basic economic force that caused the exodus from the South was the change from a primarily agricultural economy to nonagricultural. What I am talking about is the percentage of the population which is economically involved in that industry. The South, like the rest of the United States, is still a major producer of agricultural products. However, a much smaller number of people are needed to produce those goods. The sad thing is that mechanization may decrease the demand for human labor, but it does not provide jobs for those displaced by the machines. The transition from an economy made up of predominantly agricultural workers to one where less that 6 percent of the population makes their living that way is a very painful process. The change resulted in much suffering and even fatalities, and many reached the point of literally starving to death because they failed to find an alternative source of income. The free-market economy can be quite ruthless as markets shift in supply and demand, especially when we are talking about the supply and demand variables of the labor market. Those who had depended on agriculture for their livelihood have been tossed about as they looked for some new way to make a living. No doubt the greatest problem for most of them is that they needed little education to be a farmer, whereas the technology of modernization demanded people with more formal education.

This painful transition began before World War II, but it did not conclude until after the war. As of 1940, there were still 15.6 million Southerners, more than 40 percent of the population, who farmed. By 1980, the number dropped 1.6 million which was much closer to the national average with only 6 percent or less working in that industry. Technology produced the machines that replaced the people, but the cost of these machines made it difficult for the small farmer to compete. The number of farms declined from 2.9 million to 949,000. This change affected black and white Southerners alike, though the whites did have a little more money than the black ones, which made it a little easier for them to make the needed move to search for new jobs.

The difficulty and pain of this kind of change comes from the lag in income as the displaced workers migrate into some other job. Many turned to the big cities of the North in their search for work, and thus, we have the Southern Diaspora. Roosevelt was aware of the fact that the South was even more economically strapped, and even though the entire nation was in a depression, he saw to it that more military bases and defense plants were put in Southern region. This may have slowed the mass exodus, but more jobs were available in the port cities on either coast or in the manufacturing centers to the North so that displaced Southern farm workers continued to move out in search of work. Throughout the 1920s and 1930s, the Diaspora continued. However, the greatest numbers were during the World War II years and immediately after.

Other industries developed in the South, but it would take a while for the number of jobs to exceed those in the North. It would also be a while before the new industries could provide enough jobs for the displaced agricultural workers thus making in unnecessary to leave the region to find work. This trend continued for almost a generation after World War II ended. Gradually, the North would begin an economic decline that would end with the once-booming industrial center of the nation being called the Rust Belt while the South continued to become more diverse. By the 1970s, the situation reversed itself so that more people migrated into the South for the same economic reasons they had left in the first place—to make a living and support their families.

There are two other changes in the South that contributed to the increased migration into the region. First, air conditioning which I will show to have a social as well as an economic impact. Second, the calming of the racial storm that left the land a much better place to live than it had been before the changes. Even though they fought integration, in the end this was as great a change for whites as it was for blacks since the end of apartheid helped to open the way for an improved economy. Both of these changes helped to lay the foundation for the improved economy discussed above. Before World War II, the South lagged behind the rest of the nation; now it is as good or better than the nation as a whole. There are still a number of Southern states that are below the national average, but to counter this, the cost of living is also lower so that the overall lifestyle is better than in some parts of the country where people make a lot more money, but they can't afford to buy a house.

The Magic of Air-conditioning

One of the most overlooked technological innovations has been air-conditioning. History books have dedicated many pages to discussions of canals, railroads, the steel-tipped plow, and the telegraph, but they rarely mention the economic impact of air-conditioning. We all know that the North has more cold and snow, and this is why the snowbirds head South in the wintertime. It has always been colder in the North; why is it only in recent decades that so many have moved to the South? Miami started becoming a refugee camp for escaping Yankees in the early twentieth century, but what we have now is more who are actually moving to the South and calling it home. More importantly, they are not just the retired but younger people with families. We Southerners have grown accustomed to the heat and humidity, but many of those from the North hate and detest the Southern summer heat, that long hot summer heat, more than the snow and cold they are accustomed to. Air-conditioning has changed all of this. They can now stay in their cool houses or public buildings when the heat is unbearable just like they used to stay indoors when the Northern cold became unbearable.

There are some historians who have explored the ways that air-conditioning have changed the South. The homes do not need the architectural features, such as big porches, large eves, or the large windows designed to maximize ventilation. This means that Southerners do not live on their front porches during the long hot summers like they used to. This has taken a toll on the feeling of community that our ancestors experienced. All of this is fascinating to think about, but I am more interested in the ways this change has affected the Southern identity. I am more interested in the fact that this innovation has brought foreigners into our region in such large numbers that much of the South is less Southern because many of the people who live there today have no Southern roots. They came from up North or from lands even more foreign than the North. When journalists poll a city to see what they think about the removal of a Confederate flag or monuments to Confederate heroes, many of those who live in the South now have no opinion. Some may even have the same negative attitude as their friends and neighbors up North. They live in the Sun Belt, not the South. Many think that concerns about such things are quaint at best while others may still possess a hatred for what they call the slaveocracy of the past. They considered the South as a place where the people are uneducated, provincial, backwards, racist, and generally culturally and intellectually inferior to the people of the North land. They hang around with fellow Yankees or those modern Scallywags who agree that the traditional ways of the Old South do not belong in our New South.

I have been making the point all along that the main reasons for the massive migration, first out of the South and then later into the South, have been economic, and so now I wish to discuss some of the ways in which air-conditioning have directly impacted the Southern economy. There have always been those who have argued that warm climates have produced civilizations which are much less productive. Back in 1915, geographer Ellsworth Huntington argued that the tropics had a "dull, unprogressive population." One of his followers argued that cities like Washington, New York, and Los Angeles were doomed. No telling what they would have to say about Atlanta, Miami, or Houston. There are some technical difficulties with the non-air-conditioned South. Before the controlled climate, cotton threads broke; cigarette machines jammed; bread grew mold; film attracted dust; pasta lost its shape; and chocolate turned gray with the fluctuation of temperature and humidity. In the late twentieth century, controlled climate became even more important as we dealt with products, such as computer chips, CDs, or the high-tech manufacturing of modern medicine.

The bottom line is that air-conditioning, whose development parallels the period I am discussing in this chapter, has contributed to changing the economy which has helped to bring in new carpetbaggers, which has helped in the decline in Southern distinctiveness. Air-conditioning was invented prior to World War II, but it was not until after the war that it became accessible to the common man. No doubt it was a major variable in creating the New South.

Our Biggest Black Eye

The frequent display of the Confederate battle flag as a symbol to the resistance of desegregation is probably the biggest barrier we have in the preservation of that flag and other symbols of our heritage. There are those who speak of slavery and the general mistreatment of black Southerners, but the images from the civil rights movement is not merely history, but for many of us living today, it is part of our personal recollections. On television, in newspapers, and magazines, we saw the peaceful protesters taunted by angry faces waving Confederate flags. I will make no attempt to write a history of the civil rights movement; that is a subject which many before me have approached, and a thorough coverage of the topic cannot be done with less than a book. I am simply addressing the ways in which this has contributed to the loss of our culture. I will discuss the topic to the extent necessary to make sure we are on the same page and to address ways in which this change has contributed to the decline of our Southern identity.

Black Southerners and the New South

As stated above, I am not going to give a detailed account of the civil rights movement. The most important thing for us white Southerners is to understand and accept that black Southerners look at our land in a different way than we do. This, of course, is a major part of the controversy I am dealing with. John Shelton Read and his friends at the University of North Carolina in Chapel Hill have done numerous surveys in which it is clear that the majority of blacks have a strong Southern identity. This is true even after the great migration. What we need to understand is that their Southern identity is not associated with Miss Scarlet, the Confederate flag, or the grand Greek revival antebellum mansions. They do share with us memories of good food, good music, and a kind of social grace that most of the time extends beyond color lines. They may have gone to churches where most of the congregation was black, but they sang many of the same songs; prayed to the same lord; and most believed that we were all brothers in Christ. Black or white, I firmly believe that most know and understand that we have many things in common, and that is Southern.

The number one thing we white Southerners need to accept is that the blacks were either slaves or second-class citizens through most of our history and that we cannot expect them to accept that with any more glee than we would. At this point, I hope I have made it clear that blacks did not find any more equality in the North than they did in the South, but nonetheless, we must be careful to avoid denial of the fact that they have much to be unhappy about in their Southern past. This is the key to why many object to what we consider to be symbols of our heritage. I believe that a large number, if not a majority, of blacks understand that today the Confederate flag, clearly the most contentious symbol, does merely represent our heritage. Our goal should be to convince the rest that this is true. The reality is that this symbol has been used in negative ways in the not-too-distant past, and that is why there are still some who see it that way today. We should follow the example of Martin Luther King, Jr., and have patience and faith that the truth shall set us free. When King first started, he was greeted with jail and violence. He even lost his life as a victim of that violence. In the end, after a relatively brief era, white Southerners realized that he was right, and they were wrong.

The Supreme Court decision of Brown v. Topeka Board of Education and Rosa Parks, and Central High in Little Rock sparked a savage era in the South to which many whites reacted with anger, frustration, and even hatred. After all of the rock throwing, church bombings, cross burnings, and other such acts of terrorism, who would have believed that within a generation, most white Southerners would not only accept defeat but also even feel an element of shame and regret at our behavior during these tumultuous days. The majority of blacks have graciously accepted our apologies, but we must realize that there are some scars.

We are far from being one big happy family. On one hand, today there are blacks who feel they have not yet achieved true equality. The fact is that the black population still has an average income below that of the whites; they are still lacking in housing, education, and in many careers they are still underrepresented. On the other hand, there are whites who have complaints with the way things are now. Some are victims of reverse discrimination as jobs and scholarships and such are awarded to people because of the color of their skin. They cannot understand the double standard which says it is okay to have a black

Miss America and not a white Miss America. It is clear that the issue of race has not gone away. However, things are much different today than they were at the end of World War II. And just as it was before the world war, these problems are an American problem, not just a Southern problem.

One way in which blacks have achieved equality is that they have political leaders who profit from the race card. George Wallace claimed that he tried to campaign on other issues, but it is the segregation issue that the public wanted to hear about, and so that is the one which propelled his political career. I have little doubt that black leaders such as Jesse Jackson are using the Confederate flag as a battleground for their personal political advancement in much the same way that George Wallace used segregation. I, for one, hope that Jesse Jackson and other black leaders today will demonstrate the same courage Wallace did when he stood before to public and admitted that he was wrong and that those who struggled for civil rights were right. The preservation of our Southern white heritage is also a civil right.

There are two main variables which have helped to make the South of today much different than it was in 1945 when it comes to race relations. No doubt the greatest advance was the Voting Rights Act of 1965 in which blacks achieved equality at the ballot box. The second was capitalism. The businessmen of the South finally understood that the money of black people could buy just as much as the money of white people. They also realized that a South in which race riots, segregation, and racial discord ruled would be a land with a large handicap when it comes to competition in the world market. By the 1970s, as whites began to return to the South, black Southerners joined them.

The Return to the South

Between 1940 and 1970, while so many people fled the South to find work, others stayed and tried to restructure the economy. It began before World War II, but it would take a generation before the migration into the South exceeded that out. After 1940, the number of nonagricultural jobs in the South more than tripled, from about 7.8 million to 25.9 million in the 1980s. This of course means urban growth, which is evident across the region. Dallas/Fort Worth went from 473,000 in 1940 to 2.4 million in 1970 to over 4 million in 1990. Atlanta went from 302,000 to 2 million to almost 3 million in the same years. Nashville went from 167,000 to 700,000 to almost a million by 1990. Several cities across the region experienced the same basic growth pattern.

This growth in nonagricultural industries is also reflected in the development of education that would be needed as the people went from being farmers to professional and skilled workers. In the 1930s, only seven universities had departments that offered doctoral degrees and only forty-two such departments of the 661 that existed throughout the United States. Likewise, primary and secondary education lagged behind the nation. They began to catch up by the 1970s. The new workers in the South would need more education and so they became more like the North in this respect.

As of 1990, there has been a trend to divide the South into what is called the inner South, middle South, and outer South. Those in the inner South remain substantially below the national average income. Most are about 70–80 percent of the national average. This includes Arkansas, Mississippi, Alabama, Tennessee, and Kentucky. Out of this group, Tennessee is the only one that exceeds 80 percent of the national average at 85 percent, mainly because of Nashville. The middle South is North and South Carolina, Georgia, and Louisiana. The latter is the only one below 80 percent of national average. The outer South includes Virginia (the Chesapeake area), Florida, Texas, and Oklahoma. The first two are actually above national average, and the latter two are in the 80 percent category. However, the low cost of living goes far in offsetting the lower income.

Above, I spoke of the decline in agricultural jobs which caused the great exodus from the South in the first place; by 1990 the South exceeded the North in many of the nonagricultural jobs. In 1963, the East North Central region (primarily Michigan and Illinois) produced 30 percent of the nation's manufacturing while the much more numerous states of the South produced only 21 percent. By 1990, the South had grown to 29 percent while the East North Central states declined to 15 percent. Since 1990, there are indications that the South even began to exceed the West, which has also prospered since World War II. Their wages are still higher but so is their cost of living, mainly housing. As a result, many of those in California would join the parade back to the land of their ancestors.

Blacks and Other Minorities Also Return

It is difficult evaluate the role that racism played in the black portion of the Southern Diaspora, and that remains true when evaluating the reversal of that exodus too. The Librevs love to talk about race and assume that all the suffering the South went through during the war and the century after was deserved. They assume that the South is much more racist than the rest of America, and therefore they believe that Jim Crow and the large number of lynches in the early twentieth century was a major factor in what they call the Great Migration. As mentioned in the last chapter, I still fail to see that race problems were any worse after World War I than before. I pointed out that a large number of blacks did flee North, but so did a large number of whites as well as Hispanic and Indian. It is a fact that the migration back to the South includes blacks as well as the other minority groups. What makes the whole thing difficult to evaluate when trying to determine the role that racism played is the fact that as the economy got better in the South, so did race relations. It is very difficult to determine whether the migration patterns resulted from racial issues. I may not be able to prove that the major variable in both the exodus and the return was economic, but I do not see that the Librevs have proven otherwise.

I have not found any statistics on Hispanic or Indian movements since 1970, but by personal experience, I am aware that at least some have. I know people of Mexican background who I went to school with out in California who have returned to Texas in recent years. I also remember when I met Wilma Mankiller, the first woman principal chief of the Cherokee Nation, that she had something in common with me other that our Cherokee ancestors. She is about the same age as me; her family moved out to California about the same time as mine; and she returned to Oklahoma about the same time I did. I know that this proves nothing, but I do feel it is more than coincidence. I will never forget something she said in our meeting. "San Francisco is a beautiful place"—the same area where I spent most of my California years—"but it was never home," she added. That expresses my feelings on the subject too.

The events that happen in history such as the migration out of and then back into the South are facts. The reason for such historical events is the material of discussion and debate for historians. We are left with what is called anecdotal evidence, such as the personal recollections I mentioned in the preceding paragraph. For more recent events such as this one, we do have access to the results of various polls to lend support to one position or another. However, it cannot really be considered "proof." There is still a bottom line result that blacks make up a smaller percentage of the Southern population than they did before. In 1940, only 23 percent of blacks lived outside the South, but by 1970, that figure rose to 47 percent. However, there is another variable which has entered the picture; there are now a lot of blacks living in the United States who have migrated from other countries, mainly Africa or the Caribbean. This is one reason I object to using the term African-American. Many blacks in America today do not fit that description.

Nonetheless, the numbers of those returning to the South has increased. Do not forget, as in the case with white Southerners, there were always a certain number who returned even when the Southern economy was bad. Louis Armstrong was not the only one who felt that way when he sang his song about returning to the sunny South. In the 1930s, approximately one black returned to the South for every five who left. Since 1955, each five-year period saw one hundred thousand black Northerners returning to the land of their ancestors. Please note that this was during the heyday of the violence of the civil rights movement. By 1970, more were returning to rather than leaving the South. About two-thirds of those who moved between 1965 and 1970 were going back to the land of their birth, and from 1975 to 1980, 41 percent were return migrants.

There are other reasons for the why than simply economics. However, the economic improvement made other reasons more viable. One survey in 1973 listed kinship as the major reason for returning. The main one of these familial reasons was to care for an aging parent. Only 20 percent of these respondents gave economic reasons for their return though this was only the beginning of the economic reversal. Other reasons included nonfamily social issues, health, or climate. I emphasize, they may not have recited economic reasons to be the main reason why they returned, however, if the economy had not improved, it may not have been possible for them to return. The crime that encouraged many white people to flee the Northern cities also influenced blacks. In 1971, Earnest Smith told one interviewer, "For the first twenty years, life in Chicago was real nice. But the last five years was when I come to gettin' scared. They killed King and the people started tearin' up the place. Crime got so bad that I got scared and started carryin' a gun."

There is also evidence that the blacks felt a bond to the land of their ancestors, just like us whites. In 1971, Atlanta businessman Jesse B. Blayton explained the reason for his return. "Grandma is here . . . Most American blacks have roots in the South. The liberation thinking is here. Blacks are more together. With the doors opening wider, this area is the Mecca." Actor Morgan Freeman said it best. He was born in Tennessee and grew up in Mississippi before living North and then west. "This is our home. This is where my roots are. . . We built the South, and we know it. What I own in the South isn't because I went and bought it. What I own is my place here because my mother, my father, my grandmother, my grandfather, my great-grandmother . . . all the way back to my great-great-great-grandmother, who happened to be a Virginian—that's where they had the farms."

We must remember that this is their land too and that they have a say in what it is all about. Just as King convinced white Southerners that they should have a better life in the land that we share, we must convince blacks that we have pride in our heritage too. They have black history month; they must realize how important the sense of history is to a culture. I have a dream that someday black and white Southerners will be able to hold hands and respect the role that each has played in making the South the land that we all love. We have put black Southerners in the history books and respect the role they have played, and this is as it should be. But now, we must convince black Southerners that we are proud of our ancestors too, even though they did not think and act like we do today.

The Evangelical and Fundamentalist Right

Some discussion of the Christian Right is necessary since this is a part of the changes in the post–World War II South. I begin by making a distinction between evangelical and fundamentalist then I will discuss the background of each followed by the Republican Southern strategy and then the discussion of the status of each today. Then and only then will I be prepared to discuss their role in the demise of our Southern heritage. As in the case of civil rights, I am not writing about history or religion, and so I will discuss these topics only to the extent necessary to evaluate what I am interested in—the preservation of our Southern heritage.

I have often considered these two terms, fundamentalist and evangelical, to be synonymous, but there is a distinction. They are similar in that they are more conservative than many Christian denominations. By this, I mean that they tend to live by a theology in which the Bible is taken more in the literal sense than some other denominations. The best example is their view on evolution. There are Christians who have been able to retain their beliefs without having any difficulty accepting the theories of evolution since they see the Bible as a book of allegory. It does not really matter how many days it took God to create the heavens and the Earth, what matters most is the teachings of how to live and how to express their faith. Those who accept the literal interpretation of the good book cannot accept the notion that it took millions of years for life to evolve when Genesis says it took only six days to create the planet and all of the life on it. In addition, all the begats reveal that the age of the Earth as being measured in thousands of years, not billions of years as the theory of evolution states. Most important, it was God that created all life forms, human and animal, and that they did not simply pop up out of the mud and ooze of a primeval world.

The main distinction between evangelical and fundamentalist, as I see it, is that the former has a tradition of political activity, and the later has been isolationist until recently. Fundamentalism is a form of Evangelical Protestantism and is thus, by definition, a minority representing about 15 percent of the Evangelicals. They appeared in the first decade of the twentieth century and started among the conservative Presbyterian academics and theologians at Princeton Theological

Seminary, which is in the North, not the South. Generally speaking, the fundamentalists are more adamant in their literal interpretation of the Bible. Some will have a difficult time accepting the fact that this genre of Christianity is relatively new in the South. The stereotype that most Americans have, Northern as well as Southern, is that the South is the Bible Belt, and that is because it is and always has been the center of conservative Christianity. The fact is that at the time of the Scopes Monkey Trial, fundamentalism was a minority view in the South with less than the 15 percent of total Evangelicals.

Fundamentalism was in its early stages from 1920 to 1960. The Churches of Christ was one of the first of the genre to appear in the South and has been around since shortly after the Civil War. It, in fact, was fundamentalist before the movement began. The Bob Jones tradition was the next major Southern fundamentalist which goes back to the 1920s. By the 1950s, their numbers in the South increased slightly. Prior to 1970, they remained separate from mainstream America. Except for a brief concern at the possible election of a Catholic president in 1960, they left politics to the world of Caesar. The change that I am most concerned about here began in the 1970s as fundamentalism spread to the Baptists, Presbyterians, and other larger denominations. They lack the isolationism of traditional Fundamentalism and have become politically active, which has fit in well with the Southern strategy of the Republican Party. It is hard to determine who influenced who.

The confusion that many of us have in making a distinction between fundamentalist and evangelicals is in part because of their political participation. The likes of Jerry Falwell, Tim LaHaye, and Pat Robertson have been labeled neofundamentalists as they abandoned the tradition of being isolationist. In the 1920s, H. L. Mencken and other modernist looked at the conservative Christians as being divisive, intolerant, anti-intellectual, and downright ignorant and foolish. When Clarence Darrow put William Jennings Bryan on the stand, the liberal press broadcast the event and made it clear to their public that Bryan looked foolish. For these reasons, those who in fact were fundamentalist began to refer to themselves as Evangelical in an attempt to avoid the label put on them by the liberal media and accepted by much of the American public.

The Republican Southern Strategy and the Christian Right

The seeds of the Southern strategy go back to the election of 1928. With the growth of Jim Crow, the influence of black Republicans declined. They simply could not vote. This left a void that the Republicans could fill with white Southerners. In the election of 1928, the Democrats ran a Catholic candidate, Al Smith, which enabled Herbert Hoover to win five of the former Confederate states which had been solid Democrat since Reconstruction. The Republican progress reversed itself with the Depression and the rise of Roosevelt. The elections of 1932 to 1944 were the only time in American history where all Southerners, black and white, voted for the same man. To this day, most of the Southern white conservative Christians who remain loyal to the Democratic Party are the elderly who remember the Roosevelt years. It is really remarkable when you realize that Roosevelt's Agricultural Adjustment Act put more of them out of their homes than the dust bowl, but regardless, many Southerners loved FDR.

The seeds of discontent for Southern Democrats actually began during the Roosevelt years as the Democratic Party became the party of civil rights. Franklin and Eleanor helped to lay the foundation for the changes that would come after the war with their rejection of the view that blacks were racially inferior. Americans were not much different from Germans in their belief in Aryan superiority. The National Origins Quota Act was designed to put an end to the growth of the non-Aryan population. The American army which invaded Nazi Germany was segregated. The Army Air Corps did not believe blacks to be smart enough to fly air planes, and that was the historical significance of the Tuskegee Airmen. It may be that Hitler did most to change this way of thinking when he went to the next logical step of exterminating the inferior peoples. I am in agreement with the Librevs who think that this may have been a major reason that many Americans began to question their racial views. For whatever reason, after World War II, much of the western world began to reject their beliefs of racial superiority. The United States were among the last to make the change, and much had to do with peer pressure from the other industrialized western nations.

By the election of 1948, the Democrats had become so much a Party of racial equality that many of the more conservative Southern population formed the Dixiecrats. They were not prepared to follow the alternative party of Abraham Lincoln and Reconstruction, and besides, the Republicans did not have an anti–civil rights platform. Eisenhower, for example, was neither racist nor segregationist, he simply did not believe it to be the government's job to legislate morality. The Southern voters wanted someone who would stop any notion of racial equality. The Dixiecrats worked about as well as most other attempts at a third party, and so Southern conservative voters muddled through the fifties and for the most part remained Democrats. In 1960, they had to choose between the Democrats with another Catholic candidate or go with the party of Lincoln. Fifteen electoral votes went for Harry Byrd—Mississippi, six of Alabama's votes, and one electoral vote from Oklahoma. The rest of Oklahoma, Tennessee, Kentucky, Florida, and Virginia went Republican, but the remaining Southern states stayed with the Democratic Party.

The sixties offered too much controversy for the conservative Southern voters. By the end of the decade, segregation had all but ended. Hippies were smoking dope; war protestors were leading the way to defeat in Vietnam; and even gays were seeking acceptance as being simply an alternative lifestyle. The Republicans would not stop desegregation; in 1965, the Voting Rights Act guaranteed black voting in the South, and so the Southern population turned to other concerns. The Republicans convinced the new breed of fundamentalists that they best represented their value system. The plan worked so that with the help of the failed presidency of the Democrat from Georgia, Jimmy Carter, the South started voting Republican. The only exceptions in the election of 1980 were Carter's home state of Georgia, along with West Virginia, and Maryland. The born-again Christians had become known as the Christian Right, and they became major players from then into the twenty-first century.

There are many who dispute the success of the Southern Strategy by pointing out that the conversion to the Republican Party was not complete. In 1976, Oklahoma and Virginia were the only Southern states that went Republican after the development of the new Republican strategy. The South has continued to elect Democrat governors, senators, and congressmen, and a large percentage of the population remains registered Democrats. The counter to this is a reminder that the Southern Strategy was aimed at presidential elections only. Also, as the older generation dies out, younger Southerners are enrolling as Republicans at a higher rate than their parents.

What This Means to Southern Culture

There are mixed signals about what this all means as it relates to the destruction of our Southern culture. That are numerous examples of the leaders of the Christian Right holding meetings at Confederate Memorials, speaking out in defense of Confederate icons that are being destroyed by political correctness, and of course many of the politically active are aware of their Confederate genealogy. It would be difficult to find examples of this political force promoting the cultural genocide that has been going on for many years now. Nonetheless, I am convinced that their emergence has been a detriment to those of us who give a high priority to the preservation of our heritage and especially to those of us who still consider ourselves to be unreconstructed.

I find myself in agreement with a well-written article by Sam Hill, Professor Emeritus of the University of Florida. He wrote, "Despite its reputation, the advent of Fundamentalism into the South in recent decades has brought with it significant disruptions to the traditional religious order, and has challenged the established Southern culture as no other social movement this century." He went on to say later, "What the fundamentalist-minded Baptists and Presbyterians and their third force compatriots . . . have wrought is the supplanting of being true to the South. Now being the right sort of church person and citizen comes first." They may not even be aware themselves of the impact they are having, but as Hill says, "The old tribalism of Southern life, a product of its history and its heritage, has been dissipated by the recent developments in these central and stalwart denominational organizations." They are more concerned about social issues, such as abortion, same-sex marriage, and prayer in school. As summed up by Hill, "Briefly stated, the old base on which unity and identity rested that was social-cultural-historical has given way to a new base that is ideological, theological, and ethical."

Conclusions

Most of my life has been lived in the last half of the twentieth century, and the America that exists today is not the same as that which I was born into. The South is probably the most changed region in all of the nation. We should be grateful for some of the change. Although many blacks complain of the continuation of racial injustice, things are much better today than they were at the end of World War II. The poverty, disease, and ignorance which ran rampant throughout the region have been replaced with prosperity, improved health, and thriving institutions of learning. It would be foolish to deny that these changes have marked an improvement for most of the population, black and white.

What I resent is the loss of our Southern culture and identity. The tragedy of the war and Reconstruction served to strengthen our resolve, so much so that the Librevs claim that this was actually the birth of our regional identity in what they call the "lost cause myth." The century of poverty and hard times after the war ended up driving many of our people from their homes and into the cities of the North and West, but they took our Southern culture with them. Rather than having a negative impact, they spread Southern culture throughout the land with the introduction of Southern music, some of our fine though unhealthy cuisine, and our folksy ways.

There are a number of variables which have taken its toll on our heritage. With the growth of business combined with the invasion of foreigners into our land, from the North and other countries, the merchants have been willing to sacrifice our heritage for their profits. The Christian Right has given priority to their social conservatism and are more interested in preventing gays from getting married, and from unwed mothers having abortions, and in reforming the education system that teaches evolution and at the same time bars religion. Those who have embraced racial equality are willing to submit to the forces of political correctness in denying the heritage of American racism by scapegoating the sins of our American past to the symbols of the Confederacy and claiming that America has always been a land of equality and freedom. They accept the Northern view of the truth and blame the South for those things that were bad in American history.

The greatest change that has come about in the last half of the twentieth century is the near extinction of unreconstructed Southerners. Most of our people drive around with "United We Stand" bumper stickers and are willing to sacrifice our heritage for the good of the United States. As I have said before, you cannot serve two masters. It may work in the short term, but in the long term, it will fail. The crises comes when one master gives orders contrary to the other master. That time has come with our Southern heritage. The United States allowed us to keep our identity back in 1877, as long as we were willing to accept our military defeat. Now, more than a century later, they are telling us that we must give up the only thing we had left after they conquered us—our Southern identity. The Librevs do their part by claiming that our identity was never real in the first place, that it only came about in the years after the war. They give fuel to the fires consuming our culture by trashing our respected leaders and endorsing the idea that the war was a necessary evil in order to abolish slavery. Now they say that we should be willing to hide our Confederate heritage for the sake of racial harmony. The Southern businessmen and the Christian Right comply. I am sure that most would object to being called scalawag, but that is what they are. They are reconstructed. If we are to be united Americans, we must leave our Confederate past in the dust. This I am not willing to do, and this is why I call myself unreconstructed.

CHAPTER TEN

Conclusions

I am an unreconstructed Southerner. I define this as someone who is Southern first and American second. I do not accept what the United States has wanted us to accept since 1865, that they were right to invade our land; destroy our farms; burn our cities; rape our women; and kill our people because in doing so they freed the slaves. The reasons for the war are debatable; however, it is a fact that the North did not invade our land to free the slaves. At the time of the invasion, Abraham Lincoln and his friends said they did not threaten the institution of slavery, and we know that neither Yankees nor politicians lie. If I accepted the distorted and convoluted arguments made today to show that the war was fought to free the slaves, even though they said it wasn't when they started, then I am even more outraged. This is the only country in the world, of the very large number who had slavery in the past, which found in necessary to kill hundreds of thousands and possibly as many as a million people in order to end slavery.

I do not apologize for the fact that some of my Southern ancestors owned slaves. Things have changed in many ways over the centuries. Catholic hierarchy no longer tortures, kills, or imprisons those who resist the authority of their church. Aztecs no longer make human sacrifices to their gods. Scandinavians no longer make goblets out of human skulls. Once Cannibal cultures no longer eat human flesh. Southerners no longer own slaves. Of all of these cultural traditions that we now consider unacceptable, why is it that only those in the Southern United States cannot be forgiven for living by a different code in the past that we live by today?

The Catholic Church is a respected institution, and crowds number in thousands when the Pope visits. The cross is not barred, and Catholics are not expected to deny their heritage. The Aztecs are acceptable as the name for a college team at California State University in San Diego; are not barred from using an Aztec warrior as their mascot like the University of Mississippi; or other such schools have been intimidated into banning their rebel soldier mascots. It is simply ignored that some people in Africa or various other countries around the world practiced eating human flesh. No one expects those in the Scandinavian countries to eliminate the symbols of their Viking ancestors just because some of their pagan customs are consider cruel and unacceptable by today's modern standards. No one objects to sports teams using Viking mascots. Why is it that everything Confederate and many other symbols of the Old South are targeted for removal? Is it because some of our people owned slaves? Why aren't all of the other previous slave-owning countries, including the United States, despised for their sinful past?

The way that I see it, the United States government endorses the attitude toward our Southern culture today just as they did toward our ancestors in 1865. They not only wanted us to accept defeat, but we must recognize that the United States was right for what they did. From the beginning of the war, there have been Southerners who did not agree with secession. After the surrender, some were proud to be American again and endorsed the occupation of our land by the United States. These people were called scallywags. With the Compromise of 1877, the majority of our population were allowed to maintain our Southern pride despite military defeat. The Librevs now call this the "lost cause mythology." They accept as proven that our people did not even have a separate identity until after the Compromise of 1877. As long as the United States government endorses the extermination of our culture, I cannot accept calling myself an American. I see myself as a Confederate living in occupied territory.

Today the majority of the Southern population are patriotic Americans. Many of them would resent being called scallywags, but that, in fact, is what they are. They complain about the political correctness that dooms our heritage to extinction, but they seem to be willing to make the sacrifice for the sake of a united America. I, for one, as well as many of the unreconstructed, have a sympathy for the victims of American imperialism as we realize that we too are victims of that same imperialism. We have been conquered by the United States, and as is often the case, we are expected to be grateful for the fact that they have made us like them. I am not.

I am a realist and know that the Confederate States of America will never regain its independence. I think about the fact that Ireland was occupied for eight centuries when it finally won its freedom from the British Empire, but there are some major differences for us. The most critical is that we have finally achieved some prosperity. With that prosperity came a great number of non-Southerners who have immigrated into our nation. Some come from India, some from Latin America, and some from New York. In cities like Atlanta, Miami, and Houston, the majority of the population are foreigners. They have no desire to be independent from the United States and have little interest in the preservation of our heritage.

What motivates me to write this book is that I hope to gain some recognition for the fact that our people did exist, that at one time we did have our independence, and that we are proud of our heritage just as most others are proud of theirs. I have a hope that our fellow Southerners, the black Southerners, will realize that this is all that we ask for. I not only accept their contributions to our Southern heritage but am proud of the influences they have had in making us different from those to the North who insist that our uniqueness is a myth. It is not a myth. I feel more of a cultural bond with many of the islands in the Caribbean in comparison to those of New England. No doubt it is because of the shared plantation background complete with the African influences. I hope that when the black Southerners see the truth in what I am saying that they will stop leading the attacks on our shared heritage. Their politicians appear to be leading the attacks under the name of political correctness. I do not believe that this accomplishes anything in bettering the life of African-Americans, but it does much for the black politicians. They fool many of the black people into thinking that they are doing something for their heritage, when in fact all that they are doing is destroying ours. There is room for their culture and Southern culture, which includes African influences.

I have tried to give my fellow unreconstructed Southerners the weapons to defend the attacks against us. The liberal Northern dominated academic historians seem to be on the side of political correctness. They like to think that they are objective and that only they can write the true history of the South. This is typical of the arrogance that the United States has displayed toward those that they have invaded and occupied. The Indians, the Japanese, and even the Vietnamese, whom they failed to conquer, should be grateful for the American way of life that has been given to them upon the conquest. What is ironic is that most of the time, the liberal revisionists have been critical of this attitude and American imperialism in general. In our case, they are convinced that it is only the conquest by the United States which could have ended slavery and the ways of the Southern civilization which they despise.

I do not believe this is true. I am not grateful for having been conquered by the United States. I do not feel that they have greatly improved our civilization. That is why I am unreconstructed. If an apology is owed to anyone for the past then it is the United States who owes an apology to the people of the South. After hundreds of years, the United States government finally accepted that the conquered Indians had the right to preserve their tribal heritages. All that I ask for is the same respect for the South. Many cultures throughout the world honor and respect their ancestors. This is the foundation upon which cultures are built. I love the diversity of cultures that abounds on our planet that is why I have traveled and visited many nations on every inhabitant continent. I love my culture too, Southern culture, and do not want to see it exterminated.

BIBLIOGRAPHICAL ESSAY

The following is not intended to be a complete bibliographical essay on the subjects of Southern history but rather is aimed at the defenders of Southern heritage. I am covering the more essential books that we should be familiar with; some because they will help us defend ourselves, others so that we can better understand the Librev mind. The basic idea that I have employed is that we should be prepared to defend our culture by defending our history, and in order to do that, we need to know the enemy. Most of these are the books generally accepted by the academic liberal revisionist community of professional historians, many of whom at least appear to take the position that the symbols of our Confederate and Southern heritage are offensive. Many could be called "anti-Southern," but they should be considered for their own merits as history. I do not mean to imply that these historians are all wrong and that they have evil intentions toward our heritage. Remember, these books were written by professional historians. Most of their work is simply historical research. Some of the revisionism is good. For example, I value learning more about the black population who had been all but ignored in earlier American history. Like all of human knowledge, present generations build on the foundation left to them by past historians, just as those in the future will improve on our efforts. However, historians have their interpretations and this means that they can be wrong. They have their bias just as we do. My only objection is against those biases which are being used to make the claim that our Southern culture is any less noble than any other. Our people are no worse than any of the others who make up the population of the United States today, whether they be American Indian, of African descent, or even those from the North. Just like in that war so many years ago, my basic strategy is one of defense. It is the other side which is the aggressor. They are conducting another War of Northern Aggression.

Southern Identity

The basic issue related to what the Librevs call the lost cause myth revolves around the question of Southern distinctiveness. Those of us who object most to this myth are in agreement with Grady McWhiney and his book *Cracker Culture: Celtic Ways in the Old South*. His basic assumption is called the Celtic fringe theory. The idea is that the South is predominantly a Celtic culture while the North, especially New England, is Anglo-Saxon, and thus, the conflict between the two cultures is older than the English colonies. He has been given support by some others in journal articles: Rowland Berthloff, *Journal of Southern History* (November 1986) and Forrest McDonald and Ellen Shapiro McDonald, *William and Mary Quarterly* (April 1980). This appeals to me personally and much of my interpretation of history is based on the acceptance of this assumption. I do not agree with the full extension of his thesis which is the basis for a book he wrote with Perry D. Jamieson, *Attack and Die: Civil War Military Tactics and Southern Heritage*. I do not believe the notion that the South is more militaristic because of their Celtic heritage. Academia in general accepts the reality that McWhiney is a professional and published historian, but they almost always preface any reference to him as a "controversial" historian.

Very important to the question of Southern identity is the colonial background. As stated above, I personally accept the assumption that the South is basically a Celtic culture, but even if one cannot accept this, I see that the South has differed from the North, especially New England, from the first days of the colonies. This is the main reason colonial history is so critical. One of the more widely accepted histories on the early South is Wesley Frank Craven, *The Southern Colonies in the Seventeenth Century, 1670–1689*. Though published in 1949, it is still widely acclaimed. Some other volumes include: T. H. Breen, ed., *Shaping Southern Society*, a collection of articles; Edmond S. Morgan, *American Slavery, American Freedom: The Ordeal of Colonial Virginia*, noted more for his thesis that the land of slavery gave birth to democracy because with slavery, there emerged a feeling of equality among the white population. Carl Bridenbaugh, *Myths and Realities: Societies of the Colonial South* deal with those myths not related to the Confederate flag controversies since it was published in 1952 before this became a topic. See also Wesley Craven, *White, Red, and Black: The Seventeenth Century Virginian*, Gloria Main, *Tobacco Colony: Life in Early Maryland, 1650–1720*, and Rhys Isaac, *The Transformation of Virginia, 1740–1790*. The emphasis on Virginia and Maryland is justified by the fact that much of the population in the western states and even the Deep South states, including the Carolinas and Georgia, migrated there from the Chesapeake colonies.

Through the years, many have assumed that the South resisted modernity while the North spread the capitalist economy and ended slavery, and this is what justifies their actions. For this reason, the topic of the Southern economy is important. Some of the more widely accepted books related to the economy will be discussed later under the New South.

Many of those who love to hate the South see it as a land where the Anglo-Saxons dominate over all non-Anglos, especially those with darker skins. The reality is that before the War, the South was more diverse than the North, especially New England. Not only was it more diverse but most of these non-Anglo, or what should be called non-Celtic, helped to defend the Confederacy. There is no denying that they quite often had lower status than the white population, but they seemed to do as well or better than their counterpart in the North. This included the Indians. Though they are older books, two that are still good were written by Annie Heloise Abel; *The American Indian as Slaveholder and Secessionist*, 1915, and *The American Indian in the Civil War, 1862–1865*, 1919. Some others on Indians include Wiley Britton, *The Civil War On the Border*; Kenneth W. Porter, *The Black Seminoles*; W. Craig Gaines, *The Confederate Cherokees*; Angie Debo, *And Still The Waters Run*. Jeffrey Burton, *Indian Territory and the United States, 1866–1906*, covers the period after the war. See also *Africans and Creeks: From the Colonial Period to the Civil War* or *Africans and Seminoles: From Removal to Emancipation* and *The Cherokee Freedmen: From Reconstruction to American Citizenship* by Daniel F. Littlefield and *Slavery and the Evolution of Cherokee Society* by Theda Perdue. A good one on Jewish Southerners is *The Jewish Confederates*, by Robert

N. Rosen. Some others are Leonard Dinnerstein and Mary Palsson, eds., *"Turn to the South": Essays on Southern History*, Eli Evans, *The Provincials: A Personal History of Jews in the South*. John O'Donnell-Rosales has compiled list of *Hispanic Confederates*. Some other sources on Hispanics in the South include Silvia Pedraza-Bailey, *Political and Economic Migrants: Cubans in Florida*; and Alejandro Portes, *Latin Journey: Cuban and Mexican Immigrants*. There are some books on French and Spanish colonies; *The Spanish Frontier in North America* by David J. Weber; *Africans in Colonial Louisiana: The Development of Afro-Creole Culture in the Eighteenth Century*, by Gwendolyn M. Hall.

Slavery

There are many books on slavery; I will discuss only some of the more popular. On the slave trade, there is Philip D. Curtin *Atlantic Slave Trade*, and one that I find objective is *The Slave Trade*, by Hugh Thomas, an English historian. His book is well-researched, and I like it because he is not out to find someone to blame. Ulrich Phillips wrote one of the first books on the subject of slavery in 1918, *American Negro Slavery*, but the Librevs have their students read it so they can see the racism that was America at the time. Winthrop Jordan sums up the Librev view with *White Over Black*. For generations, Southerners have been guilty of justifying slavery by claiming that the slaves were happy. For this reason, many liberals like to discuss slave resistance. Since they know there were not many slave rebellions in what became the Confederate States of America, the Librevs like to show other ways of resistance Some books on rebellions and resistance include: Gerald W. Mullin with *Slave Resistance in Eighteenth-Century Virginia. From Rebellion to Revolution; Afro-American Slave Revolts in the Making of the Modern World* by Eugene Genovese and *Gabriel's Rebellion: The Virginia Slave Conspiracies of 1800 and 1802* by Douglas R. Egerton. Stanley Elkins is considered one of the more influential on Librevs in a 1959 book *Slavery: A Problem in American Institutional and Intellectual Life*. Many of the Librevs like to study the preservation of African culture, which I also admire. Some of the better known are Eugene D. Genovese, *Roll, Jordan, Roll: The World They Made Together*; Herbert G. Gutman, *The Black Family in Slavery and Freedom, 1750–1925*; Lawrence W.

Levine, *Black Culture and Black Consciousness: Afro-American Folk Thought from Slavery to Freedom*; George P. Rawick, *From Sundown to Sunup: The Making of the Black Community*, and, John Blassingame, *The Slave Community: Plantation Life in the Antebellum South*. Paul D. Escott compiled some interesting statistics from the *Slave Narratives* in his book *Slavery Remembered: A Record of Twentieth-Century Slave Narratives*. Some books on the economic aspects of slavery include Paul A. David with *Reckoning With Slavery: A Critical Study in the Quantitative History of American Negro Slavery* and Eugene Genovese, *The Political Economy of Slavery: Studies in the Economy and Society of the Slave South*. One which attracted a lot of criticism from the Librev community is *Time on the Cross*, by Robert W. Fogel and Stanley L. Engerman. I highly recommend this book. These men were from the liberal Mecca of Madison, Wisconsin. However, they compiled statistics and showed how the slaves were part of the Southern economy. David, mentioned above, was one of many who attacked them so that they found it necessary to write a sequel in which they did not change their position but emphasized how slavery was still evil. I have always liked the book by Mechal Sobel, *The World They Made Together*, which stressed the impact that each culture has had on the other.

The War of Southern Independence

There are more books written about the war than any other topic in American history. I will make no attempt to identify the best, or even the ones I recommend, but rather only those that are most admired by the Librevs. When it comes to the causes of the war, they like to defend that position that it was still over slavery. They know all the things that I and others have written, and they cannot deny the many quotes from Lincoln and Union military officers in which they said they were not fighting to free the slaves. Nonetheless, they still see slavery as the cause. I wish South Carolina had not backed down in the 1830s and then we could clearly state that secession was over tariffs, not slavery. One of the approaches they use is to try to show that the movement for secession was by the planters and was not supported by the poor. The middle class who did support the war, even those who did not own slaves, since they know that the majority of Southerners did not, did so because they either wanted to profit from the system in the future or their racist attitude wanted to keep the blacks subservient. Some of the books on the war and its causes also like to push the idea that Southern identity did not exist before the antebellum era. With this in mind, the following are on the Librev "must read list" relating to the causes of the war or on those supported secession: Daniel Crofts, *Reluctant Confederates: Upper South Unionists in the Secession Crises*; Eric Walther, *The Fire-Eaters*; Eric Foner, *Free Soil, Free Labor, Free Men: The Ideology of the Republican Party before the Civil War*; David Potter, *The Impending Crises* and *Lincoln and His party in the Secession Crisis*; James M. McPherson, *Battle Cry of Freedom: The Civil War Era*; Charles Royster, *The Destructive War: William Tecumseh Sherman, Stonewall Jackson, and the Americans*; E. Merton Coulter, *Confederate States of America, 1861–1865*; Emory M. Thomas, *Confederate Nation, 1861–1865*; Shelby Foote, *The Civil War*, Drew Faust, *The Creation of Confederate Nationalism*; Paul Escott, *After Secession: Jefferson Davis and the Failure of Confederate Nationalism*, Douglas B. Ball, *Financial Failure and Confederate Defeat*, and Frank Owsley, *State Rights in the Confederacy*. James McPherson did one that they all love, *What They Fought For, 1861–1865*, which is very interesting and suggest that Southerners did not fight simply to protect slavery. Again, I only suggest these books to gain an understanding of the more popular interpretations of the events among the academic community which I have labeled the Librevs.

Reconstruction

As stated in my essay, Reconstruction is one of the most critical areas of controversy between us unreconstructed and the Librevs. They use the work of William Dunning who wrote *Reconstruction, Political and Economic, 1865–1877* in 1907 as the bench mark for what they now call the "lost cause myth." Though Dunning was with Columbia University, he took the position that it was the North rather than the South which was wrong in Reconstruction. They even admit that Northerners were as accepting of this interpretation as Southerners were. The first ones to dispute this view were Kenneth M. Stamp in 1965 with *Era of Reconstruction, 1865–1877.* In 1982 came James M. McPherson's *Ordeal by Fire: The Civil War and Reconstruction.* I would say the most important book representing the Librev view today came in 1988, Eric Foner's *Reconstruction: America's Unfinished Revolution, 1863–1877.* Perhaps the most important aspect of this book is that he looks at Reconstruction as the end of slavery and thus saw the beginning as beginning with the emancipation proclamation in 1863. Richard N. Current defended the Northerners with his *Those Terrible Carpetbaggers: A Reinterpretation,* and Thomas Holt objected to the view of the black politicians as incompetent with his book *Black Over White: Negro Political Leadership in South Carolina during Reconstruction.* George R. Rable saw the violence of the time as an attempt to keep blacks in their place in his book *But There Was No Peace: The Role of Violence in the Politics of Reconstruction.* There are many others but these are the most important to the academic elite.

The New South

The New South debate began in 1951 with C. Vann Woodward's *Origins of the New South, 1877–1913.* Woodward saw the Redeemers as "new men" who rejected the agricultural South in favor of economic diversity. Since then there have been numerous books defending or disputing this view. Some of the more popular have been Numan V. Bartley in an article in the *Georgia Historical Quarterly* titled "Another New South." Also important have been Jonathan Wiener, *Social Origins of the New South: Alabama, 1860–1880*; David L. Caroton, *Mill and Town in South Carolina, 1880–1920*; Edward Ayers, *The Promise of the New South: Life After Reconstruction*; Gavin Wright, *Old South, New South: Revolutions in the Southern Economy since the Civil War*; and Paul M. Gaston, *The New South Creed: A Study in Southern Mythmaking.* Related to this topic are Blaine A. Brownell and David R. Goldfield, eds., *The City in Southern History: The Growth of Urban Civilization in the South*; David Goldfield, *Urban Growth in the Age of Sectionalism: Virginia, 1847–1861*; Lawrence H. Larsen, *The Rise of the Urban South.* From discussion of the new South we can go into Populism and other economic topics. One book that connects the topics is Roger L. Hart, *Redeemers, Bourbons, and Populists: Tennessee, 1870–1896.* A good one on populism is Steven Hahn, *The Roots of Southern Populism: Yeoman Farmers and the Transformation of the Georgia Upcountry, 1850–1890.*

More specifically on Populism, though it dates back to 1931, is John D. Hicks, *The Populist Revolt: A History of the Farmer's Alliance and the People's Party*. Getting into southern economics often leads to discussion of the Depression years. Some good books here are James C. Cobb and Michael V. Namorato, eds., *The New Deal and the South*. About the new South since 1945 see Bruce J. Schulman, *From Cotton Belt to Sunbelt: Federal Policy, Economic Development and the Transformation of the South, 1938–1980*; Peter Applebome, *Dixie Rising: How the South Is Shaping American Values, Politics and Culture*; Dan T. Carter, *From George Wallace to Newt Gingrich: Race in the Conservative Counterrevolution, 1963–1994*; John Egerton, *The Americanization of Dixie*.

Race Since 1865

I cannot think of anything new to say. The South was segregated; Black Southerners were second-class citizens until recent times; and I see no reason for us to feel proud about the way our ancestors treated black folks. My only objection is to the attitude that this is a Southern thing is it was not much different up North. We cannot deny the way things used to be, and there is nothing the Librevs can add to make it worse. This is one of the main reasons that there are those who want to wipe out our heritage, and the fact that many of our kinsmen used the Confederate flag as a symbol of resistance to the civil rights movement is why that banner is most despised. The only thing I can say is we should be as knowledgeable as possible on the subject. The defense of our heritage can only be based on the conviction that this is not the whole story of our heritage, and it is not what we are about today.

Many people think of the South as having always been segregated. However, if we think about it, we would realize that under slavery, blacks and whites lived together and worked together. The Jim Crow South came after the war. The foundation book on this topic would have to be C. Vann Woodward's *Strange Career of Jim Crow*, a fourth revised edition was published in 1974. John Hope Franklin would be on the same level of respect. He wrote *From Slavery to Freedom: A History of American Negroes*. Some other related volumes include John W. Cell, *The Highest Stage of White Supremacy: The Origins of Segregation in South African and the American South*; J. Morgan Kousser, *The Shaping of*

Southern Politics: Suffrage Restrictions and the Establishment of the One-Party South, 1880–1910; Joel Williamson, The Crucible of Race: Black-White Relations in the American South since Emancipation; Leon Litwack, Trouble in Mind: Black Southerners in the Age of Jim Crow and Howard N. Rabinowitz, Race Relations in the Urban South, 1865–1890.

Some books that cover a more general approach to the story of black Southerners in the twentieth century include John Hope Franklin, From Slavery to Freedom; August Meir and Elliott Rudwick, From Plantation to Ghetto, Herbert G. Gutman, The Black Family in Slavery and Freedom; Lawrence W. Levine, Black Culture and Black Consciousness; and, Gail Williams O'Brien, The Color of the Law: Race, Violence and Justice in the Post–World War II South. An interesting view is offered in Willard B. Gatewood's Aristocrats of Color: The Black Elite, 1880–1920. Some focusing on the violence toward blacks is Scott Ellsworth, Death in the Promised Land: Tulsa Race Riot of 1921; W. Fitzhugh Brundage, Lynching in the New South: Georgia and Virginia, 1880–1930; George C. Wright, Racial Violence in Kentucky, 1865–1940: Lynchings, Mob Rule, and "Legal Lynchings"; and, Stephen J. Whitfield, A Death in the Delta: The Story of Emmett Till tells the story of a 1955 lynching that probably played a key role in the changes that came in the next two decades.

There is no definitive general survey of the civil rights revolution that came after World War II though the books on the subject are quite numerous. Some of the more important include Adam Fairclough, To Redeem the Soul of America: The Southern Christian Leadership Conference and Martin Luther King, Jr.; David R. Goldfield, Black White, and Southern: Race Relations and Southern Culture, 1940 to the Present; Hugh Davis Graham, The Civil Rights Era: Origins and Development of National Policy; Aldon D. Morris, The Origins of the Civil Rights Movement: Black Communities Organizing for Change; and, Juan Williams, Eyes on the Prize: America's Civil Rights Years, 1854–1965. Of course Martin Luther King, Jr., has become synonymous with the movement; for more on him see David J. Garrow, Bearing the Cross or Taylor Branch, Parting the Waters: America in the King Years, 1954–1963. There were whites who helped create the change and they are covered in David L. Chappell, Inside Agitators: White Southerners in the Civil Rights Movement, and Elizabeth Jacoway and David R.

Colburn were editors of a volume that discussed *Southern Businessmen and Desegregation*. A good one that shows that the civil rights movement was an American thing not just a Southern thing is Thomas J. Sugrue, *Sweet Land of Liberty: the Forgotten Struggle for Civil Rights in the North*. There are those who question the end of racial problems, see Michael V. Namorato, ed, *Have We Overcome? Race Relations since "Brown;"* William Julius Wilson, *The Declining Significance of Race: Blacks and Changing American Institutions*; and any book from John Hope Franklin should be given great credence, see his *Race and History: Selected Essays, 1938–1988*.

The Lost Cause Myth

My conclusion is that we have convinced the professional historians that we are not racist, that the interest we have in preserving our heritage has nothing to do with a desire to bring back slavery, etc. They cannot abandon the liberal cause, and so they have taken the position that things Confederate are not really symbols of Southern heritage but rather of what they call the "lost cause myth." The books most related to this point of view are Charles R. Wilson, *Baptized in Blood: The Religion of the Lost Cause , 1865–1920*; Gaines Foster, *Ghosts of the Confederacy: Defeat, the Lost Cause and the Emergence of the New South, 1865 to 1913*; David W. Blight, *Race and Reunion: The Civil War in American Memory*; Karen L. Cox, *Dixie's Daughters: The United Daughters of the Confederacy and the Preservation of Confederate Culture*; Gary W. Gallagher and Alan T. Nolan, *The Myth of the Lost Cause and Civil War History*; and, Grace Elizabeth Hale, *Making Whiteness: The Culture of Segregation in the South, 1890–1940*. Of course they cannot go without attacking the greatest symbol of the Old South—Robert E. Lee. The latest to do this is Elizabeth Brown Pryor, *Reading The Man: A Portrait of Robert E. Lee Through His Private Letters*. It has gotten to the point where most graduate students and academic historians speak of the "lost cause myth" as if it were a proven fact.

Religion and the South

Religion has become even more important in the liberal interpretations of the South as the new Right, especially under George W. Bush, formed an alliance with the Republican Party. An overall history of religion in America is in Sydney E. Ahlstrom, *A Religious History of the American People*. Samuel S. Hill, Jr., is a good source on religion in the South with *Encyclopedia of Religion in the South; Religion and the Solid South*; and, *The South and the North in American Religion*. The role of religion and politics is covered in John C. Green, Mark J. Rosell, and Clyde Wilcox, eds., *The Christian Right in American Politics: Marching to the Millennium* and Samuel S. Hill and Dennis E. Owen, *The New Religious Right in America*.